Eleanor Hulley

The Concise Herbal
Encyclopedia

Books by the same author:—

HERB GROWING FOR HEALTH

HERBAL TEAS FOR HEALTH AND PLEASURE

HOW TO DEFEAT RHEUMATISM AND ARTHRITIS

HOW TO KEEP YOUR HAIR ON

HERBS FOR COOKING AND HEALING

TEXTBOOK OF BOTANIC MEDICINE (8 VOLS)

DEGREE COURSE IN PHILOSOPHY

ASTROLOGY, PALMISTRY AND DREAMS

A COMPLETE GUIDE TO ALTERNATIVE HEALING

HANDBUCH DER HEILKRÄUTER

LUONNONVARAISTA TERVEYSTEETÄ

THE YOUNG PERSON'S NATURE GUIDE

THE YOUNG PERSON'S GUIDE TO WATER SPORTS

The Concise Herbal Encyclopedia

Donald Law

Ph.D., D.B.M., Psy.D., Dip.D.
D.Litt., M.N.T.A., phil.med.D.

John Bartholomew & Son Ltd
Edinburgh

First Published in Great Britain 1973
by John Bartholomew & Son Ltd
12 Duncan Street, Edinburgh EH9 1TA
and at 216 High Street, Bromley BR1 1PW

This reprint 1975

ISBN 0 85152 905 4

Printed and bound in Great Britain by
REDWOOD BURN LIMITED
Trowbridge & Esher

Contents

Introduction

Herbs have always occupied a very special position in Man's life, being used in medicine to heal his ills and pains; having their place in myths which were the precursors of written history; and having special significance in the magic rites which Man used in his desire to work his will upon the world.

The further one goes back into history the more these three branches of learning become intermixed, and one sees that many things accepted today as fully proven by the leading medical authorities were common knowledge to ancient herbalists two or three thousand years ago, but because their value and relationship were not clear at the time the wisdom was lost for centuries.

This work sets out first of all to present some of the mysteries, magic, myths and medicinal values of herbs so that the man in the street can benefit. Secondly, in order that seemingly unconnected pieces of information shall not be dispersed, neglected and lost when they might be of inestimable value to scientists in a more enlightened world, I am deliberately including the details which modern writers tend to omit 'as of no practical use'.

One of the reasons why I have recorded this lore is that some months previously I received a cutting from a German newspaper in which an electronic engineer claims that a major breakthrough in television technique has been made possible by studying illustrated inscriptions on an Egyptian tomb! *We cannot foresee what use knowledge will be to generations which are to follow us, but we can preserve it for them.*

There is one other reason which added weight to my decision. In all the ancient books of magic there is continual reference to a 'magic wand' and it is usually laughed away, but a detailed study of radiesthesia and radionics under Dr. Copen (the leading authority on the subject) convinced me that the *wand* was almost certainly a radiesthetic detection instrument.

Many of the details about herbs which seem irrelevant to us or which are described as magic may provide irrefutable fact to generations with more efficient means of research and analysis.

Herbs are man's oldest method of healing disease and curing pain; their use for such purposes goes back to the absolute beginning of recorded history, and some of the oldest writings list herbs which can be used for medicine and tell us how to identify them and employ them.

Today we tend to speak too lightly of 'weeds' so let me quote an anonymous wise man of a previous century who said : *'What right have you, O passer-by-the-way, to call any flower a weed?*

Do you know its merits, its virtues, its healing qualities? Because a thing is common shall you despise it? If so you might despise the sunshine for the same reason.'

The layman outside the field of Botanic Medicine has little idea how many of the drugs in everyday use come from 'weeds' he is probably rooting up from his garden all the year round . . . and then paying to buy them back in another form !

A lady of my acquaintance spent a considerable sum on medicines which she could have made for herself for next to nothing since the contents were growing in her own garden. This book will tell you how to make simple herbal preparations at very little expense.

Life on earth could not continue without vegetation, and yet man knows correspondingly little about the plants of the planet, and it seems that he is only now beginning to take a serious interest in their functions.

Only plants can absorb inorganic material and turn it into organic stuff; plants turn dead matter into live matter—a process which men find it virtually impossible to imitate. The tiny, almost invisible, root hairs of a plant can exude strange chemical acids which can melt mineral substances so that the plant can absorb them; this is an everyday act for plants !

Joseph Priestley (1733–1804), a world-famous research worker in chemistry, proved by experiment that one single sprig of the herb peppermint can produce enough oxygen for a fullgrown mouse to live on. When you next enjoy a ramble over wild heaths or a climb on the lonely hills you will remember whence comes all that wonderful healthgiving air you love to breathe when you are in the country—from the plants ! Those of you who have been in arid, vegetationless country will soon notice the dreadful lack of oxygen. Even the bracing oxygen of the seaside is related to the enormous oxygen production of the countless forms of algae which live just below the surface of the water. Is it any wonder that throughout the whole world our ancestors associated herbs and flowers with the gods? Somewhere in their lore there is a wisdom of which *'we see through a glass darkly'*. Gotama, the Enlightened One, obtained his priceless spiritual knowledge sitting under a species of pipal tree, the Bo tree or *Ficus religiosus*. On the other side of the world Omacatl, the Mexican god of festivity, was always fêted with flowers and herbs. Is it any wonder that Tennyson wrote :

> *'Little flower, if I could understand*
> *What you are, root and all, and all in all,*
> *I should know what God and man is.'*

This is a time of great disillusionment. Apart from instructive works such as Rachel Carson's *Silent Spring* thousands of men and women are finding out that the over-advertised wonder-drugs, and anti-biotics, may seem to heal what they claim to heal, but they bring new, undefined side-effects in their wake, and no salesmanship can out-advertise bad results, sickness and death. Never before has there been such a resurgence of simple, trustworthy herbal medicine, the method of healing proven safe over the entire history of mankind. Long ago, wise Brahmans wrote down the *Ayur Veda* in Sanskrit, they listed Aloe juice to cure some forms of constipation, Rauwolfia to cure some forms of insanity, and it has taken a long time for the irrefutable truth of their teaching to be recognised. Margaret Kreig, the great American scientist, says in her *Green Medicine* that what the Brahmans called *Sarpa gandha* is now being marketed by major pharmaceutical firms as an irrefutable cure for mental disorders caused by chemical imbalance in the brain; it reduces the need for shock treatment, brain surgery and insulin treatment for these patients. BUT THAT KNOWLEDGE WAS THERE ALL THE TIME, waiting for 3,000 years for somebody to trust and try the herbal treatment!

Over 700 herbs were listed in the Ayur Veda, and over 2,000 remedies are in the Charka Samhita which is about the same date; I remember hearing how some doctors laughed their heads off when a Chinese claimed to be over 200 years old, and attributed this to his use of a plant he called *Foh tih*, which was found to be *Hydrocotyle asiatica*, but very recent research has shown that there are two plants of this name, one the *Major* which was well known and easily available, and the other the *Minor* which has only recently been distinguished; this latter contains some very strange chemical constituents which defy analysis. Unfortunately the old man has now died. Knowledge that is not recorded can become lost forever. Do you know the story of the Romans and the last Picts? The legend has it that the Romans were desperate to discover the recipe of making the Honey Mead which the wild Celts enjoyed and which had such miraculous properties. They caught the last two Picts alive, the old one professed to hate his son and said he would tell them the secret recipe if the Romans would kill the lad; they obliged, but when the son was dead the old man sneered at them : 'My son was weak, he might have told you, now he is dead; from me you will never learn it', and so the secret was lost forever.

We may, in our self-styled superior wisdom, laugh at the *Doctrine of Signatures* which Theophrastus von Hohenheim (1493–1591) taught (under the name of Paracelsus) because his medical teaching was deeply tinged with occult knowledge, but may not some future generation have the means to prove him right? He said that for those with eyes to see, God had already shown mankind which medicines to take for such and such an illness; he claimed that all plants which healed heart conditions had either on leaf or flower the sign of a heart (just as a lover might carve it on the bark of a tree), kidney shaped leaves would cure nephritic diseases, etc. We do know that in several cases this is correct, but our present knowledge does not *yet* enable us to concur exactly. There is, by the way, a tree found in the Himalayas which shows on its various leaves, when in full bloom, all of the letters of the Sanskrit alphabet. Thus we come to understand what Wordsworth meant when he asserted :

> *'To me the meanest flower that blows can give*
> *Thoughts that do often lie too deep for tears.'*

I recently read *The Long Walk* by the Pole, Slavomir Rawicz, who escaped from a Siberian prison camp across the Black Gobi desert; the hardships which he and his gallant companions endured could have been greatly alleviated if they had known which herbs were edible, and how they could have used many of them for medicine. The desert abounds with thistles, these make a nourishing food when stripped of their prickles; *Carduus silybum* is commonly eaten in many parts of the world. Until the advent of Mao Tse Tung there were still many Chinese peasants who prayed to Sheng Noong for a good harvest; this deity was an emperor *c.* 2838–2698 B.C.) who suffered apotheosis upon his death, and was regarded as a god ever since; he compiled the first Chinese herbal, listing 365 clearly identified herbs.

Some people doubt whether the herbs our forefathers used were effective. History reminds us that many ancient kings would reward a good physician and execute a bad one. In modern days a physician experiences no such risk, so I think it is reasonable to accept that any herb recommended under such circumstances had effective use for the condition prescribed.

Men often risked their lives searching for rare herbs; indeed, a fragment in the Royal Library of the Babylonian king Ashurbanipal relates how a man called Etana died trying to get a herb which would guarantee his wife safe delivery of the herbs needed for the birth of their expected son.

The Irish Celts told of Diancecht, their god of healing, who with herbs and pure water could heal any man of any wound. The flat, mineral-less, secondhand liquid which we call water in our towns today is far removed from the crystal stream full of mineral salts which Man drank when Odysseus roamed the earth, and its healing properties have to be experienced to be fully known. Elsewhere we learn of the Hindu physician to the gods themselves, Dhanvantari, who brewed an immortal nectar of herbs, after drinking which the gods were able to defeat the evil Asuras. Not so strange when we learn that in World War II and subsequent conflagrations troops are often drugged before they go into battle. Sir Edwin Arnold, that great poet who produced the 'Light of Asia', wrote :

> *'Shun drugs and drinks which work the wit abuse,*
> *Clear minds, clean bodies need no soma juice.'*

We perhaps know Soma from Aldous Huxley's novel *Brave New World*, a very brilliant work; Huxley took the word *Soma* from the drink made from herbs for the Vedic gods, a potion which made them divine and put them above all men. Nonsense? Well, does not Maeterlinck show that the queen bee sups on a special food which is allowed to no other bee? Again the royal jelly is constructed entirely from herbs. A Roman legend tells how Glaucus turned into an amphibious man by eating of a certain herb. Can there be some germ of truth in this? Is there, perhaps, some herb which would work chemical changes in man so that he could absorb oxygen from water as fast as fish do with their gills? I do not want to be like the young lady in the Saki story of the *Open Window* of whom it was said : '*Romance at short notice was her speciality*', but to present known facts and legends in a form which might make them coherent to research workers now and in generations to come. Horace Smith declared : '*Flowers are living preachers each cup a pulpit, each leaf a book.*'

Justus von Liebig (1800–82), one of the most famous names in chemical research, insisted that God was a scientist, a super scientist. Surely one of the greatest things Socrates said was : '*The more I know the more I know how little I know.*'

Every day men and women are exploring the universe, risking their lives in search of knowledge, but too often losing their lives (such was the lot of the Frenchman Raymond Maufrais) or getting into difficulties (as did Gino Watkins round Lake Ossokmanuan when he was exploring possible air-routes in Labrador) because they may be able to identify plants but do not know how to USE them. In my book *Herbgrowing for Health* I showed that the Woad rubbed on their bodies by the Ancient Britons was not just to paint the body blue and frighten the enemy but it was a first-class antiseptic and styptic; in effect, they were more advanced in warfare than we because they prepared their bodies to heal up a wound before they risked getting one.

In the early nineteenth century the Hon. Charles Augustus Murray recorded in *The Prairie Bird* that the Red Indians of the Missouri region never smoked tobacco on its own but always mixed it with equal parts of sumach leaf and the inner bark of the white willow; have we lost something from pipe smoking by making our tobacco the sole ingredient of the mixture? Is this why we find Europeans getting pulmonary diseases which the Amerindians never suffered? The fields for research in herbal medicine are limitless. This is an obvious line of research, and one which is easy to follow, but who can fathom the relevance of the flowers carried by Coatlicue, mother of Huitzilopochtli—the Mexican god of war? What psychological mystery linked the patroness of flower-sellers with the god of war? Were the flowers she is shown with used to drug warriors?

The psychological significance of the old Graeco-Roman legends and myths is alarmingly profound. Dewdrops are the tears of the Dawn for her son, Memnon the beautiful, sired by Zeus, slain by Achilles. It has a meaning.

There is an ancient Welsh tradition that God has given men the instinct which leads their hands to the herbs which will cure them of their hurt.

I do not think that it is a coincidence that Mahomet taught that heaven consisted of gardens, as did the ancient Slav pagan priests who taught the tribes about *Raj*; even the Viking Valhalla was centred around Laeradhr, a mighty tree.

The life of plants amazes us, Redwood trees can live 2,000 years or more, many Yew trees live over 1,000 years. Varieties of the Eucalyptus and others reach over 200 feet in height. Bamboo shoots look so frail but grow over an inch a day, pushing their way right through a human body to do so; binding a man down on a bed of growing bamboo shoots was a torture in Japanese prison camps.

Next time you are at the seaside look at the massive rocks and beetling cliffs beside the surging main; it is the tender, helpless-looking plants that prevent them from being washed away by the angry tides, or being blown away as dust by the spring gales. Feuerbach teaches us : *'In the perishable petals of the flower there resides more spirit and life than in the lumpish granite boulder that has defied the tear and wear of thousands of years.'*

In a work of this nature it is unwise to 'gild the lily' by adding material which, although researched, is purely repetitive and so I have specifically avoided the temptation to fill the text with Graeco-Roman myths, etc., but have carefully included as many as possible from other sources—Babylonian, Egyptian, Aztec, Hindu, Norse, etc. In some cases the planetary influence governing a plant is known; where it is disputed I have given both alternatives; and I have tried to present the information without fear or favour. For example, it is highly probable that the magic potion used by Circe to turn Odysseus' sailors into swine was a form of Hemp (Cannabis) but there is no proof; other sources indicate the root of Mandrake, again no proof, but the description does fit *drug addiction*, a problem which we have come to understand more realistically than previous generations. Hemp was probably used by the Delphic Oracle. An eminent expert on Tibetan affairs revealed that one of the 'State Oracles' got himself into his frenzied trance by taking a mixture of Hashish and Red Pepper; need I add that most Tibetan 'State Oracles' died young?

It is a bit of an exaggeration for Kipling to tell us :

> *'Anything green that grew out of a mould*
> *Was an excellent herb to our fathers of old.'*

Such opinions blind the man-in-the-street to works such as the Ebers papyrus, the herbal compiled in Ancient Egypt *c.* 1536 B.C., listing well over 600 herbs, many of which are clearly identifiable and are still used by practitioners of Botanic Medicine today, and still giving excellent results.

Are herbs safe to use? Well, the answer is yes because no plant that could have any possible unpleasant effects is ever recommended by any botanic physician nowadays. We have not centuries but millennia of experience behind us, we know thoroughly the effect of the medicines we use; no doctor using the latest supplies from the pharmaceutical industry (many change every month) can say the same thing. Galen (A.D. 131–201) boasted just before he died that in all his life he had never lost a patient, never prescribed nor diagnosed wrongly. It sounds a brag, but when we remember that he was physician to such masters as Septimus Severus, Commodus, as well as to the cultured Marcus Aurelius, a mistake could have cost him his life, and none of the emperors was likely to allow him a second chance.

The secret of success is in DIAGNOSIS. Never treat yourself unless you are positive your diagnosis is accurate, spend a lot of time on diagnosis; remember to take every symptom into consideration, and you won't go wrong. Never exceed the dose recommended, don't try to rush the healing process, let the human body deal patiently with the condition; the object is to strengthen the body to heal itself. Herbalists do not generally subscribe to the dramatic and violent theory (it is no more) about killing germs because there never has been any 'magic bullet', in spite of Ehrlich's dream, which would kill cells a, b and c, but not harm cells d, e, and f in the body.

Do not let complicated medical works worry you to death. Find out slowly and patiently what is not working in your body, put one thing right at a time, stick to it, and the results will always satisfy you. Constipation must be always cleared at the earliest possible moment; if you don't like living with choked drains in your house, don't choke your own body.

A great deal of benefit may be had from radiesthesia for medical diagnosis, it is quicker and more reliable than most other methods I know. Some works on the subject are included in the bibliography of suggested further reading matter at the end.

I write this work in the firm belief that it will help men and women everywhere to attain better health, and provide a fund of curious and useful knowledge for many generations to come.

DONALD LAW
Ph.D., D.B.M., Psy.D., Dip.D., D.Litt., M.N.T.A., phil.med.D.

1. *The History of Herbal Medicine*

From earliest times Mankind has passed on to a younger generation such knowledge and wisdom as he has established to the best
of his ability.

Herbalism is the oldest form of healing the sick in the world; it
is widely practised not only in the jungles of the lesser known parts of
the world, not only in the mountain villages of Macedonia, but also
in the most elegant cities of the world, among the élite of Society,
for although many of these people gain their living from patent
medicines they are rarely foolish enough to take them. In recent
decades the more accurate term 'Botanic Medicine' has been increasingly employed for several reasons, but the most significant is
that 'herb' denotes plants, other than bushes, trees and marine
plants, which are increasingly used by practitioners of Botanic
Medicine.

The Chinese emperor Fo Hi and his son Sheng Noong are
credited with establishing herbal medicine about 5,000 years ago.
The Chinese herbal *Pen Tsao*, containing over 1,000 herbal remedies, was produced about this time.

The Ebers papyrus records many herbal remedies in use in Ancient
Egypt. We all know the word *Pharmaceutic*, referring to drugs and
medicine; it is not so widely known that the word is not of Greek
origin but comes from Ancient Egypt. Phar Ma Kee was the god of
healing, sometimes called Thoth. Among the herbs used by his
priests was Castor Oil.

The Edwin Smith Papyrus, written *c.* 3000 B.C., is the oldest-
known surgical treatise in the world; in it the ancient Egyptian
herbalists describe the membranes of the brain and analyse fits. Also
3000 B.C. the herbalist Imhoteb was the first man to explain the
circulation of the blood. By 2600 B.C. the Babylonians were detailing
herbal medicines.

The decipherment of their cuneiform clay tablets by Sir Henry
Rawlinson *c.* A.D. 1840 showed that herbal medicine was widely
practised in ancient Assyria and Babylon; furthermore, herbs were
being used for all cosmetic purposes.

Much of the earliest recorded trading concerned medicinal herbs.
Places such as Arabia, towns such as Alexandria, important for
their value astride trade routes, became famous centres throughout
the chequered history of Man.

Herbs such as Myrrh, Cinnamon, Rhubarb and Cloves have been
used continuously since biblical times, and still heal the conditions
for which they were prescribed when Jesus walked the hills of
Galilee. Myrrh was one of the costly items carried on the ships of

Queen Hatsepsut (*c.* 1500 B.C.) when they returned from what is now the coast of Somalia.

Herbal medicine is the most reliable, the most tested and proven form of healing in the world. If the herbalist prescribes Calamus or Cinnamon for a patient it is comforting to know that they were used to cure the sick as long ago as the reign of Ptolemy II, and recorded as healing herbs then—2,200 years ago! Many conditions can be helped by massaging in some Olive Oil—as did the followers of Hippocrates in Athens during the time of Pericles—when the Parthenon rose to glorify her Hellenic magnificence.

Which of us would tell a lie about medicine to our children? Which of us would fail to take every precaution before passing on knowledge that held the key to life and death?

About 300 B.C. Theophrastus, the Greek philosopher, herbalist and scientist, called the *Father of Botany*, compiled his book which remained a great source of knowledge for many generations.

The herbalist Aretaeus of Cappadocia (*c.* A.D. 200) was the first to describe diabetes accurately.

The vastness of early knowledge on herbal medicine astounds us :

> '*How wise I was in infancy,*
> *I then saw in the clearest light*
> *But corrupt custom is a second night.*'
> Thomas Traherne (1634–74)

To understand how enormous herbal medicine is I cite the National Apple Register, compiled by Muriel Smith. It took 19 years to create, runs to 652 pages, names 6,000 varieties and has 22,000 entries in all—only for Apples found in Britain alone. The compositae family has over 10,000 species; grasses run to nearly 4,000 species.

If you think about it for a while you will soon realise that Mankind tends to change the names of very modern ideas, but rarely if ever alter simple and ancient names for things. For example, words such as Son, Daughter, Father, Mother, Goat, Sheep, and so on can be traced right back to the dawn of history, and their equivalents can be easily recognised without any special training through Greek back to Sanskrit! It is not surprising that plants such as Almonds, Basil, Cabbage, Cinnamon, Coriander, Elder, Fennel, Figs, Mint, Parsley, Sage, Thyme, etc., can be easily recognised when they occur in ancient manuscripts. An historic event was the work of Linnaeus, the great Swedish Botanist who founded the system of Latin international nomenclature (I visited his old home when last in Sweden). He used many of the common Latin names for plants—which had been in use for over 2,000 years—when he created the international classification, thus preserving them for all time.

Hippocrates (477–360 B.C.) was the 'Father of Medicine' but his writings were the codification of observations made from 500 to 900 years before his own time. Hardly a decade goes by without some new discovery being revealed to prove Hippocrates correct! The *Phrenosophical Medical Journal* (March 1966) kindly pointed out that the idea of using sheepskins to avoid bedsores was not an A.D. 1966 discovery but is mentioned in the extant works of Hippocrates (Loeb Edition).

The Greeks were too good at logic to have made the fatal and costly blunders that 'established' medical men made in the fourth and fifth decades of this twentieth century. *The part that allopathic doctors played in the frightful experiments in Nazi concentration camps is something no freedom-loving man dare forget (vide: 'The Death Doctors' by Mitscherlich).* Nor did the Greeks need animal-vivisection! I quote Hippocrates : 'In Medicine one must pay attention not to plausible theorising but to experience and reason together.'

By the time of Hippocrates treatment included dietetics, hydrocures and psychosomatic medicine. I quote Farrington : 'The Hippocratic doctor took into consideration the food a man ate, the kind of water he drank, the climate he lived in and the effect on him of Greek freedom or oriental despotism.' *Hippocrates taught men to treat the whole physical condition; to treat the whole personality not just a few symptoms; to examine not just the man on the sickbed but the life and habits of the man; above all, to treat for the latent capacity of the human body to heal itself.*

It has taken us nearly 2,000 years to get as far forward as Hippocrates in such matters.

Roman medicine revolves round three great figures. (i) Celsus (Floreat A.D. 14–37) 'De Medicina' (8 vols. see Loeb Edition), consisting mainly of translations from the Greek rather than original collations. (ii) Dioscorides (fl A.D. 55), a work on 'Materia Medica' detailing drugs and the plants from which to make them. The influence of Dioscorides is still noticeable in every pharmacopoeia today. (iii) Galen of Pergamum (A.D. 131–201). His surviving volumes astound us with their knowledge of herbs and biology.

In his monograph on Moslem Spain J. A. Lawrence refers to the Moors' development of botany and herbalism : 'Their botany books were beautifully illustrated, and some ran to 50 volumes.' Between the eighth and eleventh centuries the Moslems developed herbalism to a high degree. They introduced spices, camphor, rhubarb, nux vomica, liquorice, senna, myrrh and ginger. I quote Lawrence again : 'The Arabs produced the first scientific pharmacopoeia, and what is more they were the first people in Europe to use soap regularly; they initiated cotton underwear and handkerchiefs.' The Christian schools of medicine at Salerno and Montpelier were founded and first instructed by Arab doctors. Only in recent years have scholars revealed the lost magnificent botanical gardens of Moslem Spain, destroyed by the Christian conquerors.

In Germany the Abbess *Hildegard von Bingen* (fl. A.D. 1150) laboriously compiled her *Book of Healing Herbs* which comprised herbal medicine, the origin and treatment of disease, and natural history. Her descriptions of plants and of symptoms are very good.

Paracelsus, whose correct name was Theophrastus *von Hohen-heim*, lived A.D. 1493–1541 and contributed greatly to our knowledge of herbalism, carefully codifying plants according to their healing properties. He was a critical scientist at heart but never forgot the body-mind relationship in his discourses on healing.

In England the Royal College of Surgeons was founded *c.* 1460. In 1540 the barbers were amalgamated to the R.C.S. as one company.

In 1511 Henry VIII decreed : 'No person within the City of London, or within seven miles of the same, shall take upon him to exercise or occupy as a physician or surgeon except he first be examined by the Bishop of London, or by the Dean of St. Paul's, calling to him four doctors of physic, and for surgery other expert persons in that faculty.'

Further monopolistic extensions of this Act were made law in 1518, and 1523 and 1540. They resulted ·in such a persecution of herbalists that poor people could no longer afford any treatment at all, because as the physicians' power grew so did their fees.

By 1542–3 the scandalous state of affairs produced royal condemnation in the famous 'Act that persons, being no common surgeons, may administer outward medicines' (Henrici VIII Regis Cap. VIII).

'Be it ordained, established, and enacted, by Authority of this present Parliament, that at all time from henceforth it shall be lawful to every person being the King's subject, having knowledge and Experience of the Nature of Herbs, Roots and Waters, or of the Operation of the same, by Speculation or Practice, within any Part of the Realm of England, or within any other the King's Dominions, to practise, use, and minister in and to any outward Sore, Uncome Wound, Apostemations, Outward Swelling or Disease, any Herb or Herbs, Ointments, Baths, Pultess and Emplaisters, according to their Cunning, Experience and Knowledge in any of the Diseases, Sores and Maladies beforesaid, and all other like to the same, or Drinks for the Stone, Strangury, or Agues, without Suit, Vexation, Trouble, Penalty, or Loss of their Goods; the foresaid Statute in the 34th Year of the King's most gracious Reign, or any other Act, Ordinance, or Statutes to the contrary heretofore made in anywise, notwithstanding.'

This act not only refers to 'Outward' Medicines in its title but to 'inward' treatment by the words : 'Drinks for the Stone, Strangury or Agues', etc. It is known as the *Herbalists' Charter*.

The most prominent figure in Herbalism in England was Nicholas Culpeper (1616–54), his *Complete Herbal* (first published 1652) has been a source of knowledge for over 300 years now. I first read it when I was about 15; many times before I was 25 I had myself proved how very effective herbs were in restoring health. Many have criticised Culpeper because he included much astrological lore with his herbal *materia medica*; two points however are very significant: (i) Most of Culpeper's prescribed cures work effectively. (ii) Culpeper's herbal helped countless poor families to survive disease. In view of which it is puerile to criticise him on grounds which we have neither disproved or proved.

Samuel Hahnemann (1755–1843) wrote in 1810 his *Organon der nationellen Heilkunde* which founded Homoepathy. Unlike the subsequent 'non-poisonous' herbalism (shortly to develop in New Hampshire, U.S.A.), homoeopathy permits some use of certain poisonous substances—albeit in extremely minute quantities (when they are, it is claimed, non-toxic in effect). This system also uses non-botanical substances and is outside my terms of reference.

The great medical reformer Samuel Thomson (1769–1843) is the real father of Herbalism as we know it today. As a child he began to learn to identify plants and their uses from an old lady in his district; by the time he was 30 he had gained a reputation by virtue of his herbal cures.

He was the initiator of 'Non-Toxic Herbalism', in which plants of any toxic tendency are excluded from therapeutical treatment.

Thomson was the first to attack allopathic medicine and show it up as a sham; he was bitterly hounded and persecuted (the doctors bribed the New Hampshire Legislature to pass a bill especially against him—by name forbidding him to heal people for nothing). Thomson triumphed mightily, for his denigrators have sunk into the oblivion that is their due, while Thomson is honoured and revered.

Dr. A. I. Coffin (1798–1866) brought the Thomson non-toxic herbalism to England. By his healing, his lecturing and his writing he did much to revive scientific herbalism which under ruthless persecution by the clique of allopathic doctors had suffered a decline.

Concurrently, Samuel Westcott Tilke (b. 1794), was prevailed upon by Lords Howden and Seymour to give up his successful business and devote himself to healing the sick, which he accomplished with phenomenal success—his earnings reached £3,000 per annum, which in the mid-nineteenth century was a fabulous figure! His books *Family Medical Adviser* and *Autobiography* reveal a profound understanding of disease and its cure. He gave very freely of his services to the poor.

Tilke was on good terms with the leading doctors of his day; he was accepted as a serious scientist and his exceptional cures (and titled clientele) could not be ignored. It is the only recorded occasion when the herbalist has received outside recognition from those who were anxious to share his knowledge. Tilke introduced hot medicated baths and vapour baths; the ancients also used baths with herbal essences.

In Germany Vincent Priessnitz (1799–1851), of Graefenberg, was introducing cold-water cures and shower-baths. He was followed in his work by the priest Sebastian Kneipp (1821–97) who so developed the hydropathic cure that hundreds of 'Kneipp' style institutes exist throughout Europe. Even before Kneipp died about 20,000 people a year were being treated.

Friedrich Ludwig Jahn (1778–1852) had started the enthusiasm for bodily exercise in 1810 (and from free-exercises to apparatus); his was a direct contribution to natural health.

Returning to the more familiar World of England and America we see a great upsurge of enthusiasm for herbal medicine. In 1893 the British Board of Trade granted a certificate for the 'General Council of Safe Medicine' which followed the Thomsonian tradition. About the same time there was a 'People's League of Medical Freedom' which fought off the many encroachments of the increasingly jealous allopathic medical profession.

The number of institutes teaching herbal medicine increased on both sides of the Atlantic, but there were two general directions: one retaining the individual freedom which herbalists have cherished for so long; the other tending to become restrictive and exclusive in imitation of the allopath clique.

In the long-term aspect the 'free' herbalist is the most likely to survive; there is no sure way of cutting off supplies of products which cover the earth, his costs are minimal, and his greatest problem—diagnosis—can be solved by a careful study of government approved textbooks.

> '*The Sweet fields do lie forgot*
> *Where willing Nature does to all all dispense*
> *A wild and fragrant innocence.*'
> Andrew Marvell (1621–78)

ECOLOGY AND ALTERNATIVES

Within one or two decades many beautiful country herbs have become extremely rare, e.g. Lady's Slipper Orchid. The cause is the unrivalled ignorance of those circles who wrongly claim that to produce more wheat you must destroy every other plant that grows in a wheat field, and liquidate every insect and animal found near the field.

The great American Luther Burbank demonstrated that if one grew roses in a wheat field you got better wheat and better roses. It is incredible that his research was not followed up nor better understood. The ancient Chinese collected nests of predacious ants and placed them on valuable citrus fruit trees. The importing of Mynahs from India to Mauritius in the mid-eighteenth century stopped the spread of locusts—upon which those birds feed. The great German scientist Albrecht Köbel saved the big Californian orchards from total disaster when in 1880 he took ladybirds to breed there and feed upon the insects which destroyed citrus fruits (cotton cushion scales). The Australians used the *Cactoblastis* moths to rid their lands of the prickly pear parasitic plants. None of these biological methods of control upsets the balance of Nature. Because these simple and extremely cheap methods have been displaced by slick and often misleading advertising, farmers and horticulturists have been tricked into using lethal chemicals and hormone distortants. The well-known journalist Cassandra wrote in the *Daily Mirror* of London (October, 1966): 'Nothing can live under the fearful blight of these pesticides that not only scorch and destroy all vegetation but affect every living bird, animal or insect with which they come in contact.'

Before my time no farmer or gardener ever had to wear rubber gloves, a face shield, protective clothing and special boots such as are worn by the workers who now spray chemical pesticides and herbicides over the land. If such materials are *harmless* why must workers not touch their mouths or skin until they remove the protective clothing? Many such products have had an untold effect upon bees, birds and wild animals. What happens to the nervous systems of those who eat food grown in such fields? Well, medical sources reveal that anybody who gets one of the bipyridyls *on his skin* is likely to experience blurred vision, mental disturbances, difficulty in breathing, vertigo, head pains, stomach cramps and uncontrollable spasms of muscles, particularly of the face. I suggest that when the herbs die (don't call them weeds) Man may well be nearing extinction himself—for these lowly and simple plants are so rich in nutritional elements that the soil will starve without them.

This view is corroborated by Professor Barry Commoner of Washington University who warned the world, way back in 1968, of an impending BIOLOGICAL CATACLYSM. Facts which support such a claim come from baby foods containing simple healthy spinach; there was only one thing wrong; the plant contained 40 milligrams of nitrate—four times the amount any baby could tolerate and live through! Producing more food helps no one if the food is no good. That the world is using more than 20 times the amount of artificial fertilisers and sprays that were used 15 years ago explains the death of lakes such as Erie—whose 9,930 square miles have become a dead mass of refuse, sewage and chemical wastes. Neither fish nor children dare swim there! Some chemicals facilitate the development of toxic bluish algae, such as at Storm Lake, Iowa, where in one year over 8,000 birds and animals perished miserably because of Man's greed and ignorance. Such is the alternative to simple herbal medicines and the natural biological, ecological approach to Man's problems. The result of applying man-made chemicals to our plant cultivation is more readily recognised than is the menace of man-made medicines to our bodies.

Our basic fault is the total unwillingness of some graduates to believe that anybody without a university education is capable of intelligent thought and observation. This is why some of the ecological progress is being made by countries which we have neglected—in Romania they accepted the countrymen's observation that pelicans feed only on unhealthy fish, and bred these birds to clean up their fisheries—with excellent results. When fishermen say that seals kill off the fish we must ask whether any seal can catch a healthy fish so easily as an ailing one? Scientists and lay public alike have been making decisions on *evidence* which would never pass in any court of law. The popular concept of nutrition is founded more upon sheer bulk than upon the quality of mineral salt and vitamin properties contained in food. When we talk of feeding the starving millions of the world we should get our facts right. When are we going to investigate fully whether a field of millet will feed more people better than one of wheat? In northern climes we often go to endless trouble to cultivate wheat when rye would serve better—and feed better. We must question the wisdom of scientists who created a man-made disease to destroy millions of rabbits (good quality protein meat) so that wheat farmers could fatten their purses if not our bellies. Cereals are primarily carbohydrate goods (incomplete foods) but rabbits' meat provides protein which the body can convert to carbohydrate when the protein needs have been fulfilled. The body cannot convert surplus carbohydrate into protein—the chemistry works only one way.

We eat too many soft and sweet foods so our teeth get bad. The logical answer is to modify the diet and take precautions as to how we clean our mouth, massage our gums etc. Instead we add sodium fluoride to water. In Britain one part per million is added as a rule—Professor Taylor of the Clayton Foundation, Texas, reported that this amount shortened the life-span of test animals by nearly 10%. Two scientists at the Churchill Laboratory, Oxford, reported that one part sodium in 10,000,000 killed human cells! Professor Steyn of Pretoria has stated that sodium fluoride can lead to malformation and, indeed, deformation of children in the mother's womb. Herbal medicines are safer—they always have been.

Health is a positive condition in which all the body works harmoniously; one wants to run and jump for joy. Once it was sought from the meadows and brooksides on sunny summer walks; now it is hunted in lifeless laboratories as we *'tread the narrow way, by tophet flare to judgement day'* by way of thalidomide cripples to a dying planet. In the immortal words of H. D. Thoreau (1817–62):

> *'Our Icarian thoughts returned to the ground*
> *And we went to Heaven the long way round.'*

The alternatives to botanic medicine represent a menace and a threat to Mankind's further existence on this planet. In Britain and other countries hospital doctors may authorise *experimental* work on patients. New man-made drugs are having terrible side-effects. In 1967 Dr. Jurand of Edinburgh University showed that mothers given cortisone treatment can produce abnormal babies—robbed for ever of a normal life before they enter this world.

In place of the experience of 5,000 years of continuing oral and written traditions allopathic medicine offers us trial and error. In Britain alone 5,580,876 experiments were performed upon helpless animals, most of them without anaesthetic, during 1970. Apart from the immorality of this system the results hardly justify it, especially when men such as Prof. Dr. Aygün of the University of Ankara has demonstrated that cell tissue and organ cultures may be used in medical research far more effectively than any other method.

One peculiar known characteristic of bacteria is that *they are harmful only in certain conditions*; should the conditions change they can just as suddenly cease to be dangerous. In the same way the growth and condition of plants relates to the condition of the soil in which they exist—as any gardener may easily discover for himself.

Deficient soil means deficient plants (and animals) for our diet, which in turn means deficiencies in human foodstuffs, and shortages of mineral salts. The work of Dr. Schüssler, founder of the Bio-chemic school of healing, is not so far removed from herbal medicine : he emphasised the structure, nourishment and life-rhythm of human cells and related these facts to the twelve established mineral salt combinations he discovered in human blood.

Every organic substance has ideal environment, without which it withers or fades 'like the damask rose you see' as Elgar's song reminds us. While research now centres on how to kill germs from without by alien substances,. only herbal medicine has developed along its traditional path of strengthening the body up to Restore its own natural forces and vigour. A much more logical approach ! Dr. D. C. Jarvis of Vermont, U.S.A., emphasised the facility with which germs multiply when the body provides alkaline comfort, and shows how acid conditions make unfavourable media for most bacteria—hence the popularity of Apple-Cider vinegar, a by-product of herbal medicine, very rich in mineral salts and nutrients.

Although State-protected and subsidised medicine costs British taxpayers some £2,000,000,000 yearly, a growing number of people prefer to pay for their herbs (when they cannot get them from the fields themselves) as well as paying the taxes because the herbal medicines are safer and without side-effects. As Anne Boleyn wrote to Henry VIII : *'Yea, let me receive an open trial, for my Truth shall fear no shame.'*

2. *Some Commonly Used Herbs*

AGRIMONY *Agrimonia eupatoria*

Sacred to Jupiter whose name derived from the Sanskrit 'Dyaus Pitar' meaning Father of Heaven. It is said to be governed by the zodiac sign of Cancer, its name comes from the Greek Argemone, probably with reference to the silver colour of its leaves. It was a charm used to ward off snakes, the old English name was Stickle-wort, hence :

> *'He that hath sticklewort by*
> *Knows no snake shall draw him nigh.'*

Ancient Greek physicians used it against cataract of the eye. I have found it helpful against liver disorders, especially jaundice; it can also be useful to combat bronchitic complaints.

ALDER *Alnus glutinosa*

I was rather pleased to note that Hampstead Heath has still plenty of alder trees, just as Culpeper recorded three centuries ago. It is a tree which has a gloomy history in many sagas and stories, not least in Goethe's *Erlkönig* describing the Alder-king with his terrible daughters, waiting to snatch up innocent children—the music written by Schubert for the poem is very chilling. The old Saxon word was Eller and this resembles the word Erle more closely. It has always been associated with the planet Venus, but is governed by Cancer. I recommend the user to keep it FOR EXTERNAL USE ONLY, applying the bruised or moistened leaves directly to any burn.

> *'If thy handmaid hath a burn*
> *'Tis to alder she should turn.'*

Older works insist that a tea made from alder leaves can be effectual against dropsy, but warn of severe vomiting which often follows such treatment. Once used by witches to induce trances.

ALEHOOF *Nepeta hederacea*

It is said to take its name from the Tuscan town of Nepete which had some prominence in Roman times. The herb is held sacred to Venus, the goddess of love identified with the Greek Aphrodite; after the Punic wars a cult worshipping Venus-verticordia (turner of human hearts) became popular. April was considered a month sacred to her. The juice can be used to wash out the ears. As a tea it is a pleasant cordial which can clean the liver.

ALEXANDER *Smyrnium olusatrum*

The scraped and washed stems were considered a great delicacy and eaten just like celery stems. The plant was sacred to Jupiter. It has warming properties. The name comes from Alexander the Great who was born 356 B.C. This exceptional genius was taught by Aristotle (one of the greatest intellects of all times) and as a soldier he conquered the then known world by audacity, strategy and strength, reaching the Indian Ocean about 326 B.C. The influence of the Greeks on Indian sculpture is clearly noticed. His conquest brought Greek ideals of freedom to many of the peoples whose kings were defeated by the young general. Before him they had known no hope but slavery. It is little wonder that this plant, named after him, is called 'Defender of Man', its use goes back directly to the time when he was alive on earth.

ANEMONE *Anemone nemorosa*

The Greek word 'Anemos' meant the Wind, and as such the plant is oft called Windflower in old herbals and by old poets. Pliny tells us that this flower never opens its buds when the wind blows. Adonis was a youth beloved by the goddess Aphrodite. He was killed by a wild boar while out hunting and the flower sprang out of the ground from his blood—at the command of Aphrodite. Arthur Findlay in his 'Psychic Stream' reminds us that this was not just another beautiful love story but that Adonis was Adonis Tammuz, one of the saviour gods of the ancient world, and as 'Tammuz' he was mentioned in the Bible (Ezekiel 8, xiv). The word may be translated as meaning Occult or Hidden. A medieval legend says that the plant turned red with the blood of Jesus dripping down from the cross. In classical times it was held sacred to Mars.

The layman had better keep this herb FOR EXTERNAL USE ONLY and will find it helpful to make it like a tea but to use that liquid for washing ulcers, sores, etc., or as an effective eye-lotion.

APPLE *Pyrus malus*

Adam's apple was probably not an apple at all, in Greek the name is 'To karuthi tou Adam' which means Adam's walnut; other sources claim it was the quince, but there is no need to change the English language for all that. I found this fruit the source of many myths and legends, such as this :

> *'If sun do shine on Christmas day*
> *Full crop o' apples come thy way.'*

For every apple you eat in a neighbour's house one day of good luck shall follow; so never refuse the invitation.

The legend that Newton observed the Law of Gravity after an apple fell on his head was related first by his niece, and it seems well authenticated. In Rome the apple was sacred to the goddess Pomona, patroness of all fruit. In the Norse legend Idhunn kept the apples of eternal youth in a box for the sole use of the gods, but Loki the evil one tricked her and Thjazi the eagle got the apples; Idhunn was changed into a nut, and eventually Thjazi was burnt to death by the gods. The Saxon word was Aepl and they believed that :

> 'Bonfires lit on midsummer night
> Shall fill the apple lofts up tight.'

Rub half an apple over a wart and then burn the half apple, said a famous witch recipe for warts.

If a maiden can peel an apple without breaking the skin into pieces she has only to turn round three times and throw the parings over her left shoulder; as it falls on the ground it will fall into pieces and form the initials of the man she'll marry. Pliny listed over 20 different sorts of apples; now we have identified about 6,000. Eris, goddess of discord, threw an apple into a crowd of the gods, saying it was the prize for the beautiful goddess there. Minerva, Juno and Venus hotly disputed who should have it. The simple and beautiful shepherd Paris was deputed to decide which of them was the most lovely. Each offered him bribes, but Venus offered him the most beautiful woman on earth for his bride, so he awarded her the prize. He later eloped with Helen of Troy (whose face launched a thousand ships) and thus started the Trojan war.

The apple which Wilhelm Tell shot off his son's head started the Swiss war of independence. A statue to Tell stands in the market-place of Altdorf today. The golden apples which Atalanta stooped to pick up, thus losing the race, were probably not apples at all. The apple is extremely rich in mineral salts, and eating apples benefits the gums and seems to break up gravel in the bladder, etc.

ASH *Fraxinus excelsior*

As Yggdrasil, the World Tree, the steed of Odin, it occupied an all-important place in Norse and Germanic mythology. Hanging on this, pinned by his spear, Odin received his enlightenment. The ash draws down lightning. Vipers are supposed to be terrified of ash leaves or ash keys. The keys were once pickled in the same way as walnuts. The ash has exceptional germ-killing qualities, and there is some connection probably between the herbal tradition and the custom of hanging a bunch of ash keys over a baby's cradle or cot to ward off evil. Many countrymen carried a walking stick of ash to keep snakes away. When Mary was brought to labour in the stable of Bethlehem the only fire Joseph could make was with the wood of the ash, and therefore it is bad luck to burn it on Christmas Eve.

Man, said the Germanic myth, was created by the gods who carved him from the wood of an ash tree. The branches of Yggdrasil covered the entire universe, one of its roots reached through to the Aesir (the gods); another reached to the Jötunn (the giants) the source of evil; the third root reached down to Nifleheim (the underworld); the Norns (the Fates—Past, Present and Future) cared for the roots of Yggdrasil; of these Urdhr—the Present—sat at her fountain where all men were judged after death and provided Yggdrasil with sacred water from her fountain. When the Twilight of the Gods—known as Ragnarök—takes place and Heaven and Earth pass away, the new race of men to come shall emerge from a sacred ash grove Hoddmimir which shall be untouched, and Lif and Lifthrasr the founders of the new race are protected by the ash. The Ragnarök may relate to the Velikovsky theory of the capture of a second moon. In most legends of prehistoric date reference is made to a world-shaking cataclysm and flood. The ash was held to be governed by the Sun.

ASPEN *Populus tremula*
The legend that the aspen trembles before every storm comes from the crucifixion when, because the cross was made of aspen, it trembled when Jesus was nailed to it. A similar legend says that because the aspen failed to bow its head to Christ it must tremble for evermore. The powdered inner bark was considered a specific against worms, it is very strong and half the usual dose is enough.

ASTER *Aster acris*
This is not taken internally but was often carried as a charm against snakes, in fact there is some indication that snakes don't like the plants. Traditionally the aster is sacred to Venus.

BARLEY *Hordeum vulgare*
One of the plants most mentioned by Robert Burns, its juice is rich in vitamin B. It is very relaxing and good for the nerves. It was sacred to Saturn, whose festival—the Saturnalia—was the origin of the celebration of Christmas during December when all the traditions pointed to Jesus being born either in April or October. Saturn was the founder of civilisation and social order, his temple was on the Capitoline Hill: He was sometimes identified with Chronos.

BASIL *Ocymum basilicum*
Governed by Mars, influenced by Scorpio. Indeed, some old practitioners of black magic taught that they could create scorpions by crushing basil between two stones and reciting a spell. Some followers of white magic employ basil for its influence and aroma. It is said to be able to resist electricity but this is not proven as yet. The Brahmans held it as a sacred plant which brought both spiritual and physical protection to the wearer.

In Boccaccio's *Decamerone* there is one story of Isabella watering with her tender tears the basil which grew above the head of her murdered lover.

Mixed with a little sage it makes an enjoyable, refreshing drink;

Basil

don't use too much basil, it is very sweet indeed. Fresh basil juice can be placed on wasp stings. As a drink it cleans out the intestines and relieves flatulence.

BAY *Laurus nobilis*

The plant falls under Leo and is governed by the Sun. It is said to guarantee safe and pleasant dreams if a leaf or two are placed under the pillow. During severe thunderstorms many Roman emperors wore chaplets of bay to protect them from harm.

A girl who wants to see the face of the man she will marry must put bay leaves under her pillow on the 14th February and recite:

> *'Saint Valentine be kind to me*
> *This night may I my true love see.'*

This is the true laurel which was placed on victors' brows, and which was sacred to Apollo. The legend is as follows:—Apollo was enamoured by Daphne, the daughter of the river god Peneus, and when she found she was hotly pursued by the excited Apollo she prayed for escape and was changed into a bay (*Laurus Nobilis*), so that the poet Waller wrote: 'He caught at love and filled his arms with bays.' From that time on the bay tree became sacred to Apollo.

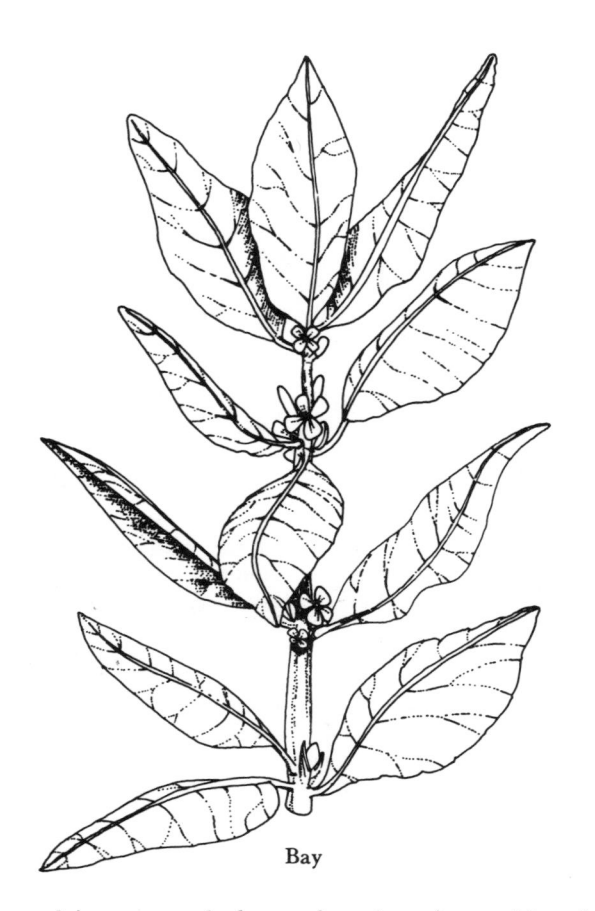

Bay

The wood is very rarely burnt, but there is an old saying I got from my grandparents :

> 'If you hear fire crack loud with bay
> Much kindness soon shall come your way.'

The leaves can be put one or two at a time in wine, or some tea; they are very aromatic and very strong. They increase the flow of urine, and are slightly astringent.

BEECH *Fagus sylvatica*

Under Saturn. Winners of the Pythian games were crowned with beech leaves. The tree is known as 'Mother of the Forests', it is extremely beautiful, especially in Spring and Autumn, it often reaches 100 feet or more in height, and 20 feet in sheer girth; it can grow in extremely poor soil, often thriving on a crag where no other tree could survive. It likes a lime soil and can exist with widely distributed but very shallow roots.

The nuts have been found very nourishing by grazing animals, and the Anglo-Saxons fattened their pigs on them. From the leaves or the nuts useful cleansing and cooling lotions can be brewed.

BIRCH *Betula alba*

In most of the northern lands it is held efficacious against evil spirits and witchcraft. Its medicinal uses are better known in Scandinavia than in more southerly countries.

In the famous Finnish *Kalevala*, the epic poem assessed as 3,000 years old, the birch tree is frequently referred to in many senses. The Finns always regarded the Lapps in the North as workers of magic and mystery; it is reputed that the last known Lapp shaman died only about 1905.

> 'Siitä vanha Väinämöinen
> Ajoa karittelevi
> Pimeästä Pohjolasta
> Summasta Sariolasta.'

Some sensitive musicians have found the *Kalevala*-inspired music of Sibelius very eerie, one eminent violinist declared he couldn't remain alone in the room when *Tapiola* was played.

A tea can be made using only half a dozen leaves or so; it is helpful for many feverish conditions, strongly astringent, and makes a good skin lotion.

Some forms of rheumatic ailments benefit from the drinking of birchleaf tea. Many poets have written charmingly about it. To see the birch growing in Springtime reminds me of Walt Whitman's line : 'No man has ever yet been half devout enough'.

BLACKBERRY *Rubus fruticosus*

I remember my grandmother singing a song at parties :

> 'It's a starry night for a ramble
> Among the woods and dells,
> Over the bushes and brambles,
> To kiss and never tell.'

The Anglo-Saxon word was Bremel, and most of the older herbals speak of the bramble. We must remember that when the university scholars came to influence the people and language of England most of them were so dominated by Latinity and Greek thought that nothing Saxon was good enough for them, and they introduced many new words to cover up their own ignorance of their mother tongue. The bramble had value in forecasting a good harvest :

> 'If the bramble bloom in June
> Harvest bounty follows soon.'

(I had better add that follows was always pronounced 'follers').

CHICORY

The leaves are often eaten with salads.

The plant is under the sign of Aries but held to be subject to influence by Venus. Walt Whitman in his 'Leaves of Grass' said : 'The running blackberry would adorn the parlours of heaven'; when seen in full blossom it is a very beautiful plant.

Some legends say that witches feared the brambles but the reason for this is not clear.

The fruit is very nourishing and rich in mineral salts, it has been used for anaemic cases with some success. The unripe berries were said to be a witch cure against snake bite.

BLACKTHORN *Prunus spinosa*

Have you ever heard the adage :

> *'Plight your troth by a blackthorn tree*
> *Happy ye twain shall ever be.'*

The word 'twain' is the masculine form of 'two' which is a survival from the neuter form of the number in Anglo-Saxon. Chaucer mentions this tree and its fruits. Nowadays many people still make sloe gin from the fruits. In the time of my grandparents the fruits were *roasted* and then eaten. Gypsies often had their walking sticks made of the blackthorn to ward off evil from their path.

Many people in Britain know to their cost the terrible winter that the 'Ice Saints' bring, their dread names were Mamertus, Pancras (the child martyr, to whom a small Norman chapel stands north of the London railway terminus bearing his name), Servatius and Boniface; their holy days fall between the first and third weeks of May, and too frequently these days show a bitterly cold return of winter that the blackthorn is said to pressage :

> *'If 't be warm when blackthorn flowers*
> *In May come winds and long, cold showers.'*

Many legends say that cold winds blow when the blackthorn blooms; this, of course, reminds us that Tolstoy told how the Russian peasants believed that the Spring winds were cold *because* the acorns came in bud on the oaks.

The blackthorn is said to be governed by Saturn. The fruit, known as *bullies* in some parts of England, was used by wise women to fasten loose teeth in the head.

BOX *Buxus sempervirens*

This was long held to be a living symbol of the resurrection of Christ; it flourishes as a proper tree best in Surrey, Kent, and Buckinghamshire. Elsewhere it seldom attains full height. Its wood is popular with wood carvers and engravers because of its fine grain and hardness. The nautical and mathematical instruments of Nelson's time were usually made from the box tree. The word 'box' in the English language, according to Professor Skeat, comes from the tree and at first boxes were made only from this—just as chairs were usually made from beech, and arrows from ash or willow. The word still retains its original Saxon spelling. I found only one reference which indicated that it was avoided by witches.

BURDOCK *Arctium lappa*

In the north of England a mixture of dandelion and burdock is still a popular drink, used as a blood purifier and tonic, and one with a very pleasant taste.

Wise women used to put burdock leaves on the head of a mother to prevent a miscarriage, or put them at her feet to draw down a child out of the womb.

A witch cure for burns was to crush burdock leaves until the juice ran, then apply this mixed with white of egg—and suitable incantations, to heal burns.

Concerning witchcraft incantations I noted with considerable interest that at the turn of the century the exact words of a very ancient charm to magic warts away were : 'Orpra nobs' repeated three times. This is very clearly ORA PRO NOBIS, the common Latin prayer to the saints from the days of Catholic England. The men and women of the towns always seemed to think that their country cousins, being so simple (?) believed and accepted everything that they were told and were far too stupid to hold their own opinions in secret. The research work of Thor Heyerdahl (*Aku Aku*) and Francis Mazière (*Fantastique Ile de Paques*) on Easter Island show that a primitive people may keep the secrets of their ancestors inviolate from prying eyes and scientists for centuries and decades; Mazière produced legends which confirmed the Greek story of the Titans; and suggested that the first inhabitants of the mysterious island had mastered the control of anti-gravity, of telekinesis and radiesthesia ! Some of the legends of Easter Island mention space travel quite casually, and refer to the inhabitants of the planets we call Jupiter and Venus.

The herb burdock is governed by Venus. The tea is cleansing and often used to relieve stone in the bladder or kidneys.

BUTTERCUP *Ranunculus bulbosus*

Many traditions insist that it is lucky to see buttercups flowering. Many of the *Ranunculus* family are poisonous and this is one reason for the story that it is unlucky to pick them : the Latin word means 'Little Frogs' because many types are found in watery meadows or near streams—near frogs; once upon a time farmers liked to see buttercups growing in their meadows because some of the buttercups were said to give a deeper colour yellow to the cream and butter. Most of the *Ranunculus* family are rich in nectar and as such popular with bees. They are said to be under the influence of the Sun or Mars.

Many old ladies made a bit of money by claiming to charm the creams or butter, knowing that the cows were feeding on buttercups and would produce a good yellow colour.

Chamomile

CHAMOMILE *Anthemis nobilis*

This herb has been in use since the civilisation of Ancient Egypt where the priests devoted to healing used it in the 'House of Life' where sick patients were sent to be restored to life abundant; there was usually such a building attached to the major temples. It was even then considered a plant sacred to the Sun. It is very calmative and good for many women's complaints. In my book 'Herbal Teas for Health and Pleasure' I recommended this herb for nervous disorders.

It has been long valued for its use in lightening fair hair, many modern shampoos still contain chamomile flowers.

The ancient Romans used it widely; modern Italians use it perhaps even more so.

CAMPHOR *Camphora officinarum*

This plant seems to have originated in what is now called Viet Nam, and Chinese records show that it was imported into China for use in the temples. The wood was also valued for building because it retained the strong perfume for which the products of the plant are known. Leaves from the plant were used to crown the brows of heroes and champions, it was considered a plant sacred to the gods, but so many are named that it does not seem to be specific to any one in particular. Formosa is now one of the most valuable sources of pure camphor. It is applied externally more than internally, and has been known to restore victims of very bad heart attacks to health, and furthermore to improve the breathing of patients with congested lungs or bad respiratory conditions. There are other products which pass as camphor, but the lack of the strong scent betrays them as far from the genuine article. It has the peculiar property of being able to deflect vibrations for most radiesthetic diagnosis, and is usually kept away from any instruments or pendulum activity.

It is sometimes used as an antispasmodic agent.

CANTERBURY BELL *Campanula medium*

Although this plant was once considered to be sacred to St. Augustine, who brought the Roman form of Christianity to Britain (as opposed to the existing Celtic form), the name is said to have some links with the unfortunate St. Thomas of Canterbury who was murdered in the cathedral at the command of Henry II. Thomas à Becket (1118–1170) was essentially a statesman first and a cleric second, as many of his contemporaries were. His efficiency as a statesman influenced the King to appoint him to the see of Canterbury, but his character underwent a significant change when he took on the power of his new office. In 1170 the breach between the court and the church was so wide that the prelate was murdered. Two years later the King had done public penance and the popular prelate had been canonised by the Pope. Almost instantly pilgrimages were started, such as the one which Chaucer describes, and many references were made to Becket and Canterbury. It is said to be very lucky to see Canterbury Bells, but unlucky to pluck them. There is one more problem, there is some indication that the original plant bearing this name was the humble *Campanula trachelium*, now called 'Nettle-leaved Bellflower'; the present plant so designated (*Camp. medium*) seems to have been imported first into this country in 1597.

Neither of these plants is recommended for use in medicine now.

CARAWAY *Carum carui*

A plant subject to Mercury and one prized in ancient days. It is most helpful in many digestive complaints and is frequently given to small children with stomach troubles. It is a useful addition to a plain cake. Some hepatic conditions are alleviated by a regular course of a drink made from caraway.

CARNATION *Dianthus caryophyllus*

An old tradition says that these pleasant flowers were formed by the tears that fell from the Virgin Mary as she stood at Golgotha watching the crucifixion. In my youth, I remember I came unexpectedly on an entire field of red carnations as I descended from the high Apennines to the coast. I do not know which shocked me most—the broad slash of blood red on the landscape or the mighty power of their perfume in the hot sunshine of Italy, but it remains one of the unforgettable scenes of my life. The flowers signify fascination, especially the power of a woman to attract a man; for a woman to throw a man a carnation is to invite him to her bed, hence the madness which *Carmen* excited in Don Jose in the Bizet opera of that name, based upon the marvellous story by Prosper Mérimée (1803–70), one of the greatest short story tellers of all times. He wrote this tale in 1846 and it is full of potent atmosphere and tension.

The carnation is not suitable for medicinal use but is very popular in perfumes. Wise women of Italy and Spain sometimes used the flowers in love potions. The carnation is universally regarded as a symbol of, and bringer of, good luck and happiness.

CEDAR *Cedrus libani*

Even in England this stately tree can attain 100 feet in good conditions. The name has remained unchanged from its original Semitic root word which signifies 'power' or 'strength'. The oil from the cones is very useful for application during massage to rheumatic joints. The tree is clearly mentioned in the Gilgamesh Epic which goes back long before the only known version which is a mere 4,000 years old (*c.* 2000 B.C.). From the ruins of Ashurbanipal's palace the archaeologists brought clay tablets in Akkadian, written in cuneiform script (with the sharp and blunt ends of a reed while the clay is still wet; after writing the tablet was baked). In a simple four beat rhythm the epic reveals man's quest for immortality and it is one of the earliest esoteric poems of the world; the hero Gilgamesh seeks a spiritually enlightened being called Etnapishti who knows the secrets by which a man may achieve whole enlightenment and join the glorious who sit in the presence of the Divine. The familiar flood story is given in book eleven of the series. In the Old Testament the cedar is specifically treasured for building purposes; as far as we know today the wood tends to warp badly, and will often shrink—even in the Middle East, so it is no longer popular for massive construction, but rather for small boxes, ornamental use, etc. It is symbolic of undying faith.

CELANDINE *Chelidonium majus/minus*

These are often passed over as buttercups (q.v.) but strictly speaking, although similar, they are not identical. The celandines were a favourite flower of Wordsworth. The *Majus* is under the influence of the Sun, but the *Minus* is under Mars.

The botanic name means 'swallow' and the plants were said not to bloom until the swallow comes. The gypsies used to put this herb (the *Majus*) in their shoes and keep it there when they walked, they claimed that it kept the feet fresh and one old herbal suggests that this was a remedy against jaundice; in view of the new therapeutical theory of Dr. Fitzgerald concerning *Zone Therapy* (which maintains that every part of the human body has a corresponding pressure point on one of the feet) the gypsy remedy may be wiser than we think. George Borrow was one of the first to show the connection of the gypsies' language with Sanskrit (they are the last of the wandering nomad Aryans and have absolutely nothing to do with Egypt). Their original home lies close to China and Tibet whence the system of acupuncture was evolved.

Modern Botanic Medicine sometimes uses the *Chelidonium Majus* in a drink to relieve jaundice and allied liver conditions. As it is very powerful I recommend that it be kept FOR EXTERNAL APPLICATION ONLY. All herbs contain mineral salts and certain chemical combinations which the body can frequently absorb through the skin. If, for example, your body has an iodine deficiency and you paint iodine on your hand or leg the colour and odour go within a few hours but the part so painted feels considerable relief.

The herb was used in magic but chiefly to effect healing as above.

CENTAURY *Erythrea centaurium*

Sacred to the Sun. It is mentioned by the poet Ovid (43 B.C.–A.D. 17), a lawyer who devoted his later years to writing of poetry. Unfortunately he seems to have intrigued at the court of Augustus with the emperor's grand-daughter Julia (banished in the same year) and was sent into exile to Tomi, a forsaken township on the delta of the Danube. His *Metamorphoses* is a marvellous, poetic recital of ancient Greek legends etc. Among these is the tale of Chiron the Centaur, the wisest and greatest of all his race (the Centaurs were probably the horse-breakers of the Thrakian plains) : Chiron had been taught by Apollo and Artemis and knew all the arts of healing save how to heal himself from the poisoned arrow of Hercules that finally killed him. Before he died he taught mankind to use the plant that is still named after him (see the botanic name above). It has tonic properties but is slightly acrid to taste; several hepatic disorders can be relieved by taking the tea made of it. Wise women called upon to rid some village child of worms would frequently administer the drink made from the leaves as a magic potion, recite their piece and collect their fee. It usually worked very well as an anthelmintic. In my researches I have been rather surprised to find how many of the magic potions prescribed by masters of the black arts were little more than simple herbal preparations which seem to work as well without any psychological persuasion. However, from the angle of psychological study I must admit that there are many patients who insist upon an atmosphere before they 'let themselves be cured' !

CHESTNUT *Castanea sativa*

This delightful tree is regarded as the domain of Jupiter. The nuts of this tree are edible, those of the horse chestnut are not, but then in spite of its English name that belongs to a totally different family—*Aesculus Hippocastanum.* Returning to the true chestnut tree :

> *'Maidens name your chestnuts true*
> *The first to burst belongs to you.'*

The custom was for a girl to name each of the eligible bachelors of the village (or county if she were ambitious) and put the nut which represented him on the fire (unfortunately she was supposed to put all the named nuts on the fire at the same time) then she had only to remember which carried which name, and when it burst open she would know that the man was bursting with love for her !

The nuts could at one time have been regarded as a virility symbol :

> *'He that would ha' manly blood*
> *Leaves not chestnuts i' the mud.'*

Like the prophecies of Nostrademus, it is so vague in the original that it begs for some interpretation.

The chestnut was sometimes used in gypsy veterinary recipes, but as the nuts are constipating if taken in large quantities there is some need for caution in prescribing it in any medicinal work. The powdered, roasted nut was frequently given to cure pulmonary and bronchitic ailments.

CINNAMON *Cinnamomum*

It was sometimes included in Eastern love-potions. The fabled Phoenix was reputed to make its nest in a palm tree and collect cinnamon, myrrh and spikenard for the magic fire in which it would immolate itself in order to be reborn.

It is one of the finest antiseptics in the world, and can be used in cooking quite freely, especially in recipes for invalids. A drink made of cinnamon, lemon juice and honey is an excellent remedy for most colds and catarrhal conditions; I have included several suggestions for its use in my work 'Herbs for Cooking and for Healing'.

CINQUEFOIL *Potentilla reptens*

The plant is under Jupiter and is mentioned very frequently in magical formulae, for love potions, for influencing people and much else. One or two sources suggest that witches are afraid of the herb. Its power was supposed to be greatest at full moon because the night was supposed to be a time of spiritual power. This originates in pre-Christian cults such as that of Diana the huntress whose symbol was the moon; many groups of men had good reason to frighten their neighbours from stirring abroad by night, especially those whose business was defeating the Customs and Excise in the smuggling game. Endymion, the beautiful youth loved by the moon goddess Selene (Artemis), fell into a perpetual sleep. Sailors who sleep on deck in the tropics know what it is to become 'moon-struck', their faces twist with the movements of the moon above them and contort the muscles which do not relax until well after sun-up.

It is said that cinquefoil will bring sound sleep if hung over the bed, but this falls more within the realm of psychosomatic work rather than of magic. It is the sort of thing Coué understood well.

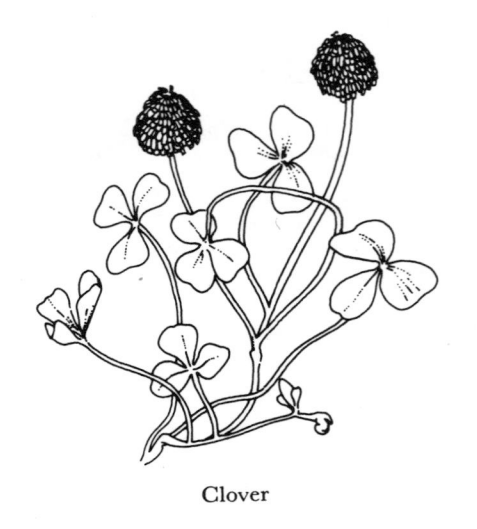

Clover

CLOVER *Trifolium pratense*

If you find a four-leafed clover you will be married within the twelvemonth. It has long been considered a charm against witch-craft and black magic. Pliny referred to the plant, and it was popu-lar among the Anglo-Saxons who practised Leechcraft—their name for medicine, they called the plant 'Claefra'.

Do you want to find a true love for yourself? You could try this :

> *'Wear thy clover on thy right*
> *Thy true love shall come in sight.'*

Again there are references to wearing clover in the shoes. One reason that our forebears could have had for this custom was that their shoes were probably wooden-soled and very uncomfortable without some plant stuffed down them. I know that as late as the 1940s some Swiss mountain folk took off their boots as soon as they got out of town and climbed the rocky mountain paths bare-foot.

COLUMBINE *Aquilegia vulgaris*

The plant was sacred to Venus. To carry the flowers was to attract sincere affection from the one you love. One is forced to observe the appalling lack of self-confidence which must have been epidemic among our enamoured ancestors—who needs charms to love?

Well, of course, it was never as simple for them as it is for us. If any reader is acquainted with that superlative Italian prose classic 'I Promessi Sposi' by Alessandra Manzoni (translations in English are available I believe) the innumerable difficulties which beset young love are clearly shown. Many of them were limited in their movements, entirely at the disposal of squire or parish priest and unlettered enough not to be aware of their dependence. For such as these, little charms such as columbines were a boon.

Comfrey

COMFREY *Symphytum officinale*

A herb of Saturn under Capricorn. A plant with extraordinary properties, and one which has put many of the medical profession to shame. Supremely confident of the value of their man-made pharmaceuticals doctors expressed contempt for the claim that this herb could mend broken bones, restore fractures, etc. The old country epithet of 'Knitbone' was scoffed at until comparatively recently it was shown that this plant was very rich in silica, which is needed for all such cases, and furthermore it was shown to be rich in natural supplies of alantoin, an ingredient known to speed up growth and repair bones. The tradition of herbalists since the days of Hippocrates and Galen had *once again* been fully justified. In the case of contusions (bruises), sprains, fractures, suspected bone damage, take a tea made of comfrey, and wrap the injured part round with crushed comfrey leaves, the results are signally impressive. It figured in many recipes from wise women, gypsies, and books on the magic arts as a cure for human and veterinary cases of bone damage.

CORNFLOWER *Centaurea cyanus*

This was reputedly the favourite flower of the great composer Beethoven (1770–1827) whose tremendous love for the simple countryside is shown in his Pastoral Symphony and some of the six hundred Lieder he composed (he is not too well known as a Lieder composer outside of Germany). The flower is supposed to bring luck to anybody who sees it, and a Greek legend says it was originally a very handsome youth who was in love with Flora, the goddess of flowers and Spring (her festival was from April 28th. until May 3rd.) and he was changed in a flower to be with her always.

Virgil mentions Camilla, one of the swift-footed maidens of Diana, who could walk so delicately across a field of corn that it never bent a single ear beneath her step. A tea made of the flowers is often found relaxing and restful for neurasthenic conditions.

COWSLIPS *Primula veris*

Straight from the old Anglo-Saxon Cuslippe. The flowers are said to represent the keys of Heaven bestowed upon Simon called Peter when Christ said *'Tu es Petrus'*, consequently the plant is consecrated to St. Peter.

They sometimes represented safety and security, hence Shakespeare's 'In the cowslip's bell I lie'. The plant is typical of the English countryside 'The cowslip is a country wench', wrote Thomas Hood. The plant is said to be subject to Venus under Aries. Milton spoke of them thus: 'Cowslips wan that hang their pensive head.' The flowers have long been used to soothe extreme nervous complaints such as epilepsy. They are now usually used to make a lotion which is very good as a skin cleanser.

CUCUMBER *Cucumis sativus*

The plant is under the moon. Culpeper recommends it for an ulcerated bladder. It is still used by leading cosmetic houses for many skin lotions and preparations. It seems to have a good effect upon some liver conditions, and can be eaten as part of a salad, and with rind and all. The hard green rind should not be too dark in colour but can be eaten unless it is slightly bitter or tough; then it is better expectorated. The plant has been considered by some wiselings as a symbol of male fertility and is occasionally eaten for that reason.

CYPRESS *Cypressus sempervirens*

One more tree of which the true cross was supposedly made; in fact the crucifix seems to have been made of marquetry, so many woods are attributed to it. 'And in sad cypress let me be laid' claims one Shakesperian character; the tree has a sad reputation which originates with it having been sacred to Pluto, the god of the underworld, the fierce and inexorable, to whom only black sheep were sacrificed (this is the origin of the words 'black' magic) he had to be propitiated, but the worshipper must never look directly at him. His only virtue consisted in the generosity with which he yielded up metals to man. He was not very lucky in his love affairs because his wife, Persephone, changed the nymph Minthe into the plant Mint, and the girl Leuce into a White Poplar, perhaps that is why he was always represented as being in a bad temper. He lived in Hades. The cypress tree has a peculiar trait—once it is cut it never grows again—but the leaves or branches cut off take longer to die than those of any other tree. In Tudor times the tree was considered under the domination of Saturn. The cones were used to make a liquid with astringent and styptic properties, which was used for inward and external bleeding.

DAFFODIL *Narcissus pseudonarcissus*

The gypsies have always regarded this flower as unlucky, but among most other races the flower seems to be regarded as a luck-bringer. It was the flower which Persephone wore (or carried) when she was captured by Pluto and made his bride. One legend says that the daffodil was always white until Pluto touched them upon seizing Persephone. It was a flower much favoured by Drayton, Herrick and Wordsworth, the latter's poem about them is famous indeed, it ends :

> 'They flash upon that inward eye
> Which is the bliss of solitude;
> And then my heart with pleasure fills
> And dances with the daffodils.'

The herb comes under Mars. The first man to see them bloom in Spring shall be rich ere the summer come. The juice cleans wax from the ears. The powdered root was held to be a cure for some forms of insanity.

DAISY *Bellis perennis*

Chaucer explains to us 'the daisie or the eye of the day', it opens its flower with the break of the day, and closes at sunset, it is the Bairn-wort of Scotland. It is under Venus in Capricorn. Since mediaeval times young maidens have risen early to be out in the meadow at dawn; gazing at the rising sun they placed their right hand down upon the ground without looking at it, and then they lifted the hand and counted how many daisy buds were beneath it—one for each month until they would be married. One imagines that the old wise women of the village were careful to choose a meadow which grew plenty of daisies. Some witches used to administer the roots to babies of people they hated, to stunt the child's growth. Schoolgirls play 'he loves me, he loves me not' with the flowers, picking off one delicate petal after another—a laborious exercise in destroying one's self-confidence! The name Marguerite is said to come from the saintly wife of St. Louis of France, not himself so good in spite of his later canonisation; sometimes the larger flowers are called marguerites. A further legend says that the alternative name is from St. Margaret of Antioch. The custom of knotting long stalks together and making daisy chains goes back into dim antiquity. Remarkable as it may seem archaeologists and historians are beginning to realise that a great deal may be learnt from the study of children's games because whatever else changes these show very little alteration with time. In the British Museum one may see Greek and Roman toys indicating that children in those days played games which were practically identical to those played 2,000 years later. Do you know this adage?

> *'Girls who weave a daisy chain*
> *Grow up pretty never plain.'*

The herb was frequently used as a drink to break up congealed blood.

Dandelion

DANDELION *Taraxacum officinale*

A plant subject to Jupiter. The French *Pissenlit* still recalls the familiar Tudor name for the plant 'piss-a-bed'; the medicinal drinks made from this herb promote an increased flow of urine, and greatly cleanse the body in this way. When the flower has blown and only the thin gossamer down remains many children play 'she loves me, she loves me not', blowing once at each turn. The poet speaks of :— 'the Spring's first dandelion shows its trustful face', and these simple flowers are one of the lovely herbs of Springtime, their brilliant yellow petals turn many a wasteground or rubbish dump into a thing of beauty. The flowerheads make a really marvellous wine which is very nourishing and retains most of the curative properties for which the herb has been famed throughout Europe. The leaves are pleasant in a green salad, and after rinsing with clean water can be used straightaway like lettuce leaves. At least five mineral salts and two vitamins have been discovered in the dandelion, and there is no doubt at all about its nutritional properties. A drink made of the flowers or the leaves of the plant is very beneficial for bladder, kidney, liver and genital-urinary ailments.

Dill

DILL *Antheum graveolens*

This is a herb madly popular among all witchcraft circles because of its fame as a love potion or aphrodisiac. Certainly the herb is most useful for clearing flatulence, relieving hiccoughs and relieving pains originating in digestive disturbances. The herb is safe enough to be administered to children, and dill water made from it is frequently used for this purpose. The herb is said to be under the domination of Mercury. There is an old Icelandic word *Dilla* which means to soothe a child. The herb is used universally throughout Europe; the seeds are most used, but cooks use the leaves for seasoning. Some old wise women gave dill water to expectant mothers to make the parturition easier.

DITTANY *Origanum dictamnus*

The name comes from a mountain district called *Dikte* in Crete although it spread from this area to many places throughout the Mediterranean lands. The popularity of the plant comes from its fragrant and volatile oil which endeared it to many people. Virgil mentioned it as a herb to apply to wounds. Witches used to mix it with verbena and pennyroyal as an aphrodisiac; this seems to have been harmless if not credulous; the same mixture is considered useful for mothers in labour, being recommended to bring an easy, painless delivery. The plant was sacred to the Moon.

Dock

DOCK *Rumex acquaticus*

The name of this plant is the same in Anglo-Saxon as in Ancient Greek, and was pronounced almost as in modern English; the plant was once cultivated as a medicinal and culinary plant. All the Rumex family were considered as being under the influence of Jupiter. They were used medicinally for cleansing properties, and the powdered root makes an admirable tooth-powder; cleansing and strengthening the gums, it should be massaged round with a finger rather than with a toothbrush. Cases are known in which ulcers of the mouth have been healed by regular use of powdered dock in a mouthwash. It can be drunk and seems to have some peculiar healing properties, formerly believed to exist only in sarsaparilla.

The large red leaves were sometimes worn to keep witches away. Culpeper asserts that any meat boiled with dock boils more quickly.

> *'When bairns' fingers nettles find*
> *See old Red Dock is close behind.'*

A charming couplet which reminds us that wrapping a dock leaf round a painful sting from the stinging nettle is a speedy and certain cure; peculiarly enough the docks and nettles always live near each other, yet one more instance of the ancient herbal lore that

> *'Where the hurt shall bring you woe*
> *God made the healing herb to grow.'*

And it is extremely strange how many herbs grow in just the places where Mankind is most likely to need them. Plants containing heart medicines grow in mountain districts where climbing might produce strain in older citizens; cures for rheumatism abound in damp places; where there is a heavy calcium concentrate in the water supply it is usual to find herbs with a suitable phosphorous content growing and a profusion of honey bees—whose products, used properly, offset the effect of the concentrate. The list of so-called coincidences is exceptionally long, and the fact has been known to herbalists for over 2,000 years. On plains where men might easily tend to fight battles there are masses of herbs growing which could be helpful to staunch blood. Growing in the Nevada desert, where atomic tests were made, is a simple herb from which American scientists have developed an antidote to radiation sickness!

ELDER *Sambucus nigra*

The true cross was made of the Elder tree, runs one legend, and therefore it is either a sin or just bad luck to burn it. Some old writers call it 'Holy Wood'. Records insist that this is one tree never struck by lightning; legend says that this is either because Christ died on a cross of elder, or because Judas Iscariot, according to Langland's Piers Plowman, hanged himself on an elder—all very confusing. Talking of hanging, I wonder if you know the tale of a court jester whose jokes got a bit too personal for the wrathful king? He was forthwith condemned to death, but with presence of mind he begged a boon, that he might be allowed to choose the tree upon which he was to be hanged. Unwittingly the king acceded to this reasonable request; the wily jester chose a little seedling, barely up to the height of his own knee : 'But that's not big enough' roared the king; 'no matter your majesty' replied the jester 'I'll wait for it to grow.' The king was so amused that he forgave the fool. See what a ready wit can do?

The elder is dedicated to Venus. Exorcists of an early age used a cross made of elder, and walked three times round a fire in a clockwise (sun) direction, crying 'Evil avaunt' three times (the invocation was probably a Latin prayer before the Reformation). There is a common superstition that no elder should be used to make a baby's cradle (the Judas legend). To beat a child with a withe (stick which flexes) was to stunt its body forever :

'A child that's beat with elder withe
Will fade away and never thrive.'

Witches are afraid of an elder tree (because Christ was crucified on it according to most sources), but in areas where the other legend (Judas) was common they liked it—no accounting for taste. The berries of the *Sambucus Nigra* make delightful wine, warm drinks for winter evenings, jams and jellies; they contain many valuable, established nutritional elements prized by dieticians, and can be recommended in such pleasant forms for coughs, colds, and respiratory conditions. The flowers can be gathered and dried to make a very good remedy against hay fever and asthmatic conditions. Weavers' shuttles, meat skewers, and the wooden pegs that shoemakers used instead of metal nails (which rot leather more quickly) were all made of elder wood.

ELFWORT *Inula helenium*

This is a much more English name than Elecampane which is often used by later herbalists. The flowers sprang up from the tears of Helen of Troy according to legends, but what did she have to weep for? Paris was considered the most attractive and eligible young male of his year group by the goddess Aphrodite herself. The magicians were united in their belief that regular drinking of the medicine made from leaves or roots brought immortality. Medicinally it helps relieve all manner of bronchitic ailments, it is slightly tonic and has some ill-defined curative properties which herbalists call 'alternative' because they *alter* sick conditions to a state of health. The concept of physical immortality is related to Man's fear of death and the unknown. Many warlocks and wiselings have made a good living from the credulous searching for a miraculous panacea to prolong life. There is a story of a Roman Emperor who was asking all the oldest men what they did to preserve their life and vigour. One ancient assured his imperial majesty that his fitness was due to his eating three cloves of garlic every day; another still more

FIELD SCABIOUS

This herb has been used in the treatment of diseases of the skin and blood.

BINDWEED

Some bindweeds are edible because of the sugar content, but
they are used mainly as a tonic for intestinal and liver complaints.
Its climbing stems and white flowers are found mainly
in areas with chalky soil.

ancient declared it came from drinking three skinfuls of wine a day; then the most haggard and ancient-looking man of the city was brought to the emperor and asked how he kept fit. 'I chase three beauteous maidens round the forum every day, your majesty', was the reply. 'How old are you?' demanded the emperor—' "30" was the reply'.

Elfwort can be used after being boiled slowly in olive oil, it makes a very soothing and useful massage oil—when cooled. Elves were supposed to live under the plant.

ELM *Ulmus campestris*

The true cross was made of elm wood (among a score of other trees) and it is so ashamed of this that it always sheds a branch whenever it remembers the tragic deed.

Some legends say that lightning will never strike an elm, but I was taught as a child that to stand under an elm during a thunderstorm was to beg for annihilation because the lightning would always go for an elm first! There is some evidence to show that elms *are frequently struck by lightning*. As they do shed their branches very easily in a storm I never stand or camp near them. There is an interesting detail about *St. Elmo* who was the saint invoked by Mediterranean sailors during a storm. The similarity of the saint and the tree would be very noticeable to mediaeval priests from Italy or France, but the saint whose 'elmo's fire' often appears on ship's masts, umbrellas or pointed objects has no etymological connection with elm which is an Anglo-Saxon word related to the Icelandic *almr* and Latin *Ulmus*. The wych elm was, as the name infers, favoured by witches, who could make the best broomsticks from it; unfortunately for this facile explanation the word *'wych'* has nothing to do with 'witch' but refers to the old English word *'wice'* meaning wicker work, and the tree was mainly valued for the excellent wickerwork it provided.

Such totally misleading pieces of information, handed down 'from one generation of witches to another', are too often shown to be wholly false or misleading, and it is a pity people who often claim to know past, future and present do not attend more neatly to history, etymology and fact.

What happened in English spelling was that the military superiority of the Normans and the French-influenced students cast aside old and genuine English spellings and words as 'uncouth' or 'barbaric'; the Cockney 'yeah' is much more correct than 'yes', the past tense of the verb 'swing' is *swang* (swing, swang, swung); by forgetting old forms of words we easily distort and misunderstand meanings and add to confusion. In Old English there was a word *'wicce'* meaning a person who could work magic or claimed to; another word was *'wice'* sometimes spelled 'wych' and this was the verb *to bend* or droop so that wych elm or wych hazel are trees that can be used to twist or bend into useful objects.

The elm proper is subject to Saturn.

Powdered elm bark was considered to be an efficacious remedy for gout—applied in poultice form externally.

EYEBRIGHT *Euphrasia officinalis*

Under the Sun in Leo. The juice of the pretty plant is still used to heal a host of eye ailments, particularly such as catarrhal conjunctivitis—which is common in big cities.

Culperer thought that it was a plant that would strengthen the brain. I found no reference to this herb in witchcraft lore.

FERN *Pteridium aquilinum*

This is Bracken, and a plant which drives witches into a paroxysm of fear; they detest it because every stem bears within itself the Greek letter Chi, the first syllable of Christ's name. If you break a stem of bracken you will see it forms at once the large X (Chi in Greek) pronounced like Ch·in the Scottish *Loch*. If a man walks into the bracken on Midsummer's Eve he will find a buried treasure. I often used to walk into the long bracken when a young man, but usually I had a girl friend with me, and I couldn't have been less interested in buried treasure. Some traditions insist that bracken seed when worn can give the wearer power over all things on Earth —one is only terribly sorry for individuals who were, psychologically speaking, so mentally maimed that they wanted such power. Bacon said that '*Power corrupts and absolute power corrupts absolutely*', which is why all dictators fall sooner or later, no man can fill the role of God, this is what the Ancient Greeks taught us with their legend of *Phaeton* who gained permission to drive the chariot of the sun for one single day across the heavens *but brought the entire earth to the brink of disaster*—Zeus killed him with a flash of lightning, his audacious sisters who yoked the horses for him were changed into poplar trees, their tears turned into amber and the rash man became the river Eridanus. The lore of the Ancient Greeks is morally instructive to a high degree. Bracken is used for bedding down cattle and storing potatoes. I do not recommend it for home medicinal uses. Under Mercury.

FIG *Ficus carica*

A plant associated with many historical, magical and medicinal uses. Once figs were eaten on Palm Sundays to celebrate the entry of Jesus into Jerusalem. There was an ancient saying about 'Attic figs' which meant the same as dreamy ideas, castle in the air (*Chateaux en Espagne*). Judas Iscariot is said by some to have hung himself on a fig tree. Plato the great philosopher was known to be fond of figs, and, indeed, most of the Ancient Athenians ate figs for breakfast during the highest period of their culture; this point is very significant because the fig is very rich in mineral salts and essential nutritive elements. Isaiah used figs to heal skin troubles. One famous work on Black Magic promises its adepts that an infallible way of taming a wild bull is to tie it to a fig tree, but omits to explain how one gets the bull to allow itself to be tied up. The fig is held to be under the dominion of Jupiter. Figs have been cultivated in England since Tudor times but they do not ripen so easily as those in the lands of the Mediterranean. The Ancient Egyptians used the wood of the *Ficus Sycomorus* to make mummy cases. The juice of fresh figs was used to cure some forms of deafness, to charm away warts, or to relieve toothache. The fruits are mildly laxative, they relieve some forms of dropsy, cure a number of dermatic ills and alleviate internal ulcers.

FIR *Piscea alba*

A tree much used by herbalists in olden times and which I have recommended in my book 'Herbgrowing for Health'. The tree is under the dominion of Jupiter. Cybele, the mother earth goddess, worshipped in Ancient Phrygia, fell in love with a beautiful but faithless shepherd called Atys; when she discovered his lack of loyalty she first drove him mad and then changed him into a fir tree. When the British missionaries went to Germany they found their pagan relatives still worshipping the oak, which had sacred connections with Thor and Odin; by some convenient miracles they managed to turn their attention to the Christmas Tree—fir, since when it has been decorated with presents ever since.

Another legend says that there were once two poor people living in the forest, they had saved enough money to buy their sick and only child a meal for Christmas Day. During the night of Christmas Eve a starving beggar child came to the door of their hut, they let the child in to keep it warm, and seeing how hungry it was they gave it all the food they had saved for their own boy. In the morning when they awoke the stranger child had gone and they were glumly contemplating what they could do for their own boy when there was a knocking on the door again. They went to the door and found the risen Christ outside standing in all his glory, behind him two angels were planting a glistening fir tree laden with food, good things and every kind of present. 'For your love and kindness to me last night when I came as a helpless child I give you this reward', he said, then he vanished. Their child was healed and they were able to feast from the richly-laden tree. The Germans call a Christmas Tree '*Christkindbaum*' or Christchild Tree because of the legend, and in Germany the tree is usually decorated with silver strips of lametta which they call '*Engelhaare*'—angels' hairs— to commemorate the silver hair of the angels that got caught up in the tree's branches. In the old Norse-Germanic legends the mother of Loki the evil one was turned into a fir tree (his father was the storm wind). From a tea-spoonful of the fir needles a pot of tea can be made which will relieve many chest conditions and muscular aches due to rheumatic or arthritic origin. For those who find it too strong to drink there is the alternative of using several spoonfuls in a bowl, pouring on hot water and bathing the feet in it, this is most refreshing for anybody who has got tired, cold and wet on a bad winter's day; if you are not certain which type of fir you have available use only the external application.

FLAG *Iris pseudacorus*

Probably this was the plant originally referred to under the name 'Fleur de Lys'; some sources indicate that this is the famous 'Lily of the field' unto which Solomon arrayed in all his glory could not compare. The Old English name was *'Segg'* which means 'small sword' referring to the shape of the leaves. Under the dominion of the Moon the plant has become associated with Iris, the messenger of the gods in classical mythology; she showed her passage through the heavens by leaving the rainbow in her trail. The powdered roots were very popular in the making of perfumed balls—pomanders, once carried around by persons of wealth. A little of the powdered root was used by witches to produce an abortion.

FLAX *Linum usitatissimum*

Culpeper says it is under the dominion of Mercury but other sources say Saturn. Linen cloth has been found in Stone Age settlements which date back beyond 4000 B.C. Throughout the ages men have poetically compared a field of waving blue flax flowers to a pool of rippling water; a classical tradition tells of a tribe pursued on to a cliff by their enemies, mistaking the flax fields below for water they flung themselves down to escape but were killed as they hit the hard soil below. Both the Egyptian and Roman sections of many museums can provide evidence of the fine weaving which the ancients could produce from linen made from the flax plant. The oil from the plant is called linseed oil, favoured by artists who paint in oils; long used to massage the chests of bronchitic sufferers; and taken orally to relieve gravel in the bladder.

FORGET-ME-NOT *Myosotis palustris*

The symbol of friendship and loyalty, recognised in most European countries where it has the same name *Vergissmeinnicht, Nezaboravak, Forglemmegei*, etc. Country swains and their lasses have worn it in devoted determination to remain constant to each other. The Greek word Myosotis means 'mouse-ear' and describes the shape of the leaves. Not much used medicinally.

FOXGLOVE *Digitalis purpurea*

All sources conclude that it is lucky to see foxgloves growing. The plant comes under Venus. The herb has been used for many cardiac and sedative medicines; some forms of heart disease show a link with kidney disorders and it has been found that foxgloves are especially helpful in such. The tolerance of different human beings to foxgloves varies most considerably, and for some they are quite poisonous. DO NOT USE THIS HERB FOR INTERNAL ADMINISTRATION WITHOUT EXPERT ADVICE! The usual boiled leaves with water can be used safely as a cleansing and antiseptic lotion for washing sores, ulcers and wounds, etc. Some witches used it to produce trances, although where a drugged illusion begins and a true spiritual trance ends is more clearly understood today.

GARLIC *Allium sativum*

This was the antidote which Odysseus used to counteract the magic of Circe, the witch who had turned his young sailors into swine. The legend probably indicates in modern parlance that she made drug addicts of the men, which is what a number of reputed witches did for profit. The plant, which is under Mars, is said to destroy the power of a magnet; the enterprising student could test this for himself. A clove of garlic carried on the person was a sure talisman against evil and witches (clearly not even they can stand the smell of it). An ancient manuscript discovered by archaeologists at Mingat, East Turkestan, dating probably to 500 B.C., refers to garlic as a cure for a very large number of illnesses. The truth of the matter is that this herb is a formidable antiseptic and germicide. Cases have been recorded in fairly recent times of garlic inhibiting the growth of cancer, curing glandular disorders and very efficiently toning up lymph in the human body—no mean archievements. Centenarians in the Caucasus and one or two I have met in Bulgaria attribute their great age and vigour to chewing garlic every day. Currently the *Hydrocotyle asiatica minor* is the most highly recommended preserver of life and prolonger of years for the aged. Garlic is frequently used to cure asthmatic, bladder, liver and even some arteriosclerotic conditions. Professor Walter Starkie in his 'Raggle Taggle', a book of his wanderings in Hungary and Rumania between 1929 and 1930, relates that bunches of garlic were still to be found hung up in many doorways against witches and vampires. Mediterranean sailors have carried a clove of garlic for thousands of years to ward off shipwreck. Talking of shipwreck, there is an interesting Danish custom which descends from Viking days—when you eat an egg you should, having finished it, make a hole in the bottom of the shell because every time you do it this prevents a ship from being holed and sunk—in view of the small number of shipwrecks today the tradition would appear to be most effective !

GENTIAN *Gentiana lutea*

Gentius was a king of the Illyrians in the land that is now called Yugoslavia, and he and his people were conquered by the Romans about 168 B.C. From him men and women learnt how to use the plant called after him. For centuries it was mixed with honey or treacle and given as an antidote to poisons. It is very strengthening indeed. All climbers and walkers through mountain country are enheartened to see the yellow or blue flowers of the gentians brightening up the landscape. The herb comes under Mars. In alpine lands of Europe a spirituous liquor is made flavoured with these herbs (yellow or blue) and highly recommended for digestion, keeping out the cold, and to kill germs.

GERANIUM *Geranaceae*

There are about 70 varieties, of which the *Ger. Pratense*—and several of the red kinds—are native to Britain. The plants are found throughout Europe, especially planted in windowboxes and round cottage doors to keep away evil. As the *Zrdavac* the plant is mentioned a lot in Serbian poetry. Witches don't like it.

> *'Where the Cranesbill grows up spry*
> *Nary a witch durst ever fly.'* (Nary=not one)

Cranesbill was the wild geranium.

Most geraniums have styptic properties in their leaves and will stop bleeding of a cut. Cranesbill made a drink against cholera.

GOLDEN ROD *Solidago virgaurea*

A plant subject to Venus. Said to have been highly treasured by the Great Saladin (1137–93), the poor boy who rose to be Caliph of Egypt and campaigned against Richard the Lion Heart in the battle for Jerusalem, he helped make the truce of 1192. During 1188 a tax to finance the third Crusade was levied in England; it was called the Saladin Tithe. From those days until now golden rod was cultivated in all the lands under Turkish dominion as a most valuable medicinal crop. There are about 100 varieties, but most of them are easily recognisable. The leaves allay nausea, improve digestion, and can be placed directly on wounds or cuts; they are rich in mineral salts and nutritive elements, etc.

Taken as a tea this is a delightful-tasting concoction which has medicinal virtues helpful in bronchitic and even tubercular cases. The many uses of the plant for a varied number of ailments bring it as close as any plant gets to being a *panacea*.

When it was used by witches it was invariably for curative properties, to bring about the healing indicated above. Once or twice there is mention of its psychosomatic value in a love-philtre.

GORSE *Ulex europaeus*

Under Mars. The old stems of the bush have been used for fuel for many centuries, the young shoots are eagerly sought by some grazing animals, making a nutritious fodder. Witches didn't thrive on it. This plant is also called Furze. On Midsummer's Day in some parts of Britain torches were made of bunches of this plant, and farmworkers walked in the direction of the sun's motion round the stables, byres, etc., chanting various phrases to keep evil at bay. Drinks made from the flowers cleanse the kidneys and relieve jaundice.

GRAPE *Vitis vinifera*

A book could be written upon the magic ceremonies, medical uses and the myths of the Grape and the leaves and roots of the vine. If one were to include the laudatory eulogies of Omar Khayyām about the grape and wine that would fill one chapter alone.

According to Persian traditions, it was Jamshid the ancient Iranian king who discovered the secret of winemaking. *In Vino Veritas* says the Latin tag when a man is drunk he will speak the Truth, from this idea comes the use of drugs and much else to rob a man of his senses, alas, so many new ideas are little more than new words for old ones. The Celtic goddess Berecyntia, virgin deity of the vine and fire, became the patroness of the Brigantes tribe, some of whom had settled in Northumbria and others in Southern Ireland. It is strange to relate that after the appearance of Christianity as an established religion there appeared a Saint Brigit whose shrine was tended by exactly 19 virgins; no male was ever admitted to the shrine, and there was a fire there which was never (before the Reformation) allowed to go out—the identical details found in Roman records of the worship of Berecyntia. Generally, the wine has been seen as symbolic of the blood of Jesus, who said 'I am the true vine', both vine and grape are frequently depicted in the architecture and paintings of Christian art down the ages. The Mandan Sioux declared that originally all men lived beneath the ground, but one day some curious men climbed up a massive grapevine and discovered a rich, bountiful and beautiful world so nearly all the tribe ascended them to colonise the earth, but the weight of a very fat old woman broke the vine, and some of the tribe were obliged to remain underground; all the dead return to the land under the ground. The story is so similar to the legend of Jack climbing the beanstalk that one is obliged to ask whether this might be some folk story from what Jung calls the Racial Consciousness, does this legend reveal the emergence of man the troglodyte? Perhaps in some past age there was an atomic cataclysm and the survivors lived underground, possibly for generations, until the radiation-hazards had cleared away and they could emerge. The Baltic Slavs of Rügen worshipped Svietovit with offerings of wine to ensure a good harvest in the autumn.

I remember tramping down a country roadside in Northern Thrace; some laughing little Greek boys of about ten to twelve came running up to me and thrust some grapes into my hands, I plunged my fist into my pocket to give them a few *drachmai*. 'Ohi,' said their leader, 'we don't want money, we want to see you happy!' The spirit of Classical Greece is not dead, despite all that Byron wrote. The Ancient Romans planted vines in Portugal, the Rhineland, and as far north as Hadrian's Wall. Strangely enough killjoy governments in Britain sought to make the juice of the grape a subject for taxation, and grapes are not cultivated widely here. We cannot say with the disappointed fox of Aesop's fable *'omfakes einen'*—they are sour, that would apply only to governments, not the grapes.

In the Jewish Talmud the legend says that the devil came to Noah during a little festivity and killed a sheep, a lion, a pig and a monkey, which is said to mean man starts to drink like a quiet sheep, becomes as bellicose as a lion, besotted and swinelike, and finally a jibbering ape. To drink like that is to waste good wine.

Bacchus was the son of Jupiter (Father of Heaven) and Semele, who was tempted to ask her lover who visited her at night to show himself to her as he really was, doubting that he was Jupiter. Having tricked him into a promise which he could not break, Jupiter reluctantly appeared to Semele in all his glory; she was consumed instantly, and became a heap of ashes. Jupiter took their son, whom the Greeks called Dionysus, and placed him with the Hyades to nurture. In his youth Bacchus discovered the secrets of vine culture and wine-making. After some youthful wanderings he was taught some religious rites by Rhea (another name for Cybele) : these were frankly orgiastic in nature, and added to drunkenness made the worship of Bacchus a scandal even in Graeco-Roman times.

From the dithyrambic chorus of dionysian festivals came the birth of Greek drama; Bacchus was the patron of tragic art.

Many modern wines have chemical additives and are far removed from rough, healthy country wines.

The vine is under the dominion of the Sun. The fresh or dried fruit are most helpful for bronchitic conditions; the leaves are commonly employed in poultices to cool inflammations. Fruit and leaves are very richly endowed with mineral salts and vitamins. It has tonic properties and breaks up coagulations in the blood and liver and is said to be good against gravel in the bladder or kidneys. It is amazing how such some of the men in classical times knew about their own health, and how to heal themselves from sickness. Plutarch remarked : *'At forty every man is a fool or his own doctor.'*

HAWTHORN *Crataegus oxyacantha*

Under Mars. The Anglo-Saxon word was *Haege* and the word hedge comes from it, because the Saxons erected hedges all over England to prevent soil erosion by the high winds. It is unlucky to cut it down. After the time of the Reformation it was taught that it was unlucky to bring Hawthorn (May) into the house because it was a plant consecrated to the Virgin Mary and was a relic of Catholic ritual. Joseph of Arimathaea's walking stick was made of hawthorn, and one day he rammed it into the ground and it sprouted! The miracle is caught up again in the Middle Ages, referring to the Pope's staff, which when it bloomed would show the forgiveness of God to the wandering poet Tannhäuser—Wagner wrote a dramatic and thrilling opera upon the loss of the poet's immortal soul. There was really a great poet called Tannhäuser, one of his verses : *'Wan wir zwei dort in einem klê. Si leiste daz si solde, und tet daz ich da wolde'* (The two of us alone there in the clover, she knew what I wanted and gave it to me as she should).

The hawthorn was gathered on Ascension Day and its branches

were carefully preserved in mediaeval times to keep the house free from lightning, storms and calamities. Because it was said to have formed the crown of thorns it was reputed to be able to ward off evil. The mystical thorn tree at Glastonbury is reputedly made from Christ's crown of thorns, and is said to bloom on Christmas Day. Funny? Well there is a great deal of evidence that it really does bloom on Christmas Day. Furthermore it is known to be a member of the hawthorn family which normally grows only on the hills around Jerusalem. Then the tree was brought to Britain by some returning crusader, except that there are references to it long before the Crusades took place. The tree is reputed to creak in sorrow and in sympathy with Jesus every Good Friday between the hours of the crucifixion. Do you know the children's rhyme : 'Here we go gathering nuts in May'? Well, it originally ran as follows : 'Here we go gathering knots of May', the word knap or knot is related to the modern German word *knospe*, meaning bud, so the song says that they are gathering the blossoms or buds of may (hawthorn) which was so called after Mary of Bethlehem.

Ovid mentions hawthorn at the festival of the Bona Dea, the rather frightening goddess of chastity; therefore it was never worn at a wedding where chastity was sacrificed. The berries are not eaten, but from the leaves of the tree a very useful herbal drink can be made which is valuable in relieving cardiac and rheumatic conditions, it breaks up cholesterol in the blood; one source says that its regular use prolongs life.

HAZEL *Coryllus avellana*

The River Boyne, rising in Kildare and flowing into the Irish Sea below Drogheda was named after a Celtic deity Boann whose sacred well was surrounded by nine Hazel trees, and the salmon of knowledge ate the nuts which fell into the waters and became wise. I cannot promise such instant intelligence for those who eat hazels today, but the nuts are rich in mineral salts and very healthy; they are extremely popular among vegetarians and fruitarians. Magic wands were often made of peeled hazel twigs and water diviners always use a hazel twig with two branches; there is something about its rate of vibration which enables it to become a good medium for detection in the hands of a sensitive. Nowadays radiesthesia has advanced on to much more complicated and efficient methods; the pendulum is more useful than a rod in many cases, and a radionic machine, as developed by Dr. Copen, is so quick and accurate that a child could use it for diagnosis, detection or what have you. The tree is under the dominion of Mercury.

Queens of witches' covens used to weave a wreath of hazel twigs to wear on their heads when they wanted their spells to work. Then there was this adage :

> *'Hazel shoots worn in the shoe*
> *Make thy heart's great wish come true.'*

Hoops, fishing-rods, walking sticks were often made of hazel wood. The nuts loosen catarrh, ease coughs and are very nutritious.

HEATHER *Ericaceae*

Burns and Scott have written enough poems mentioning the lovely purple heather of Scotland to fill a chapter at least; it is one of the loveliest of plants; I remember one summer day walking along the coast from Minehead to Porlock; the ground was aflame with purple heather and sparkling with gorse flowers, the combined scent of these plants in hot sunshine is unforgettable. In the Introduction I have related the anecdote of the two heroic Picts who guarded the secret of the original honey mead. The monks of Lindisfarne brew a mead, but the recipe is modern. Heather is used for bedding, brooms, thatch, tanning hides, fuel for baking and for heating; knowing such simple facts makes a seeming desert wilderness habitable, not knowing such details may lead a man to starve in the midst of plenty. White heather is supposedly lucky, all the Scots and gypsies who sell it insist that it is; this seems to be due to its scarcity value for it is rarer than the purple heather.

Herbalists have found it very tranquillising for neurasthenic cases and if it is not enjoyed as a herbal drink similar results can be obtained by eating heather honey, which is fairly easy to obtain.

HELLEBORE *Helleborus niger/foetidus/viridis*

The Mongols are said to have brought this plant with them when they descended upon the civilised world under Genghis Khan (1162–1227) and again under Tamerlane (1336–1405). All the plants tend to produce extremely unpleasant symptoms when taken internally. The fact that witches had a penchant for Stinking Hellebore is no recommendation; the whole family purge the body violently and can be dangerous in the hands of a layman. Modern Practitioners of Botanic Medicine avoid such plants because there are so many others which are just as effective and safer to use. The *H.niger* is the so-called *Christmas Rose*. A liquid made from boiling the roots can be painted on dropsical limbs to bring relief.

The tendency of the hellebores to bring hysterical and hallucinatory conditions was the chief reason why witches used it so much. THESE PLANTS SHOULD NOT BE USED FOR INTERNAL ADMINISTRATION without the advice of an expert. They are under Saturn.

HENBANE *Hyoscyamus niger*

Some authors ascribe it to Uranus, others to Saturn. Josephus was well acquainted with it. It is very poisonous to domestic fowls which explains its name (bane=poison); and it is not much safer for human beings. Witches liked it if they wanted to induce paralysis (temporary or permanent), madness or death in somebody; this was in the days before medical or radionic detection and they felt they could get away with murder. Some seemed to succeed, but there is always the inevitable and immutable Law above Mankind, the Ancient Hindus called it *Karma*. I know a verse which teaches it well :

> '*Every one and each are brothers,*
> *None goes his way alone,*
> *What we put into the lives of others*
> *Comes back into our own.*'

Henbane contains alkaloids such as scopalmin which can produce very dangerous reactions in some people. The herb is mentioned in the Ebers' papyrus as suitable treatment for fits, preferably for external application.

HOLLY *Ilex aquifolium*

Never bring Holly into the house before the actual Christmas Eve—because the true cross was made of it. When one considers how many trees seem to have gone into the construction of the cross it is not surprising that hundreds of unscrupulous itinerants made a good living from selling *reliques* of it. The berries were said to have been white originally but they turned red because Christ was crucified on its wood. Further legends insist that the crown of thorns was made from holly; in fact it was said that the leaves did not really have thorns in the Garden of Eden, but that the thorns came later as a punishment for letting itself be made into the crucifix. It is considered unlucky to tread on the berries (if you've got a good carpet in the house this is true). The truth of the matter is that the tree or bush has developed spiny thorns on its lower leaves to protect itself against grazing animals—especially goats, but when it reaches sufficient height to be out of their reach it doesn't grow thorns on those higher branches! The plant is ascribed by Nicholas Culpeper to Saturn because it was brought into Roman houses at Saturnalia—their version of the equinoctic festival we call Christmas. Holly was long held to be a sure defence against lightning, I cannot find any reference to a holly bush being struck by a fulminatory flash. It is the popular symbol of the resurrection, and also has been used to represent loyal friendship because it is an evergreen. Evelyn mentions it kindly in his 'Sylva'. Spenser and Shakespeare also wrote about it in an amicable and laudatory fashion. A drink made from the leaves brings on perspiration, and has been found very useful for inflammations of the lungs, coughs and colds.

HONEYSUCKLE *Lonicera caprifolium*

Astrologically under Cancer. Milton, Shakespeare and Spenser all wrote endearingly about this very pretty, typically country cottage plant. It always evokes memories of my childhood days and a time when life was slower, happier and very comfortable. Admittedly people were poorer, there were lamplighters (!), there were muffin-men going round with bells. My mother's father once hurried me out into the garden to look at an *aeroplane*; most traffic

Honeysuckle

was horse-drawn. In summer every hedgerow seemed alive with sweet-scented honeysuckle. The herb is helpful for laryngitis, 'flu, hepatic disorders and various stomachic upsets. Its juice is quite antiseptic.

HOPS *Humulus lupulus*

According to an ancient Egyptian story it was Ra the sun god who taught man to brew beer, but the concoction seems to have been a bit too much for him because it frothed up so much that the world was flooded with beer! This is at least better than being flooded by salt sea water! The herb is under Mars. The alcoholic content of beer is about 7% and it is extremely easy to brew up at home, and more quickly ready for use than home-made wine which takes longer to complete the fermentation cycle than does beer. Hops are a tonic, induce good sleep and are wholesome for the nervous system. The reason why heavy indulgence in beer drinking often produces bellicose (if not comatose) effects lies in the additive chemicals which industrialists tend to use to speed up fermentation or make the liquid keep longer. While natural, home-made beer induces a state of merriment it rarely produces a bad head the morning after. I remember meeting a marvellous old man who lived above Minehead; he brewed his own cider and called the stuff sold in the town's pubs 'mad brew' because he said it sent the drinkers raving mad; his own home-made cider had a kick like a mule. Like many of his friends I drank a lot of it (he was a generous man) but never once did I get a bad taste in my mouth or a bad head to follow the fun. The rule is for Beer and Cider—brew your own.

HOARHOUND *Marrubium vulgare*
This is often wrongly designated as 'Horehound' whereas the original English meanings of Hoar and Hore could not be further apart. The plant is under Mercury. It was sometimes favoured by practitioners of black arts, but more specifically in its simple herbal use. I encountered it in one recipe for a love philtre, but since the herb is principally of use against colds and chesty coughs, this was, perhaps, designed to ensure that the rustic swain didn't hold back from proposing because of an asthmatic or bronchial attack.

HORSE-RADISH *Cochlearia armoracia*
When the Anglo-Saxons wished to imply a slight inferiority in use of a plant they usually prefixed it with words such as 'horse-', 'hounds-', 'dog-', etc. Principally because the root is hot to the tongue it seems to have been classified as being subject to Mars. The chopped horse-radish is well known as a condiment for roast beef. A drink made from the chopped and grated root is much favoured by herbalists to relieve dropsy.

HYACINTH *Hyacinthus orientalis*
Ben Jonson, Keats and Milton have all written of the wonders of these delicate, beautifully-scented flowers. There is an age-old story of Apollo who was in love with a beautiful youth called Hyacinthus. They were playing quoits together when the West Wind Zephyrus, jealous of their love, blew a quoit so that it hit the youth and killed him. From his blood Apollo caused the flower to bloom. On its leaves are the Greek expression of sorrow 'Ai' and the initial of his name. Hyacinthus was worshipped at Amyclae as a god, and a festival Hyacinthia was held in his honour. The juice is styptic, otherwise the plant is nowadays mostly used for perfume. It is a delightful house plant.

IVY *Hedera helix*
Never include more ivy than holly in your Christmas decorations as it will bring bad luck for the ensuing year.

> *'Like the ivy on the tree*
> *So may my true love cleave to me.'*

A couplet recited by young love-sick maidens, some say on New Year's Eve, others on Midsummer Eve, yet others say it was sung three times on Halloween, holding a piece of ivy in the hand.

Another romantic association is the custom putting a piece of ivy beneath the pillow so that you would see the face of your true love in your dreams.

'Where ivy grows, there sorrow flows'

ran another saying. I remember my mother's family using that often. Possibly because it was associated with drunkenness in folklore. It was sacred to Bacchus who is said to have charmed a shipful of pirates by turning all the baddies into dolphins and the masthead into an ivy branch. Ivy is said by some old herbalists to prevent drunkenness. It is a symbol of faithfulness says one tradition, but another asserts that to give ivy to a friend is to destroy the friendship! To administer it internally might destroy a friendship quite lethally. I ADVISE EXTERNAL USE ONLY. A poultice of the beaten and bruised leaves, placed upon a preheated cloth or piece of lint, is often very helpful for application to swollen glands, or to cysts, abscesses and the like. Renew every 24 hours. Ivy figures a lot in witchcraft ceremonies, according to some traditions, but in view of its rather toxic nature some warlocks couldn't have done themselves much good by adding it to their diet.

It has been shown as a symbol of the resurrection, probably because of its evergreen nature. Longfellow wrote :

'Ivy crowns the brow supernal
As the forehead of Apollo.'

JESSAMINE *Jasminum officinale*

This is the correct old English name for the plant which came to be called Jasmin. One of my ancestors, the financier and gay blade about town in the time of William III, John Law, was called 'Jessamy Jon' because it was his favourite perfume. Rafael Sabatini wrote a very interesting story of his life : 'The Gamester' which is fairly accurate in most of the exciting and amusing details. The herb is under Jupiter in Cancer. The flowers were sometimes included in love potions, and have always been considered a slightly aphrodisiac perfume. As a drink it relieves colic and all sorts of digestive complaints; the Chinese often add jasmin flowers to tea. More famed in European literature than in English, I recall some lines from the *'Mireille'* of the great poet of the Provençal language, Frédéric Mistral (1830–1914) :

'Veguère uno figuiero, un cop dins moun camin,
Arrapado à la roco nuso
Contro la baumo de Vau Cluso,
Maigro, pecaire! i lagranuiso
Lé dounarié mai d'oumbro un clot de jaussemin.'

(I saw a figtree once in my path, my stone-ridden path on the bare rocks close to the grotto of Van Cluso, it was so thin that even a tuft of jasmin would have given a lizard more shade).

LAVENDER *Lavandula spica/officinalis*

An ancient tradition says that Mary always laundered Jesus' swaddling clothes with lavender, and this is why the plant was commonly used for laundering right through the Middle Ages up to the time of the Tudors. The best English lavender was said to grow at Mitcham in Surrey, but although some is still grown there the fields where it was cultivated have been greatly reduced in area since my grandparents' time. The plant signifies love and long life. Under the dominion of Mercury. It was my good fortune during the roaming period of my youth to come across a whole hillside covered with lavender bushes down in the *Basses Alpes*, somewhere between Digne and Mt. Pélat (10,016 ft.). The flowers were grown for the scent factories at Grasse; the air was heavy with their oleaceous perfume in the hot midday sun, the only sound was the brawling of bees inebriated with the richness of their harvest.

The herbal uses include its exploitation as a mild stimulant, a nerve tonic, a bringer of quick relief against nervous headaches, relief from the pain of toothache, a drink which was favoured by midwives to ensure an easy childbirth, and also as a remedy against some mild forms of epilepsy.

LEEK *Allium porrum*

The reason why this is associated with Wales goes back to King Cadwaller who ordered his warriors to use it as their battle emblem. Since they won their battle the soldiers regarded it as a bringer of good luck and a national emblem.

Once it was deliberately planted in thatched roofs to protect them from lightning. These beliefs remind me of the somewhat odd gentleman who was seen going down the high street of his home town scattering lumps of salt right, left and centre. Eventually a policeman approached him and asked exactly what he might be doing.

'It's very good salt, officer, I'm scattering it to keep the dinosaurs away,' was the reply.

'There haven't been any dinosaurs here for thousands of years,' replied the exasperated officer of the law.

'I told you it was a good salt,' was the riposte.

Leeks are very nourishing and used a lot in cooking, I always enjoy a good leek soup. The plant is cleansing, slightly diuretic and very helpful against catarrhal conditions, being much easier to take than onions or garlic.

LETTUCE *Latuca sativa*

Under the Moon. A common, somewhat disregarded vegetable which is very rich in mineral salts and vitamins despite its flat taste. It does not figure in mythology much, but it should figure for the daily diet as often as possible. It is slightly aperient, good for the nervous system and for a healthy blood circulation. Its cleansing properties are remarkable.

LILOCK *Syringa vulgaris*

This is the older and more correct spelling of the plant we call Lilac which was introduced into England from Persia about 1597. Any superstitions about it are therefore not founded in antiquity so much as in human perversity. The tradition that it is unlucky to bring it in the house is a miserable Puritan conviction that anybody who took flowers inside the house was a Catholic and a Cavalier to boot. Walt Whitman mentions it in his poem on the murdered Abe Lincoln : *'Lilac blooming perennial and drooping star in the West, and thought of him I love.'* The romantic French poet said : 'At Lilac time I first saw thee' (*Je t'ai vu aux temps de Lilas*). The plant is celebrated in song and drama with young love. Its principal use is for perfume. The scent is very tranquillising. The botanical name comes from the Persian word *S'rynx*, it is a distant relative of the olive family.

LILY *Lilium album hortense*

A fairly universal symbol of purity and chastity, said to have grown from the tears Eve shed when she was driven out of the Garden of Eden. It is supposedly under the Moon. It has been held as the symbol of Juno, of motherhood and of marriage in its time. Somewhere during the history of the Christian Church the lily was adopted as a symbol of the Virgin Mary, and also associated with innocence, chastity, pure motherhood and all feminine virtues. The city state of Florence and the house of Bourbon made it their emblems. Old herbalists regarded the juice of the bulbs as a specific against some forms of venereal disease but did not specify clearly which forms, nor what quantities they used. The subject should be researched.

LILY OF THE VALLEY *Convallaria majalis*

There is a charming custom in France; when it is the time of the 'Muguets' everybody presents the people they love—mothers, girl friends, etc.—with bunches of Lily of the Valley. The plant is said to be under Mercury. One old magic formula to charm the nightingales to come and warble to you was to surround yourself with bunches of Lily of the Valley. Some herbalists claimed that its extract would restore speech to the dumb (was it so bitter that they cried out from sheer shock and distaste? Speech restoration by violent shock has been recorded since classical Roman times). I have found the flowers to be a very beneficial nerve tonic—just have them in the room to smell; the curative property of scent is only now being re-investigated. A German scientist of note has shown to the satisfaction of his scientific colleagues that the scent of roses in definitely therapeutical; I have no doubt many will follow with investigation into other plants. We must remember that a smell contains some microscopic particles of the substance from which it emanates, and as such is practically a homoeopathic dose in itself.

COMMON RED POPPY

YARROW

This common wild plant grows anything up to two feet tall and has little whitish flowers. Noted for its healing effect upon wounds.

LIVERWORT *Lichen*

There are over 300 different varieties, some said to be under Saturn, others under Jupiter in Cancer. Some witches used them somewhat indiscriminately but the results achieved were a little unclear. There are so many other herbs which are safer to use for healing humans. Rabies in dogs was often treated with a liverwort.

LOTUS *Lotus nelumbium*

The Lotus mentioned by Theophrastus was the *Lotus Zizyphus*, but the *Nelumbium* is the one that is most certainly the Sacred plant. It is the symbol of Brahma, the impersonal and abstract conception of God; of Vishnu, the second, personal, essence of God; and the symbol of Gotama Buddha to whom the daily prayer is offered : 'Om mani padme hum', meaning 'Hail to the jewel in the flower of the lotus'. A Cantonese friend presented me with a carved wooden statue of Kwan Yin, the goddess of mercy; she is depicted as seated upon a lotus. Amida, the Japanese Buddha, is always shown as seated upon the blossoms of the lotus; there is a 50-foot-high statue of him at Kamakura which is one of the principal tourist sights of the country; Kipling wrote :

> *'Ye who tread the narrow way*
> *By Tophet flare to Judgement day*
> *Be gentle when the heathen pray*
> *To Buddha at Kamakura.'*

Amida is supposed to have gained so much spiritual merit while on earth that he could take the sins of all believers upon his own shoulders, just as Jesus is represented as 'he that taketh away the sins of the world'. Hap, the god of the South Nile, was clearly depicted ensconced on a lotus, as was Horus the youthful sun god of Ancient Egypt. The flower is almost universally considered a symbol of purity and holiness. Dryope was changed into a lotus tree—*Dyospyros lotus*. Tennyson's 'Lotus Eaters' who were 'eating the Lotus day by day' are founded upon the mention of the land of the Lotus Eaters made by Homer in the Odyssey, Ernle Bradford in his fine book 'Ulysses Found' shows very sound reasons for identifying this with the island of Jerba in the Gulf of Gabes; the same author suggests that the actual λωτος was either *Cordia myxa* or the *Rhamnus zizyphus*; from the former the natives made a type of bread, from the second a type of alcoholic beverage could be made. No medicinal use is certain.

LUPIN *Lupinus perennis*

The seeds and juice contain supplies of vitamin A. The plant is said to be under Mars in Aries. A paste made from the seeds can be applied to skin blemishes to clear them up. Powder from the crushed seeds was often taken in the old days to drive worms out of the infested body. There are one or two witch recipes using lupin seeds for worming cattle.

MAIZE *Zea mais*

Sir James Frazer devoted two or three of his 13 volume book *The Golden Bough* to the legends, rites and ceremonies connected to Corn, those interested can refer to the work. The details given here relate to Indian Corn. It was a universal fertility symbol among practically every tribe of Amerindians. Its origin was said to be the teeth of the first man and woman on earth. Opochtli, the Aztec deity of fishing and hunting, was always offered maize flowers instead of human sacrifices which were common to other cults. In the cult of Omacatl bones made of maize paste were offered as a sacrament during festivals. The herbal medicament is useful as a soothing meal for people with ulcerated stomachs. It is inclined to promote urination. Maize, like wheat, barley, oats, rice and millet, is commonly associated in symbols with motherhood and birth, occasionally in association with animal symbols of fertility, e.g. cow, nanny-goat or sow. Most of the myths associated with cereals—including the modern myth (started by Goethe) about an Original mother-plant of all plants—are not supported in any way by botany.

MANDRAKE *Mandragora officinarum*

A well-known cattle poison, one with which angry witches punished unsympathetic farmers. Weird and wonderful stories were told about the plant having human form and being a botanic type of man who screamed with such a terrible cry when pulled out of the earth that all who heard it must die; witches taught that only a dog could pull the root up at the magic hour of midnight. It is suspected that the plant mentioned in the Old Testament is the *M. autumnalis* which is a pretty plant growing up to a foot in height. Although the mandrakes have often a forked root, human cupidity and incredulity led to a little sly carving to alter the appearance of the root so that it assumed human features, after which it was quickly replanted and then pulled up with much play-acting by a charlatan before one or two rich clients for use in 'magic' ceremonies. The fact that it could only be pulled at midnight and that many prohibitions were invented for it all point to deception. Lawrence Durrell, in his *'Justine'* and *'Cleo'*, mentions cabbalistic magic as active in Alexandria in the 1930s. Shakespeare is one of many other writers who mentions mandrake. The herb is quite unsuitable for medicinal use because it is very poisonous. The American plant *Podyphyllum peltatum* is sometimes, wrongly, called mandrake. The many legends about using the mandrake to 'create' a living man would imply that the believers were either impotent or unaware of the normal human procreative system.

MAPLE *Acer campestre*

From the powdered bark herbal drinks can be prepared which bring relief for liver complaints. There is an old belief, which is somewhat vague in origin, that children passed through a maple are blessed by it and stay healthy and strong for life.

Maepel was the old Saxon word, and Maepelder is found in one or two place names, meaning 'maple tree'. The ancient Gothic word *Kilthei* meant womb, and Kild was that which came out of the womb, from this we have softened the initial sound to make Child, sometimes 'Chile', plural 'childer', 'chillen', children.

> *'Follow the maple three times round*
> *that will keep thy childer sound.'*

The tree is governed by Jupiter.

MARIGOLD *Calendula officinalis*

When Kipling wrote : 'The sun was lord of the marigold', he merely stated accepted astrologica lore, the sun has dominion over Marigolds in Leo according to Culpeper. The plant was said to be the favourite flower of the Virgin Mary. It is used widely in India as a symbol of life, eternity and health. Often it adorns funeral pyres before the conflagration. The drink made from the flowers or the leaves is very good for a wide variety of nervous diseases, for many skin disorders which are difficult to heal, and also for many cardiac disorders.

Marjoram

MARJORAM *Origanum vulgare*

Lucretius started the story that pigs are afraid of Marjoram and must avoid it. The plant is under Mercury. It was often included in love potions by wise women, perhaps they knew it is a very good nerve tonic and would help hesitant and frightened young lovers to tell each other what they wanted to say. It is very healthful in cooking and as a herbal medicament for digestive disturbances. It is a useful remedy for bronchial and asthmatic coughs.

MARSHMALLOW *Althaea officinalis*

The writer Theophrastus who died in 287 B.C. compiled a list of about 500 medicinal plants commonly used by herbalists in his time, among those most highly praised was Marshmallow. The plant is very valuable in all nephritic cases, catarrhal, bronchitic, pulmonary, and similar ills. It has figured in the recipes used by wise women for purposes of healing mostly.

MELISSA *Melissa officinalis*

It was held to be sacred to Apollo, the god of medicine, and held up as an elixir of life; when Apollo fell in love with Daphne, he is reputed by the poet to have said : 'I suffer from a malady that no *balm* can heal.' The Swiss physician Phillip von Hohenheim (1493–1541) who was professor of surgery at Basel (1526–8) wrote a great deal about medicine, he was noted for his exceptional cures, and he stated clearly that he had achieved remarkable success with melissa. Feverish conditions, colds, cardiac complaints and many other ills are alleviated by taking a simple tea prepared from Balm Melissa.

MIMOSA Either *Mimosa* or *Acacia* family

Reputed to bow to whosoever seeks shade beneath its branches. It is a symbol of Eternity, a bringer of good luck, it wards off evil. The perfume is very tranquillising and cheering for cardiac patients. When I was a young man there was one place on the *Côte du Midi* where a whole forest of mimosa grew; the scent was slightly overwhelming, it reminded one of the Moslem idea of the gardens of Paradise. The softly blowing balls of yellow fluff seen against the cerulean blue are a thing of beauty. The name comes from the Greek word for imitation, the plant is said to imitate others.

MINT *Mentha viridis*

The plant is said to be under the dominion of Venus. Virgil says that stricken deer seek it to heal their wounds when escaped from the hunter. Ovid speaks of it. It often formed part of love philtres. Mint has medicinal uses for kidney, liver and stomach disorders. It is helpful for all digestive disorders. A massage oil can be made from the leaves.

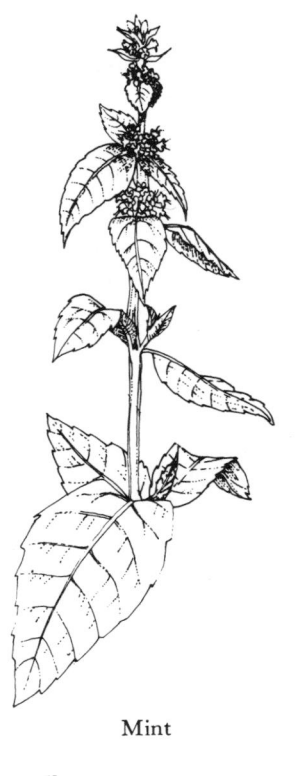

Mint

MISTLETOE *Viscum album*

The old English spelling was Misteltán, meaning twig of the mists. It was considered a symbol of fertility. Under the Sun in Jupiter. It was lucky to be kissed under the mistletoe, one berry should be plucked off for every kiss given and received. This was the holy plant of the Druids, the original 'Golden Bough'. The details of the Druid religion are somewhat conflicting. Caesar appears to be one of the principal sources of the stories of human sacrifices—he had good reasons to convince the Romans back home that the British were savages. Other sources indicate that the Druids worshipped one god, had no statues; they do not appear to have indulged in human sacrifices. The use of the herb as a medicinal drink was common, especially for what we would call today psychosomatic diseases. It seems one of the most ancient remedies for epilepsy. Frigga, the goddess, extracted a promise from every living thing that it would never harm Baldur the Beautiful, the darling of the gods, but she ignored the mistletoe, which was too small to harm anything—so she believed. Unfortunately Loki the evil one discovered this omission and tricked Hodur the blind to cast a mistletoe twig at Baldur who promptly fell down dead. The gods took their revenge and chained Loki up so that a serpent's venom should drip forever on his face; when Loki cannot endure any more punishment he writhes and an earthquake results.

MULBERRY *Morus nigra*

Originally white, the berries are said to have been dyed red by the blood of Pyramus, and purple when later Thisbas killed herself over his body. The story is told in the fourth book of Ovid's *Metamorphoses*. In 'Os Lusiadas' Camoens writes:

> *'and stained with lovers' blood*
> *the mulberries hang from pendant boughs.'*

The plant is under Mercury. The medicinal uses are laxative, and worm-killing, the berries are very suitable for patients with fevers because they are cooling and thirst-quenching.

MYRRH *Comiphora molmol*

A popular herb in biblical times, it has antiseptic, stimulating and tonic properties. It is excellent for cleansing sores, ulcers and wounds. It is under Jupiter. It was much in demand for first quality mummification processes (which could cost an Egyptian family up to £2,000 each). The Mother of Adonis was changed into myrrh according to Classical myth.

MYRTLE *Myrtus cerifera*

> *'On each side wall let myrtle grow,*
> *There's a home no strife shall know.'*

Because the plant is sacred to Venus it is worn in bridal headdress, wreaths or chaplets. It is the bringer of harmony and peace. Culpeper ascribes it to Mercury. Virgil mentions it although it would seem to have been a native of Persia which later reached the Graeco-Roman world. Phaedra, the faithless wife of Theseus, tempted her stepson Hippolytus beneath a myrtle tree, having fallen violently in love with the beautiful young man; his honour was such that he rejected her advances. Furious at being scorned she denounced him falsely to her husband who cursed Hippolytus. While the blameless son was racing his chariot along the seashore Poseidon sent a bull from the sea which frightened the horses so that Hippolytus' chariot overturned and he was killed. When the father learned of his son's innocence Phaedra killed herself, but not even the goddess Diana could (so says Horace) restore Hippolytus to life.

The eating of myrtle leaves conveyed the dubious ability of being able to detect witches. Myrtle is one of the most ancient scents recorded, and is often included in compound perfumes produced today. It has a beneficial action upon the colon and is a tonic herb of significant importance. It is invariably administered as a powder made from the inner bark. Claims have been made that it can cure cancer.

Witches seem to have either feared it or to have used it as part of the inevitable aphrodisiac drinks they made a living by selling.

NARCISSUS *Narcissus*

Many hundred varieties of this plant are known, but we have in mind the common white flowered kind. Narcissus was a handsome youth who was immune to the feeling of human love; this greatly angered the gods and Nemesis caused him to perceive his own reflection in a pool of clear water; he fell in love with his own image and pined away until he died and changed into the flower carrying his name. The flower was sacred to Ceres (Demeter) whose festival was held at Eleusinia. The juice of the bulbs can be applied externally to sprains and contusions.

NUTMEG *Myristica fragrans*

The rhyme tells us that

> *'a wife, a dog and a nutmeg tree*
> *the more you beat'em the better they be.'*

That was, of course, before wives went out to evening classes to learn Judo. Women seem to be ill-favoured by the nutmeg because if a girl should carry one around with her she would certainly end up married to an old man, and a bad-tempered old curmudgeon at that. The nutmeg gives a delectable flavour to a fruit cake. The powder given in small doses can stop fainting and sickness.

OAK *Quercus robur*

It is good luck to touch an oak but bad luck to cut it down. To have an oak growing near the house was a sure way of warding off all evil influences, sickness or lightning (in spite of the fact that oaks are occasionally struck by lightning).

It was a symbol of Thor, and called the tree of life. Needless to say the true cross was made of oak! The oak was sacred to Odin, inventor of the Runic alphabet; he is the Sun god after whom Wednesday is named (Woden's day), it was he who received the souls of brave warriors in Valhalla, and made them welcome. The tree is a symbol of fecundity, and many disappointed wives used to creep out late at night to touch some mighty oak tree and become fertile. The acorns have been regarded as symbols of good luck for centuries; they are said to keep illness at bay. In early centuries they were a source of food for men, but later just regarded as fodder for pigs; serfs, under the manorial system, had the inalienable right to send their pigs to grub for acorns in the lord's woods (in view of the rate at which pigs breed it was lucky for them that this virtually assured them costless pigkeeping). Circe was said to have fed Ulysses' unhappy, drugged crew on acorns after she had turned them into swine. In Saxon times, before Christianity made its mark in the land, young couples were often married under an oak tree by a heathen priest holding a hammer (referred to as marriage by Thor's hammer). There is one curious survival of this ancient custom at Gretna Green in Scotland where many runaway couples have fled for centuries to get a marriage blessed that their parents wouldn't sanction. The fact that it is a blacksmith who performs the rite cannot overshadow the relationship between Thor, patron of Smiths, and the magic hammer Mjölnir. *'There's a valley under oakwood where a man may dream his dream,'* wrote Kipling. Many are legends of the oak. Benevenuto Cellini in his memoirs relates that he saw an oak on fire one day, and there right in the midst of the hottest flames was a live salamander (a mythical beast reputed to be able to live in fire), alas, his veracity is open to doubt on several occasions. I knew an old man from Devonshire who taught me this :

> *'If ash bloom afore the oak*
> *Spring rains will truly soak.*
> *If the oak's afore the ash*
> *'Twon't be nought but a splash'*

(I dare not write it down with the vowels he used, they were so much Saxon as to seem a foreign tongue nowadays; try *wooant* for won't !).

The oracle of Zeus, the Father of Heaven, at Dodona was interpreted by the different ways in which the wind rustled in the leaves of his sacred oak tree there. The Japanese have a saying about another tree which is similar to this concept :—*'When the leaves sough in the pines but there is no wind this is the voice of God.'* Culpeper places the tree under Jupiter. Erisichthon hewed down an oak in which a nymph, of whom Demeter was fond, dwelt; the revenge of the goddess was swift. Erisichthon was punished with an appetite he could never fulfil, he died gnawing at the living flesh on his own limbs. Milo, the mighty athlete of olden times, met an untimely end in an oak tree. He found an oak which had been riven by a stroke of lightning, and decided he could use his strength to split it from top to bottom. As he pushed his massive body into the crack and tried to completely split the tree the oak sprang back, trapping him there so that he died of strangulation or starvation. The only other case I have read of concerning a man being killed in this way is in one of the magnificent novels of Karl May *'Old Surehand'*. When Wabble, the wicked, unrepentant villain, is caught by the vengeful Utah tribesmen they split a tree open with wedges, inserted his body and then removed the wedges so that he was crushed to death. From the inner bark of the oak one can make a most useful lotion for clearing a sore throat. The Germans have made a very good acorn substitute for coffee, which is at its best (in my opinion) when mixed half and half with the real thing.

OATS *Avena sativa*

> *'Bring thy oats home e'er cuckoo cry*
> *Harvest, her'll be wet not dry.'*

This very nutritional food is also part of herbal medicine, following the dictum of Hippocrates, 'Let thy medicine be food, and thy food thy medicine'. A Scottish friend told me of a custom which says any young couple who want to ensure that their marriage shall be prosperous and filled with harmony ought to make sure that there are oats in the pantry before the 'groom carries his bride across the threshold on their wedding day.

Oats have curative properties for skin, nervous and stomachic ills. Their calmative effect on nerves (especially when made as porridge with lots of cream, a little salt and lots of brown sugar) far exceeds the achievement of any tranquilliser made by chemists.

OLIVES *Olea europeae*

Demokritos of Abdera (*c.* 450 B.C.) an authority in his day, summed up therapy in one sentence : 'Honey inside, Olive oil outside', regarding these two valuable therapeutical agents as the total requirements for good health in his country and climate. The olive is rich in mineral salts and nutritive elements, and it has shown itself to be most reliable in the treatment of diseases of the bowels, colon, genito-urinary disorders; it is very safe in children's ailments, useful against constipation. It is one of the very few substances which it is considered safe to put into the human ear, and some forms of deafness are said to be cured by the simple administration of warm (not hot) olive oil. Noah's dove returned to the ark bringing an olive branch in its beak, it is the symbol of hope. Peisistratos (605–527 B.C.) is said to have introduced the cultivation of the olive to Greece. At night the trees seem possessed of a most intense blackness. I recall camping down on the Italian coast, far away from tourist haunts, among terraces of olive trees; there were the stars, the elfin movements of the fireflies, the sound of the sea, and the usual half-empty bottle of Chianti, a bunch of grapes, some rough cheese, a hunk of bread—it was a happy youth. When Minerva and Poseidon vied for the right to become patron of Athens it was Minerva (Pallas Athene) who won by offering the Athenians, as they were later called in her honour, olive trees as a reward for their support of her claim. Only a virtuous woman may plant an olive tree, if a harlot plants one it will wither within the year. The olive branch and a pure white fleece (later a white flag) became the accepted symbols of peace and truce; this system started, according to Virgil, when Aeneas proffered them to Pallas, son of Evander. Some botanists teach that the tree had its origin in the Punjab, and came to the Mediterranean lands by way of Persia and the Caucasus —the traditional pathway of the Aryan tribes when they left the primeval homeland north-west of the Himalayas and the Hindu Kush. Odysseus used the trunk of an olive tree to construct the connubial couch to which Penelope was true during 20 years of her husband's absence. Hercules was crowned with a chaplet of olive leaves.

ONION *Allium cepa*

Snakes are supposed to be frightened off by raw onions, witches too; if you eat too many raw onions you will scare everybody away. Still, they're not so bad as garlic for odour. They are subject to Mars, according to Culpeper. At one time a needle stuck through a small onion was used for radiesthesia purposes but this is wholly antiquated when such fine, perfectly tuned equipment is now available and cheap.

Herbalists have found out that the onion is remarkably antiseptic. They are a sovereign remedy against colds and throaty coughs. Onions lightly boiled in milk were a remedy which my mother used to apply as first aid whenever there was the slightest sign of a chill; for children a little brown sugar can be added. I have known some very nasty abscesses cured by application of a fresh slice of onion every day (one very large and bad abscess was healed within three days as I saw with my own eyes) : the stronger the onion smells the stronger are its chemicals which produce the cure.

ORANGE *Citrus sinensis*

A symbol of innocence on one hand, and of fertility on the other. Scholars believe that these are the original apples of gold from the gardens of the Hesperides. He gave them to Hera when she married Zeus. Atalanta, the proud daughter of Iasus and Clymene, refused to marry anybody who could not defeat her in a foot race—the failures were to die. Aphrodite, goddess of love, was annoyed by this, knowing that Atalanta was the most swift of all living mortals, so she helped Milanion, a nice, respectable young man, get the sacred golden apples : as he began the race he dropped one apple after another, and Atalanta, who had never before seen anything so precious and beautiful, stopped to pick them up—and lost the race. She had to marry Milanion, but then settled down and became a respectable housewife and mother. Milton is one of the earliest English poets to mention oranges in 'Comus'. They are rich in vitamin C and some mineral salts. They are thirst-quenching, suitable for several fever conditions, and can often avert a cold. The peel can be scrubbed and used for marmalade and to flavour cakes.

PAEONY *Paeonia officinalis*

Originally named after Paeon, a reputed healer of ancient times, who is mentioned in Homer's Iliad as being in the Trojan War. There was a tribe of people on the sunkissed plains of Thrace who were called Paeones and whose country was called Paeonia. In Greek myths the peoples of Thrace seem to have been credited with much knowledge concerning healing herbs. This is a herb of the Sun under Leo. The roots, seed, flowers and leaves were all used against epilepsy, St. Vitus's Dance, and nervous tic; nowadays the most commonly-used form is the powdered root.

The plant is mentioned in Theophrastus' works, and was long

regarded as an infallible bringer of luck and a talisman against evil.

PALM *Palaceae*

Unfortunately, many of the trees which look like palms are not, in the strict botanical sense, members of the *Palmaceae* family. Castor oil is a product of the *Palma christi*; it is used as purgative, and to cleanse the eyes, being one of the safest substances to put in the eye—especially useful for people who find that chlorinated water in swimming baths upsets their eyes—dab a little castor gently into the eyes before swimming. Substitutes for butter and oil can be made from several palms. The *Cocos nucifera*, called the Coconut palm, produces extremely nutritious nuts with a nourishing milk inside. The husk produces coir which is used for brushes, matting and ropes; from the dried kernel comes copra which is a source of candles, margarine, soap and cattle fodder (oil cake). The Moslems say that Allah made the palm from some oddments left over when he had finished making the rest of the world; they refer chiefly to the *Phoenix dactylifera* or the Date palm whose nutritious fruit, rich in natural sugars, is widely eaten and enjoyed. It is quite a complete food for the climate in which it grows, and Bedouin tribesmen could survive days at a time on a handful of dates— which made for light and speedy travelling. The produce of the date palm provides brooms, cloth (made from its fibres), roofing material and ropes—also the wisps of palm handed out in Christian churches on Palm Sunday. The reason why the people of Jerusalem waved palms before Jesus when he entered their city was not just as a mark of respect but as a sign of victory; the palm has been a recognised sign of triumph almost since the beginning of recorded history. In Ancient Egypt it was sacred to Thoth, the ibis-headed god of wisdom, arts and sciences, the measurer of all things, sometimes depicted as a moon-god. In the West Indies the Bakairi Caribs said that Man sprang from palm seeds sown by Mama Nono—the good mother. Do you remember Kipling's poem 'The Donkey'?

'I also had my hour, one far fierce hour and sweet,
There was a shout about my ears and palms before my feet.'

Did that donkey think it was all for him or for the rider?

PANSY *Viola tricolor (arvensis)*

The reason why Titania in Shakespeare's 'Midsummer Night's Dream' fell in love with the first *ass* she saw when Puck had dropped Oberon's juice of 'Love in Idleness' into her eyes originates in an ancient superstition that the juice of the pansy, as we now call it, had the peculiar property to evoke instant love!

The flowers were originally white, says legend, but were turned purple by Eros (Cupid) the god of love. My mother's mother always wrote her own poetry for birthday and Christmas cards; only when this remarkable woman was dead did the family realise what a shame it was that practically nothing of her writing had ever been kept. I am happy to have some of those unique pieces in precise copperplate. Here is 'To a Pansy' a poem she wrote when she was nearly 77 and suffering from her last, incurable illness :

'Walking along a lonely road, I passed a rubbish heap;
I stood and gazed at a pansy, its little face so sweet.
The sun was just a-peeping through; it lifted its pretty head
Upward, turned towards the sky; it seemed to me it said :
I've strugged through these stones and mud, and tried so hard to live
Now God has brought me through it all, my thanks to Him I give.
Take lesson from that little flower, when life seems very hard;
Turn your eyes towards the skies, and tell it to your God.
Poor little Pansy, I feel so sad, leaving you all alone,
Pushing your little, velvet buds through all those hard old stones.
I wish I could take you home with me, and plant you in the sun,
I'd watch your little buds come through, then I would say 'well done'.
I'll take a lesson from that flower, and by so do my best,
When Life is going very hard, and leave to God the rest'.

Not bad for a woman who was taught in a dame school and who left it at 12 to help on the farm with her mother.

A decoction of the herb can be used against eczematous and allied skin disorders. It is not a very pleasant drink but it does clear up some internal catarrhal conditions.

PASSION FLOWER *Passiflora caerula*

A favourite plant of missionaries because the three stils show the three nails used in the crucifixion of Christ, the ovary does look like the hammer which nailed Him to the cross; the five stamens represent the five wounds (don't forget the 5th wound made by the spear in his side); the corona is, of course, the crown of thorns and the ten petals show the ten true apostles, Judas is excluded and so is Peter for denying Christ thrice before the cock crew. The plant is, of course, native to South America, especially in Brazil; the first one brought to Britain was in 1699. It can flourish in Southern England provided it is kept out of east winds and draughts. Some species produce a nutritious, edible fruit but not usually outside their native habitat. Some medicinal use is made of the leaves as an anti-hysteric and anti-convulsant but this is definitely NOT FOR USE WITH-OUT EXPERT GUIDANCE.

PEACH *Persica vulgaris*

Under the Sun in Leo. Sacred to Venus. Greatly valued for its talismantic properties in warding off evil and disease. Even the stone wards off disease. My mother succeeded in growing a very healthy peach tree from a stone, and when it was mature we had fruit from it yearly. Peaches are so soothing to the stomach of invalids that they can be given in almost any case, particularly to people with colitis. The fruit is very nutritious and plentiful so there is little need to make use of the seed oil except for cosmetics; it is good for the skin.

PERIWINKLE *Vinca major*

A symbol of loyalty in olden times; under the dominion of Venus, and since the last decade of absorbing interest to medical research workers. When herbalists claimed that it could be used to cure cancer many allopathic doctors laughed them to scorn, but the discovery by American research chemists of over 40 different alkaloids, many of them hitherto unknown, in this small plant has made it a very important plant indeed, and one that is now accepted as a source of medicaments against both leukemia and cancer generally. There is only one other comment needed here—the botanic physician usually administers herbs as simple medicines in a natural form, occasionally requiring frequent doses which the sick body can accept and use easily. Others often wish to condense some healing powers into some quick-working pill which is frequently too strong for a sick body to absorb and use properly. The human body takes weeks and often months to become sick, it cannot be hurried ungraciously back into health by sheer brute force and violent methods without further damage occurring. I opt for safe herbal methods all the time. There is a simple example in this— cucumbers are often said to be indigestible, this is because they are eaten peeled, the actual peel contains chemical particles which prevent the internal substance from causing indigestion; wash the outside but don't throw it away! Again, powdered willow bark is good against colds, chills, headaches, to relieve menstrual pain and so on, but in the concentrated form of acetylsalicylic acid it can produce unfortunate side-effects and is a drug. Although sold everywhere in aspirin-type pills many people have no tolerance for it, some are even allergic to it.

PLUM *Prunus domestica*

The predominance of the plum tree, flowers and fruit in Japanese art dates back to a man called Tenjin who lived around the ninth century A.D. and did much to foster learning, scholarship and introduce writing into Japan; by apotheosis he was made a god and patron of writing, learning, etc. The Japanese have a tradition of gratitude, and when they feel there is nothing else they can do to thank a human being it is not uncommon for them to make him into a god. Lafeadio Hearn, probably the most learned scholar of all time in the field of Japanese life, literature and traditions, tells the story of Hamaguchi Gohei, the rich squire of a seaside village who witnessed a most extraordinary withdrawal of the tide.

The sea retreated way back, beyond sight of land; the villagers ran down on to the shore to look at the miracle, wandering far out on the former ocean bed. Hamaguchi Gohei was up on the hill, pondering what this meant, when he recalled his grandfather telling him that it had happened before and had been followed by a gigantic, monstrous wave which had destroyed the entire village. To his horror he perceived some high, moving, black thing on the far horizon. The man had no means of calling the villagers back. Suddenly he made up his mind, and set fire to his valuable ricks of rice, just harvested. He beat the gong, and the villagers turned, saw the blazing ricks, and rushed back inland to try to save the harvested rice. The last of them reached the hillside home just before the colossal wave swept in and destroyed the entire village below them. Hamaguchi Gohei was now a pauper and had ruined himself to save them. They in turn had nothing to give him for the village and all their possessions were destroyed. Very soon after this he was made into a god, and until the beginning of this century, at least, was still venerated. In Europe the plum is said to be under Venus. Eaten as a fruit the plum is slightly laxative, if eaten with unripe skin it is positively purgative.

POMEGRANATE *Punica granatum*

In spite of its name the so-called Apple of Grenada started life in India or Persia. It was introduced by the cultured Moors into Southern Spain. One Eastern tradition says that this was the original fruit which Eve offered to Adam. A similar legend says it was the fruit which Paris awarded to Aphrodite (see Apple). Because the unfortunate Prosperine ate a pomegranate in Hades she could never return wholly to live on earth but was forced to live with Pluto part of her life. For some 5,000 years it has been a source of cosmetics for women, and is an ingredient of many perfumes. It is a national emblem of Spain, especially of Granada. From its flowers herbalists make a tea which is most beneficial for many nervous disorders and which helps relieve migraine speedily. From its bark a powder is made which has been used for clearing out clogged-up bowels. It is one of the oldest plants on earth. Some pomegranate seeds have been found in late tertiary deposits. It is a universal fertility symbol. The bark can be boiled like most herbs and drunk against worm infestation. A friend from Istanbul told me that in country parts of Anatolia village brides still throw a pomegranate to the ground; the number of seeds which spill out indicate how many children they will bear. There is a Turkish proverb which is very good advice for the young :—

'Love the one who loves thee,
Though he be ruler of Egypt love not that one who loves thee not.'

(Sev, seni seveni, hâk ile yaksan olsa.
Sevme, seni sevmiyeni, mırsıda sultan olsa)

POPPY *Papaveraceae*

Under Saturn or the Moon. The Yellow Poppy is under the Sun in Leo. Fletcher in his 'Faithful Shepherd' wrote of Endymion discovered by Diana : 'His temple bound with poppy' which is signficant because in those days it was considered to be a method of hypnosis to tie poppies to the temples of a person. Mildred Cable and Francesca French described the waving poppies growing wild and profusely in the savage Black Gobi desert. Ceres used poppies to heal the son of Celeus and Metanira. Rupert Brooke immortalised the Flanders poppy with his poem about 'some corner of a foreign field', and due to this influence it was adopted as a symbol of remembrance for the fallen servicemen of the First World War.

The plant contains, in Europe at least, insignificant amounts of opium but it is NOT SUITABLE FOR INTERNAL USE because of its soporific properties. Roasted seed is sometimes used for cakes. The fresh juice is very useful to clear up warts.

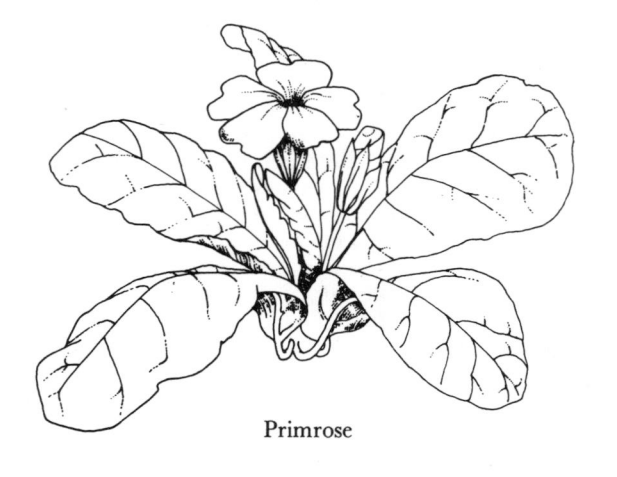

Primrose

PRIMROSE *Primula vulgaris*

Beaumont and Fletcher, Burns, Cowper, Milton and Shakespeare all enthused about this beautiful spring flower, indeed it is hard to find a poet of note who hasn't. It has long been seen as a bringer of luck. Disraeli was responsible for the Conservative Party founding the Primrose League. The leaves can be used to treat cuts and wounds while the flowers or the leaves can be boiled gently to make a drink to drive out worms, relieve certain rheumatic ailments, and, according to some old authorities, to bring relief for infantile paralysis.

ROSE *Rosaceae*

A symbol of incorruptibility, of purity, of love, a symbol of St. Teresa de Lisieux. Saadi (1184–1291), one of the great Persian poets and mystics, a sheikh and famous traveller of his day, wrote three magnificent volumes of verse, *Diwan* (lyrics), *Bustan* (Garden of fruit) and the most famous of all—*Gulistan* (Garden of Roses). In the verses of Omar Khayyām (died 1123) the rose is constantly celebrated in his lilting quatrains. The highly-sexed young emperor Elagabalus (A.D. 205–222) is said to have suffocated with roses some citizens who protested at his bi-sexual appetites; not long afterwards the Imperial Guards killed him. The mediaeval verse treasure '*Roman de la Rose*' dating from the thirteenth century is a beautiful epic poem on the art of love—in all its aspects, showing how hard it is for a young man to pluck the rose of his choice. Chaucer did an approximate translation, dating a century later. Cupid gave Harpocrates (the deity of silence) a rose to buy his co-operation in keeping quiet the amours of Venus. On the fourth Sunday in Lent the Pope blesses a 'golden' rose which is then presented to some sovereign or person of note.

In the Wars of the Roses (1455–85) Lancaster took the Red rose, and York the White rose as symbols. Henry Tudor, the Welsh diplomat, designed the Tudor rose with both white and red petals, symbolic of the end of the feud !

The word 'Dog-rose' has nothing to do with the canine species at all, it comes from the old English word for 'dagger' and meant a rose with a sharp thorn. That reminds one of Schubert's music and Goethe's words about the young boy picking a rose on the heath—'*Sah ein Knab'ein Röslein stehn*'. Attar of roses is usually made by steam distillation. The valley of the Maritza is a remarkable sight when the rose crop is in bloom. Attar of Roses haunts one all through the Turkish world; it is very hard to buy any soap, brilliantine or perfume which is NOT attar of roses. It is a very old process, and even the Chanson de Roland (eleventh century poem) refers to attar of roses.

> '*The first at mass thy rose to see*
> *Is the swain shall marry thee.*'

This refers to collecting a rose at night and wearing it to mass ('church' in later days) in the belief that the first man to admire it would be the one who would marry the girl wearing it.

Girls often used to put a rose under their pillow to see the face of their lover in their dreams.

Rose leaves were scattered at weddings to ensure a happy wedded life. Judging by the present divorce rate I think it is time we stopped using substitute paper rose petals—they don't seem to work so well. Another legend :

> '*God who in His wisdom created Light*
> *Likewise in wisdom made the rose white,*
> *Made it chaste and pure with a sweet fragrance;*
> *Thus it stayed till Adam in his vagrance*
> *Saw it spotless while it was unfolding,*
> *And the rose blushed red at his beholding.*' (Law)

CHAMOMILE

The dried flowers are used for making tea, and the flowers are
sometimes used in shampoos for fair hair. Also it has been used
as a cure for insomnia.

The word Hip in Rosehip comes from the Anglo-Saxon *Heop* and the fruit, which is rich in vitamin C, has been used for medicinal purposes many centuries.

St. Dominic (1170–1221) received the first rosary from the Virgin Mary during a mystical visitation. Some sources say that each bead was a rose, others that each bead was scented with roses. The Roman Catholics use two forms of rosary, one with 165 beads divided into groups of 15, the more common one with 55 beads; the Catholic Rosary Sunday (the first in October) celebrates the victory of the Christians over the Turks at the Battle of Lepanto in 1571. The Buddhists, especially the Lamaistic Mahayana sect, use a rosary, as do the Moslems and the modern Phrenosophists; the latter use a rosary of 21 beads and call it by the same name. The idea is that each bead represents a prayer, and the beads (roses) are an aide-memoire to keep your place during the devotions. The hips and the petals of the rose (preferably the red rose) are useful in all catarrhal, bronchial and even pulmonary disorders. As a drink they have peculiarly rest-bringing properties and are very peaceful and tranquillising to have around the house as flowers. Sir John Mandeville in his book of travels (*c.* fourteenth century) says that the rose sprang from a fire in which an innocent maiden was burned to death. In some Greek towns visitors are still offered rose jam on a clean grape leaf when they take coffee.

ROSEMARY *Rosmarinus officinalis*

Butler mentions in his *Hudibras* (*c.* 1663) that it is a useful herb for lovers. It is certainly a symbol for friendship and, as Shakespeare makes Ophelia say in *Hamlet* : 'Rosemary that's for remembrance.' It is reputed never to grow higher than Jesus was when alive in Galilee. An old saying has it : 'Where the dame is master rosemary will thrive.' It was long considered essential for a young bride on her wedding day to wear rosemary about her person. Frédéric Mistral, rejuvenator of the Provençal language, wrote : *'Un vòu de blóundis abiho que raubon sa melico i roumanin dóu gres'*—a swarm of blonde bees robbing the rosemary among the stony fields of its honey. The plant is under the dominion of the sun.

The drink made from this plant is most soothing and helpful for all headaches, even for migraine. Oil of rosemary is commonly used in many preparations for curing baldness. (*See* my book *How to Keep your Hair On* for full details), and also to lessen the pain of toothache.

ROWAN *Pyrus aucaparia*

The tree is, of course, closely allied to Germanic folklore, and all over Northern Europe there are sayings such as : 'No witch dare pass where rowans grow.' A cross made of rowan wood and carried three times round a house, farm or stable, etc., in a sunwise direction would protect it from all evil. To grow a rowan tree near the house was to keep witches and warlocks, and all things that go bump in the night, away from it. The farmers of olden times always hung sprigs of rowan round the necks of their cattle, or in their stalls and byres, to keep off diseases, sickness, accidents and all witchcraft. Later traditions were so optimistic as to say that a sprig of rowan always brings good luck in gambling.

The berries can be used to make very useful herbal medicines against influenza, sore throats, etc. They are astringent and very antiseptic, but the beginner is recommended to make this mixture at HALF STRENGTH because the acid in the berries is exceptionally strong.

The rowanberry has some use in combating deficiency diseases which affect skin and neural health.

Rosemary

RUE *Ruta graveolens*
Under the sun in Leo, called the herb of Grace because it is the symbol of repentance. It was held to be the only thing on earth

the monster Basilisk could not wither with a glance. Throughout the Christian and Islamic world it is reputed to be able to ward off the evil eye and cast out devils. It is most useful as a herbal drink to alleviate internal bruising, and was once favoured to act as an antidote to poisons.

SAFFRON *Crocus sativus*
Favoured in oriental cooking, and used as a dye for clothing. It was valued to ward off evil, and was the symbol of the marriage of Zeus and Hera. It is mentioned in the Bible and the works of Homer. It is under the Sun in Leo. Medicinally it can be used to relieve asthma and several types of convulsions. It is carminative.

ST. JOHN'S WORT *Hypericum perfoliatum*
Under the Sun in Leo. One of the most popular herbs used against witchcraft, devils, evils, ghosts and storms. To hang St. John's Wort over a house was to protect it from danger, theft, lightning and much else. The little crimson flecks are said to be the blood of St. John the Baptist when Herod had him executed at the behest of Salome (Oscar Wilde wrote a descriptive play about it). Pieces of the herb were frequently used in amulets to bring good luck. The plant is quite picturesque; *'Weeds make dunghills gracious,'* wrote Tennyson. Blended with a vegetable oil the herbal juice was valuable for application to cuts, sores, rheumatic limbs and swellings.

It was sometimes included in love philtres.

SCARLET PIMPERNEL *Anagallis arvensis*
Called the poor man's weatherglass because it closes when bad weather is approaching. The Greeks called it 'laughter' and said it could cure liver ailments and what we would now classify as psychosomatic troubles. This was the flower which the Hungarian Baroness Orczy made famous with her novel *The Scarlet Pimpernel* concerning an English adventurer who frequently risked his own life to save victims of the French Revolution. The book was first published in 1905, having been refused, it is said, by no less than 39 publishing houses before the last one took a chance and made a considerable fortune from it. So young writers, take heart. The herb is used to heal kidney disorders.

SNOWDROPS *Galanthus nivalis*
Sacred to the Virgin Mary. There is a tradition that one should never bring snowdrops into the house on St. Valentine's Day lest the girls of the house remain old maids forever. It is not used generally in herbal medicine.

SORREL *Rumex acetosa*
A herb of Venus. Some sources claim that this was the true 'Shamrock' with which St. Patrick showed the Celtic heathen how

Sorrel

the 'Holy Trinity' could exist. It is most certainly the plant intended
in the Mabinogion, that marvellous collection of Welsh tradition
dating from the 7th century A.D. : *'Four white trefoils sprang up
wherever she trod, and therefore Olwen was she called.'* It can be
used to alleviate blood pressure, cool the blood, act against rheumatism and jaundice. It has a fairly strong effect upon the kidneys.
Feuerbach wrote : 'In the perishable petals of a flower there resides
more spirit and life than in the lumpish granite boulder that has
defied the tear and wear of thousands of years.' It is sometimes
used in salads. It might have been among the herbs offered by
Baucis and Philemon when they entertained Jupiter unawares.

SUNFLOWERS *Helianthus annuus*

One of my most lasting memories of Turkey is that of fields of sun-
flowers stretching almost as far as the eye can see. In July and
August those fields of moving flower heads are incredible. The giant
heads do turn and follow the sun just as Thomas Moore tells us
in his poem. It was the symbol of St. John the Evangelist. The
seeds contain vitamins A, B, calcium, phosphorus and other valuable mineral salt traces. One member of the Helianthus family is
the beloved old symbol of the Incas who were sun-worshippers.
This mode of worship was not the simple primitive faith that some
people now think. It showed God as the Light and Giver of Life.
A very spiritual and advanced religion, using the sun as symbol of

God was taught by Akhnaten, the Egyptian monarch and reformer of the 18th. Dynasty. The sunflower is a symbol of loyalty. Ancient Turkish *Hakims* prescribed a medicine against malaria made from the leaves.

SYCAMORE *Acer pseudoplatanus*

This is supposedly the tree into which the taxgatherer mentioned in the gospel climbed in order to see Jesus. It was a tree which the Egyptians held sacred to Hathor, goddess of beauty, of love and of the sky, she it was who provided refreshment for the soul. It is a very ornamental tree. The wood is much sought after for toy-making, furniture and at one time for making type faces for printers. It is unwise to use internally medicines made from this tree. The juice, or the decoction made from its fruit, can be used to close bad cut and wounds, applying them externally.

VALERIAN *Valeriana officinalis*

Said to be under Uranus. It has been a standing ingredient of countless aphrodisiacs and love potions. It is a common ingredient of many modern nerve tonics used by botanic physicians. In many parts of the country the herb was hung up in the house to bring peace in the home and prevent the marriage partners from bickering. Chaucer called it 'Setwall', and it was known and used by the Romans. It was a favourite remedy for palpitations of the heart and for epilepsy, and may still be said to exert a benevolent influence on these conditions.

VERBENA *Verbena officinalis*

Flowers formed from the tears of Juno. This was the *herba sacra*, the one which older writers regarded as a panacea; you name the illness they said, Verbena will heal it. In many English books it is called Vervain. The Druids are known to have used it to ward off evil. Pliny says it was used to tell fortunes, but doesn't say how. Beasts for sacrifice in Ancient Rome, were decorated with verbena. Was it a coincidence that they greeted foreign embassies with verbena also? Flower festivals called *verbenalia* were often held. Herbalists used it for snake bite and variocele at one time; now it is more commonly employed to relieve ulcers, sores, dropsical conditions, jaundice, gout, various feverish conditions—for many of which it is very good—for colds and coughs. It has good use for nervous complaints. The herb is said to be under Venus.

VIOLET *Viola odorata*

Once, the story goes, this plant stood proud and erect until the shadow of the cross fell upon it, since when it has always hung its head in undying shame at the inhumanity of man. Hood, the poet (1799–1845), wrote : 'The violet is a nun.' Chaucer and Byron wrote about these delicate, sweetly-scented flowers. This is the floral

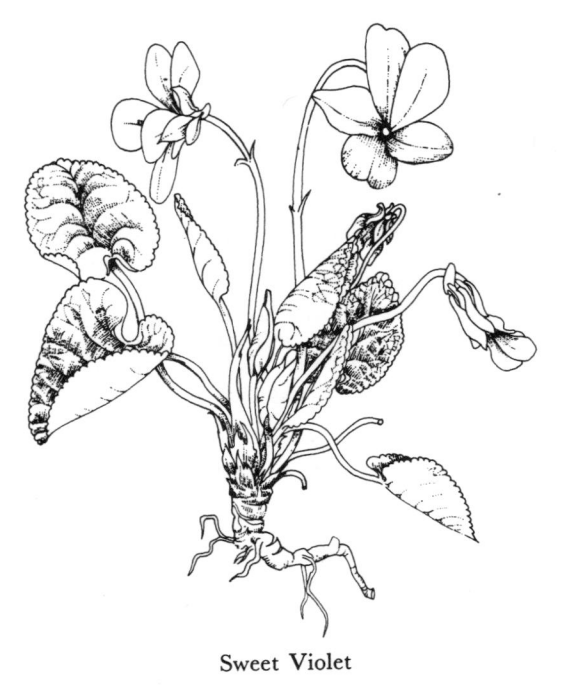

Sweet Violet

emblem of Athens, said to have sprung up purple from the blood
of the dying Ajax; it is a flower which represents faithful friendship and innocence. The flowers are said to be a powerful aphrodisiac. If we are to believe Homer the violets were the most beautiful
thing about Calypso's island. A sentimental verse from Emma Brace:

> *'Little Violet, Oh how sweet!*
> *Drooping your head at people's feet,*
> *Casting your fragrance in the air*
> *Helping to make God's earth so fair.*
> *Our lives are short the longest,*
> *So let us do our best*
> *To make this life a sweet one*
> *And leave to God the rest.'*

Culpeper said the violet was subject to Venus astrologically. This
was the favourite flower of the Emperor Napoleon. Tennyson in
'Aylmer's field' makes a reference to the story that when Nero died
(A.D. 68) some unknown used to bestrew his tomb with violets—
perhaps there was one sentient being who really could love even
Nero! Violet leaves have antiseptic properties and would seem to
have anticarcinogenic materials; several cases have been reported
to me of cancers having been *cleared up* by use of them in con-
junction with dietetic reforms and so on.

WALLFLOWER *Cheiranthus*

The Greek name comes from two words meaning 'carried in the hand' and these flowers (or some remarkably like them) are depicted in some of the most ancient drawings. One eminent authority has said that they were known to the Cretans and the Ancient Egyptians, for they do seem to be the flowers drawn on wall paintings in both lands. Sir Walter Scott (1771–1832) wrote as follows :

> '*The rude stone fence with fragrant wallflowers gay*
> *To me more pleasure yields*
> *Than all the pomp imperial domes display.*'

Galen, the great physician of olden days, advised that the yellow flowered had the best medicinal effect. They were long used to make childbirth easy and painless, to clear cataract from the eyes, and to clean kidneys and liver. Culpeper mentions that in his day a jam was made of the flowers and given to patients with palsy and apoplexy with success; this should be investigated. The flower has become the symbol of loneliness, in earlier days it signified loyalty. They are under the Moon.

WALNUT *Juglans regia*

This is another tree about which it is said beating is suitable (as for dogs and women !); alas how sadistic our ancestors seem to us. There seems one peculiarity which may be more than a legend. Flies and insects do not like walnut trees, so if one grows near the house the flies will keep away, and your cattle will be happier if you put them in a field where a walnut tree is growing. The tree was introduced into England, probably from Persia indirectly through Spain (by way of the Moors) about 1562. The Greeks call the 'Adam's *Apple*' a 'walnut'. The tree and the nut are under the dominion of the Sun, and protect the home from lightning and people from rheumatism. To carry a walnut is to attract luck to yourself. The WAL part of the name has nothing to do with 'wall' it is the same as 'welsh', i.e. 'foreign' (the Germanic Swiss call the Romantsch '*Walliser*'). The nuts are very rich in many nutritive elements and highly prized by vegetarian cooks. The wood is ideal for furniture-making.

WORMWOOD *Artemesia absinthium*

Sacred to Artemis (Diana) who had some interest in the healing art (being sister to Apollo—god of healing). This plant is a symbol of healing and health. Another myth says that it grew from the slime left by the slithering serpent in the Garden of Eden. If kept in cupboards it keeps moths and flies away from clothes. The original Anglo-Saxon was a self-explanatory language which meant that everybody could understand instantly what a thing did even if he had never heard the word before, and the plant was called 'Wer mod' meaning 'Caretaker of the Mind' (compare ware in be*ware*,

and the word *mood* as an aspect of mind); this meaning is related
to the herb being an antidote to drunkenness; it is a tonic and stimulant, but more commonly used against fevers. It should be prepared
at half the strength usually used when making herbal drinks.

Some witches used this plant to produce a heightened state of
suggestibility in their clients; the bitterness of the drink being equal
to a physical shock if made too strong. Culpeper says it comes under
Mars.

YARROW *Achillea millefolium*

Recommended to young girls who want to find themselves a
lover. Its botanical name reveals its connection with Achilles. One
story says that the plant comes from the scrapings of Achilles' spear.
There was an ancient belief, held fairly universally, and strongly
marked among the Fenno–Ugrian tribes (it is mentioned in the
Finnish *Kalevala* several times), that to heal a wound one must
touch or take scrapings from the weapon that caused it. The plant
is under Venus. The most common story is that the plant was shown
to Achilles by Chiron, the Centaur from Trace. The simple Anglo-
Saxon name was 'Gearwe' from the verb to repair; this is the great
healer (or repairer) of human bodies. Influenza, colds, coughs, fevers,
blood disorders of several sorts and many other disorders yield to
the simple of Yarrow. I try never to be without it in my home.
It is one of the first herbs I resort to, and moreover it makes a very
pleasant drink.

YEW *Taxus*

The Greek word from which its botanic name comes means 'bow'
and the Yew tree has been used to make good, strong, springy bows
for well over 1,000 years. All the Robin Hood legends relate that
his bows were made of yew. The famous longbow with which the
English archers swept their way through France—especially at the
victory of Agincourt, on October 25th. 1415—was usually made of
yew. The tree is under Saturn, according to Culpeper. It has long
been seen jointly as a symbol of death and of immortality. Most
legends refer to it as a symbol of longevity, and a protector of the
dead; the reason why yew trees are planted in churchyards is because they keep the dead from harm. The tree often lives to 1,000
years or more. The Druids favoured it and usually grew yew trees
near their temples. It is never used for medicinal purposes and
should be avoided because of its toxicity, which affects some patients
more than others. It was once used for ill-defined nervous cases and
epileptic seizures.

                                        *

WARNINGS

DO NOT TREAT YOURSELF UNLESS YOU ARE ABSOLUTELY CERTAIN
YOU HAVE CORRECTLY DIAGNOSED WHAT IS WRONG WITH YOU.
In the case of colds, coughs, etc. this is easy enough, but do not
rush to conclusions when there is a headache (which is often

a symptom of something else and not the real malady) or vague pains which you are not sure about. Consult one or more of the recommended works which will help you in diagnosis.

If you order herbs from a supplier do be sure to quote the correct Latin botanic name given beside the English name. If you want to collect herbs for yourself use one of the recommended works, and make sure that the description fits the plant exactly—this prevents any accident.

Common mallow *Malva sylvestris*

WILD FLOWERS

Chenil

Angelica archangelica

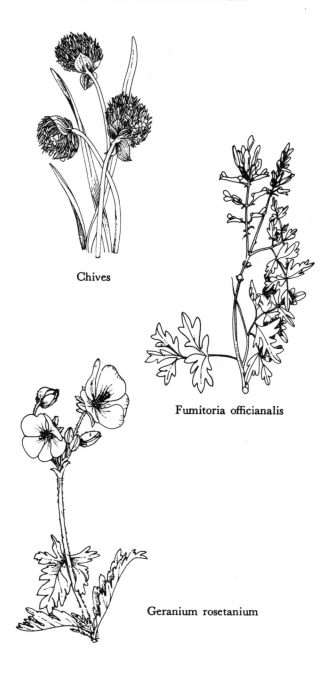

Chives

Fumitoria officianalis

Geranium rosetanium

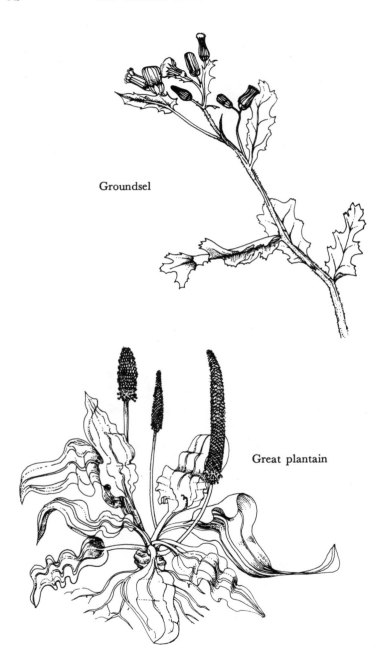

Groundsel

Great plantain

Rampian

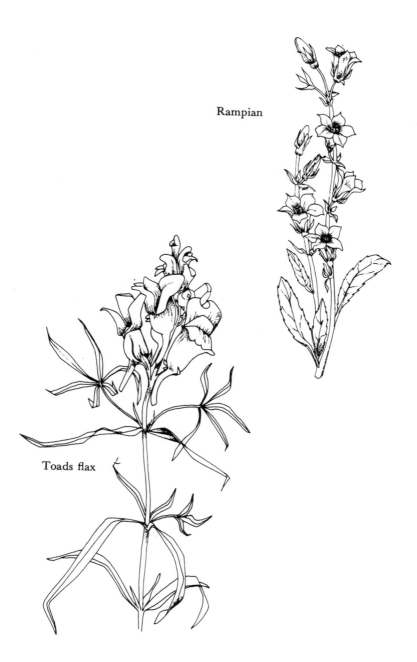

Toads flax

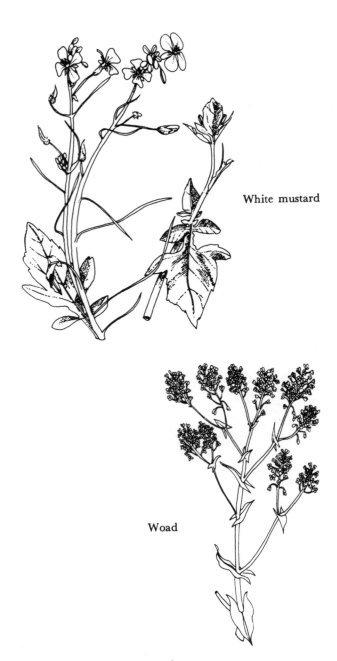

White mustard

Woad

3. Health from Herbal Wines

In the following text if no specific recipe is quoted use the BASIC RECIPE given below :

2 oz. of the herb.
3 lb. sugar.
Juice of one or two lemons as per taste.
One gal. of water.
   In metric values :
      ·057 kg. herb.
      1·36 kg. sugar.
      4·55 l. water.

Tastes vary, and by trial and experiment the reader will learn how much body (taste) is wanted in a wine, how much sweetness, etc. Avoid oversweetening wines at first. Sweetening can easily be added but not removed.

*

The making of wine has been known to Man from the misty beginnings of history, and frequently in myths the origin is said to have been divinely inspired.

Wine is one of the oldest-known ways of preserving the life-giving properties of herbs; there are indications that this is indeed the tradition of Egypt, and certainly of Ancient Greece and Rome.

It is well known among practitioners of Botanic Medicine that herbs take effect more quickly if assimilated in liquid forms. Apart from aiding in their preservation, the wine also tends to extract more of the healing property of the herb so, apart from the interesting and useful hobby of wine making, you can keep a valuable store of safe home remedies by you, knowing that they will keep for years.

This section provides you with a detailed list of herbs which you can use to make wines with, and shows useful tonic and restorative healing properties.

There are clear instructions on how to make wines if you have never tried it before—and I hasten to assure you that it is easy to make wine : really all you need is the patience to leave it to mature.

There is no need to fear alcohol. Jesus drank wine, and the prohibition of Mahomet was an isolated historical event, a law to lessen the excitable nature of the belligerent tribes he led on his *Jehad*. Phrenosophists permit the use of wine and beer but not of spirits or liqueurs. I think that while there is nothing wrong with wine there is a lot wrong with any person who can find no joy in moderation.

As a student in old Heidelberg I would often pass a delightful evening in some corner of a baroque *Weinhaus* with girl friends, enjoying the lilt of some gypsy violinist, perhaps making one or two bottles last the whole evening for two or four of us.

Wine is a social occasion, it stimulates thought, tolerance, wit and the exchange of great sentiments, it inspires conversation.

Unfortunately, nowadays there is incredible adulteration of wine by many commercial houses, and you are far safer with simple home-made herbal wines. Chemicals and additives are used to speed up natural processes, and falsify taste, etc. In 1968 there was a terrible scandal in Italy when an internationally-known firm was prosecuted for putting into their wine scrapings from banana boats, carob beans, dates, figs, *lead acetate* and invertasi (to turn cheapest quality cane sugar into a glucose) and so on. I think it is safer and healthier to make your own wines.

Herbal wines are natural, simple products, they retain the vitamins and mineral salts of the plants, and can be used socially and medicinally.

In the case of grape wines there is a heavy deposit which contains calcium, magnesium tartrates and a lot of potassium hydrogen tartrate—the precipitation increasing as the process of becoming alcohol proceeds. Grape wines are usually pale in colour during the fermentation stage, and commercial houses often add such substances as isinglass (prepared from the airbladders of fish), lime (a caustic earth), and sometimes gum (from tree resins or fish) to speed up the natural clearing process.

As if this were not enough in the way of additives there is a tendency to use plaster of paris (gypsum) to carry off the potassium hydrogen tartrates, a peculiar process which, while making a wine easier to keep and slightly dry, deposits the acid sulphate of potassium. Not too appetising is it?

Occasionally, bought grape wines have had sugar added to them to increase their sweetness, but some sulphur dioxide must them be added to prevent excessive fermentation bubbling up. Such wines are usually described as 'fortified' wines but this word is not always understood by the purchaser.

Occasionally wine merchants will add colouring matters and other chemicals to force through different effects; some are just plain deception, but others are of debatable value. For these highly chemicalised concoctions the public are often asked to pay prices which are bordering upon the excessive.

PURE WINES ARE HEALTHY

Research shows that our forefathers never drank such bottles of chemicals but used simple pure wines which brought health and strength and nothing like the hangovers which some of our chemicalised potions produce.

Well, where can anybody obtain such wines today? The answer is simple—MAKE THEM YOURSELF. If you are not going to pro-

DANDELION

Grow to a height of between 2″ and 12″. The fresh leaves may be used for salads. Dried they form a basis for herb beers etc., milky extract from root provides a valuable medicine. Dandelion wine is also a common use.

duce some overchemicalised product you need practically no equipment which you cannot afford out of a moderate weekly wage, and once you have the simple, basic necessities you will find they will last you for years—and make many *gallons* of delicious wines.

The actual amount of effort involved in wine-making is very small, the time you spend on the whole process from start to finish often being less than you could spend in the waiting-room of a doctor's surgery, if you made a couple of visits to get medicine—and at least you will know exactly what is in your own home-made wines.

This section tells you how to make wines which will not only be charming additions to your table and to pleasant leisure hours but which can bring you health—your health in every sense of the word.

It would be wrong to suggest that you cannot get drunk on home-made wines; indeed you can, but I think it is only right to say that I have never known anybody have a bad head (morning after the night before) following a carouse on even strong home-made wines—because there are no noxious chemicals to hit at the nervous system.

The instructions are simplified to help you even if you have never made wine before; do read through the chapter which is subtitled 'and how not to', it outlines the pitfalls which an enthusiastic beginner might rush into. In various part of the country herbs have different folk-names, and to make certain that you do get the correct herbs a fully detailed list of the correct botanical Latin names will make it easy to identify the right herbs, so that you could even gather them yourself. Many a glorious summer day can be spent gathering herbs which can make the wine that gladdens your heart on a cold Christmas Eve.

Properly made herbal wines keep their tonic and healing properties for years, the remedy is always at hand; no need to rush round to a chemist, just pull the cork, and pour out—health!

HOW MUCH TO TAKE AS MEDICINE

If the wine is taken for medicinal and tonic properties the usual dose would be a 3 oz. fluid glassful taken twice or three times a day; remember that a sick body often takes smaller doses and uses them far better than it can ever absorb a huge dose. Herbal healing substances are often quite powerful even when in homoeopathic doses.

A fluid ounce is an ordinary ounce of distilled water at a temperature of 16°C, or 64°F. For the reader in a hurry let us simply say that the average eggcup contains one fluid ounce.

All of the wines in the text may be taken freely for enjoyment except the wines marked * which should be treated as specifically tonic and healing drinks.

Do not imbibe immoderately if you feel unwell; temper your thirst with a modicum of reserve.

Herbal wines are often very attractive by reason of their bouquet; many charming and enticing flavours ascend to your nostrils and set your taste buds into a thrill of excitement with alluring promises.

Do show restraint in the amounts of herbs used; remember that you can always add more herb to strengthen the taste but you can only reduce an overstrong taste by adding more water and starting over again.

I have used herbs and fruit for home-made wines for many years and find them a never-ending source of pleasure and health. It is a sure way to make friends and keep them.

HOW TO MAKE YOUR OWN WINE

Under each herb mentioned are suggested amounts of the herb or fruit and recommended amounts of sugar and the water required. It must be understood that unless specifically stated otherwise the amounts of herb or fruit used to give the wine its flavour can be varied slightly and the amount of sugar can be increased when the wine is already fermenting, but *not at the beginning*—you can always add sugar, you cannot take it away.

The first process of making wine is to have around you all the things needed, so let us list the bare essentials.

You will need one large enamel saucepan or container to cook your fruit or herb or in which to seep it. On no account use aluminium, which tends to impart a horrible metallic flavour to wine and can infuse aluminium salts into the liquor. If it is only a matter of seeping the flavouring materials cold or with boiling water poured over them you could use a clean plastic container (keep it for wine and use it for nothing else). Next a winchester or any large container which can take an airlock (as described under the section on *Fermentation*) and that means you need an airlock and a rubber or cork bung which has been pierced to take an airlock (it is advisable to have a spare airlock by you). You need one large (plastic) funnel, a large sieve with a narrow mesh (this can also be made of plastic) a small bottle of Campden tablets (for sterilising bottles etc) some bottles and corks (all new corks, never re-use old ones unless you have sterilised them personally), muslin, a wooden spoon, and some petty labels which you can fill in at your leisure. My name is *Donald* so I label my wines *'Château d'On'* which amuses my friends. Every reader can think up some witty addition to the labels. Finally, to make the job easier, a three-foot length of rubber tubing (keep in a clean plastic bag) is helpful.

Now this is what we do with all our paraphernalia.

(1) Get the recommended quantities of ingredients ready.

(2) Boil, seep or cover with boiling water according to advice specified (normally we boil the ingredients or simmer them).

(3) When cool stir in the sugar until it all melts, then add $\frac{1}{2}$ oz. or 1 oz. yeast spread on a piece of freshly-made toast; in practice you can add the yeast without the toast but for the

beginner the addition of a small piece of toast guarantees that the yeast has a solid foundation on which it can grow.

(4) The initial fermentation is violent so it is usually conducted in a large container with a couple of layers of muslin tied tightly over the mouth to prevent access by vinegar fly (see section on *Fermentation*). The actual duration of the initial fermentation depends on the violence and the strength of the fermentation process (this is usually strong enough to be heard clearly without listening especially for it). You can allow anything from five days to ten days. When the mixture is no longer bubbling strongly you can put it into a winchester or similar container with an airlock (never put a gallon of newly-fermenting wine straight into a gallon winchester—the airlock is never strong enough and you will sooner or later have a kitchen flowing with yeasty wine froth pouring out of the unwelcome prison it finds itself in). DURING THE INITIAL FERMENTATION STIR THE MIXTURE EVERY 12 HOURS; use a wooden spoon in preference to a metal one.

The initial stage is also useful for testing the strength of the taste of the wine, it is this stage which is most suited for the addition of extra flavour, or modifying lemon juice etc. Use only natural products with wine; avoid chemicals and artificial products.

Once the wine is in the winchester the second process takes place, this is slower and extremely important. It is fully explained under *Fermentation*. The wine must be passed through the sieve and through a layer of muslin before it is placed into the winchester. If you don't do this your wine is unlikely to clear and give good transparent colour. When the ingredients have been boiled to extract the flavour there is usually a slight fog which may not clear; this is nothing to do with the soup-like opacity which comes from wine that has not been racked correctly!

Clearing takes from three to six months to be effective and happens automatically without any help from you. When you are racking the wine you may find it needful to add a little more water to fill the winchesters (keep them as full as possible), never add more water without *adding more sugar*; if you add a pint of water add about 4 oz. sugar.

(5) Repeat the racking procedure once a month, and for the second and subsequent racking operations use the rubber tube in this way—suck up a little wine into the tube, pinch the tube tight and place the free end into the container into which you are going to empty out the wine, then the wine will flow down by force of suction and a vacuum.

(6) Bottle any time after six months in the winchester. You had better store the wine in a temperature not exceeding 59°F. or 15°C. Cork it tightly, cover with leaden seal if so desired. Label clearly with its name, date of making and your name. You

are allowed to give wine away but not to sell it without a licence under British Law. But when you make wine you will find many friends willing to swop goods with you! Sterilise every bottle (and cork) before you put your new wine into them. The Campden tablets will do this very well; you just crumble the tablet up, add hot water and swill round the bottle for a few minutes; leave corks to soak in a solution of Campden tablet and hot water for two hours.

ESSENTIALS

(1) Do not oversweeten. If after a month or two the wine is too sweet add some more yeast (just a pinch) and start a further fermentation process.

(2) If the wine has too strong a flavour add a little sugar and the juice of one or two lemons or oranges.

(3) If the wine begins to taste and smell like vinegar act at once or you'll lose all of it. Add one Campden tablet (it will do no harm) to each gallon-size winchester. Two days later put a little dash of yeast and four ounces of sugar—if your luck holds good you'll save it. If it still smells of vinegar and tastes of vinegar a week later just use it as you would use household vinegar. See the section on *Fermentation*.

(4) If white *flowers* begin to form inside your winchester you must quickly empty the wine into another container; clean out the winchester with a Campden tablet and hot water, dry out and then sieve the wine (rack it) back into the cleaned winchester. You may use a little wad of cotton wool in the sieve to keep non-liquid matter out of the wine.

(5) Do not allow your wine to stand on a bed of used-up yeast; it will give the wine a bad flavour. After racking add a little sugar and keep your fingers crossed.

(6) Do not let your wine stand in a half-full winchester or it will get far too much air—and faults may develop; allow no more than two inches from the bottom of your rubber bung in the winchester neck and the top of the liquid.

(7) Do not use damaged fruit or any materials which are not fresh and wholesome.

(8) When boiling do not leave scum on the top of the saucepan.

(9) Do not fill the wine bottle completely, allow two inches from cork bottom to top of the liquid for expansion of gas.

(10) Lastly, once again, do not oversweeten.

FERMENTATION—the mystery of Wine

It is not quite clear at which precise time in history Man learned, either by study or by accident, to utilise the process of the simple self-reproduction of yeast to produce alcohol. From the Etruscan times of Tarquinia to the shores of Cathay men have shared the knowledge of alcohol.

If we put a quantity of yeast into water containing sugar the conditions are extremely favourable for the reproduction of yeast cells; the natural biological and chemical processes ensue provided the temperature is not wholly unfavourable.

At the conclusion of the procedure about half the sugar has been changed into alcohol and the remainder into carbon dioxide (whence come the bubbles in your wine); the yeast is a living organism which produces fermentation in the medium it inhabits.

The fruit pulp (must) is really there only to provide flavour and body for the wine, but every lovely effervescent bubble you see (particularly when you are making your own wine) has its equivalent in weight of alcohol.

I mentioned temperature just two paragraphs ago; let me explain what influence this has. Fermentation starts off best at a temperature of 70°Fahrenheit=21°Celsius (Centigrade) but above 100°F=38°C the yeast will die; below the lower level it is unlikely to survive, so temperature is important to fermentation.

Winemakers distinguish two specific stages of fermentation : the AIRED FERMENTATION, which is the first, violent and frothy stage lasting the first week or so; this is so powerful that the liquid is usually allowed contact with the air through a thin (fly-proof) cloth or close-mesh net; then comes the AIRLESS FERMENT, during which the slower and most important fermentation occurs while the wine is stored in winchester or vats. This second stage is best done at a temperature around 60°F=15°C.

All the best wines are the result of slow, unaided fermentation without any additives to speed it up. Some less reputable vineyards have been known to add all sorts of chemicals to force fermentation. From such additives come the terrible sickness and headaches which cheap bought wines often induce. Novices in winemaking (and drinking) must have patience.

There is one point which may disillusion quite a few misled enthusiasts; if the fermentation stops naturally when the alcoholic content reaches its maximum conversion capacity (see above) you simply cannot expect a wine to grow *stronger* because you keep it for years and years—and many of the impressive, romantic stories of sophisticated men-about-town having mouldy, cobweb-covered bottles of antique vintage wines brought to *their* table in the restaurant or club by faithful retainers is amusing, picturesque, but pure exaggeration.

Wines mellow up to a point when kept in *ideal* conditions, and after that, alas. . . .

> '*Golden lads and girls all must*
> *as chimneysweepers come to dust,*'

as Shakespeare so eloquently expressed the sentiment.

My late friend Herr Anton Taufenbach, so many years the fêted *Schützenkönig* of his district, put down his glass of *Lorch* one evening, looked at me with a twinkling eye and said : 'Always remember, more people ruin a wine by keeping it too long than by drinking it too soon.' True words of wisdom from a connoisseur.

Unfortunately there is a point at which the mellowing of taste stops; wine begins thereafter to degenerate into an aromatic, thin, sour liquid (however much you paid for it) and your best friends will never dare tell you that it tastes like domestic vinegar; no, they pour it on to your house-plants when your gaze is directed elsewhere, your house-plants expire next day, and your friends stay away for six months.

Happily I have a disposition and family background that make it hard to keep a wine more than two years, so I turned to making my own wines with great gusto!

The actual process of the airless fermentation is of the utmost importance to all people who make their own home-made wines, so I will describe it in sufficient detail.

There is only one easy way to achieve this secondary fermentation correctly; it is to insert an airlock or a fermentation-trap-valve in the mouth of your winchester or vat; they are usually made of glass or plastic and cost very little.

A rubber cork is hygienic because it can be washed and used again, but cork and rubber corks with a suitable hole in the centre are available; into the hole you insert the airlock or valve described above. Some water is placed in the lock or valve so that while the escaping air from the fermentation may get out no outside air or insects can get into the liquid which is in ferment.

Insects? Yes, I did use that word. Unfortunately, there is a nasty little fly known as the vinegar fly, one of the *Drosophila* family, which makes straightaway for any must (fruit pulp) or unguarded fermenting liquids, and converts them into *vinaigre*, which is only French for 'sour wine'.

The *Drosophila* are actually carriers of the vinegar bacteria but sometimes these are just present in the breeze. They are life-forms and unprotected fermenting liquid makes a fine breeding ground for them; their name is *Mycoderma aceti*.

If your wine has a silghtly gelatinous mass on top of it this is the work of some fungus-like bacteria; if this happens there are two things to do with your wine—either keep it for cleaning out the drains, or throw it away at once.

If it is a case of one or two small flies being found during a daily inspection of the home-made wine in winchesters you can strain the wine off carefully, remove the flies, sterilise the jars with a Campden tablet (one per gallon winchester). Two days later add a powerful fast-acting yeast and more sugar—in other words start all over again. But if the liquid smells vinegarish don't bother, it is lost, throw it away—especially if there is a jelly on top of the liquid. Sterilise your jars well.

I personally use only Danish plastic airlocks which are fairly unbreakable, cheaper than glass, and very effective; all winemakers' suppliers stock them. The air rises from the wine through a central tube, is forced to pass through water on the way out. Watching the bubbles rise through the air locks is one of the fascinating occupations of all amateur winemakers. When the bubbles stop rising the fermentation has finished, allow one week to pass for a safety check, then insert a tight bung to keep the winchester closed. If you want to use corks you must seal them with candle wax to prevent an attack on the cork by any of those nasty insects that enjoy it in their diet. This is why many of the expensive bought wines have those little lead foil seals to protect them during their cellarage. Your winemakers' suppliers will have these foil seals in stock if you want to use them.

Yeast is the basic factor in all fermentation and I cannot recommend readers to try so-called 'yeastless' homemade wines, which tend to rely upon uncontrolled fermentation and may be less hygienic than forms of fermentation described.

Yeast is no trouble at all, it only wants to feed, live in peace and to multiply. Homemade wine producers are its best friends.

I cannot recommend any of the specially prepared yeast cultures available to winemakers; I use only the simple, natural brewer's yeast which is obtainable from any bakery or brewery in small quantities.

I use only demerara or brown natural sugar. I advise against using white sugar; white is not a natural colour for sugar, manmade artificial agents are added to it to bleach it white; these chemicals are such that no sick person should take the risk of consuming them. Although brown sugar will make the wine slightly darker it will keep herbal wines healthier and stronger.

Artificial sweeteners should never be used. Store your wine about 50°F = 10°C.

*= Tonics and healing drinks

AGRIMONY   *

Excellent in cases of asthma, bronchitis, coughs, dropsy, jaundice and skin troubles. Strengthening in case of weakness. Leaves used.

ALEHOOF

Dyspepsia, some glandular disorders and some cases of jaundice seem to benefit greatly from this. It is a stimulating tonic. Leaves used. Add the juice of an orange.

ALKANET   *

Rich purple-coloured, was a great favourite in old days to help smallpox and measles patients. Discorides held that it was efficacious against snake-bite : it seems to be useful in certain kidney conditions. Leaves or root used.

ALMOND

Almonds are a natural source of calcium, copper, iron, magnesium, manganese, phosphorus, potassium, and sulphur. Herbalism is the oldest form of healing in the world; sources from Ancient Assyria, Babylonia, China, Egypt and Greece show that Almonds have been used for millennia to relieve bronchial disorders (especially sore throats, hoarseness, asthmatic conditions), fevers, kidney and urinary disorders. The nut is used.

Recipe: 4 oz. (0·113 kg.) almonds (ground); 2 lemons, 4 lb. (1·8 kg.) sugar; 1 gal. (4·5 l.) water.

Let us never be too proud to accept healing from the wayside flowers and 'weeds' we have too long ignored. I find it ungrateful to spend many millions of pounds on 'research' (which money could alleviate poverty and suffering) when we deliberately ignore remedies which are all around us if we will only open our hearts, believe and trust.

ANISEED

This is a gentle and pleasant carminative; it not only helps indigestion but tends to open the bowels.

Also a Tonic.

Recipe: ½ oz. (0·014 kg.) aniseed oil; 3 lb. (1·36 kg.) sugar; 1 gal. (4·5 l.) water.

Add a little more Aniseed later in the process if you feel it advisable for the taste. The oil is used.

APPLE

This can be made either as an *Apple Wine* or as a Cider. I will give both recipes below. Apples contain calcium, iron, phosphorus and potassium; they are considered very helpful against stone in the bladder or kidney. There are over 300 varieties of Apple, many different flavours are found. The Apple contains, moreover, *Malic Acid*—a potent germicide; there is much truth in the old English adage: *'An apple a day keeps the doctor away.'*

Bladder troubles, colitis, dropsy, gout, kidney disorders, rheumatic and stomach disorders are all helped by apples. The fruit is used.

Recipe: (*Apple Wine*). 7 lb. (3·175 kg.) apples; 1 lb. (0·454 kg.) raisins; 2 lemons; 1 gal. (4·5 l.) water.

Chop up apples, add raisins and lemon juice, add the water when it is boiling, then simmer very gently until about a quarter of the liquid has boiled away, then add to make up to one gallon again, cover over and leave for a month, after which proceed as usual.

(*Cider*). A special press is needed to crush the apples. The extracted juice is collected and kept at not less than 70°F (21°C), yeast is added. Fermentation is really rather violent (I've seen a century-old cider press at work in Somerset); when fermentation begins to die down treat as for any other wine.

APRICOT

In my travels I have often seen the Apricot tree in blossom. It is extremely beautiful. The fruit contains vitamins A and D, calcium, iron and phosphorus. The apricot has been treasured in many parts of the world for its nutritional properties. It has, as a wine, a charming velvet taste, comparable to a good Cream Sherry. It is an amazingly good tonic wine.

Recipe: 3½ lb. (1·588 kg.) apricots; 3 lb. (1·36 kg.) sugar; I advise you to leave any additive fruits out, use just pure apricots.

Many of those who complain about the 'backwardness' of some of the Eastern European countries miss the sturdy virility so pronounced in the character of these peoples; their attitude to old, trustworthy knowledge is not conservatism but a fundamental awareness that all things *new* are not necessarily better than proven remedies of yester-year. South and east of Ljubljana you will find herb markets in nearly every town; suffice it to say that many who cannot distinguish so well between real progress and the novelty of the moment would give their all to enjoy such health as the 'undeveloped' peoples know. Ovid warned us that *'Dress deceives us'* and I would add that the very idea of treating illness with *'old-fashioned'* herbs horrifies many of the inexperienced; so often it is only the incorrect association of ideas that render things pleasant or unpleasant.

ARTICHOKE

This contains an unusual polysaccharide—Inulin. It is rich in protein and has about 300 calories to the lb. weight; also there is a good supply of silica, a most useful mineral salt.

Recipe: 5 lb. (2·268 kg.) artichokes; juice of either 2 lemons/2 oranges or one of each; 4 lb. (1·815 kg.) sugar; 1 gal. (4·5 l.) water.

ASPARAGUS

Asparagus is very beneficial to the lymphatic system; it is cleansing and a good tonic.

Recipe: 2 lb. (0·907 kg.) asparagus shoots; 3 lb. (1·36 kg.) sugar; 1 gal. (4·5 l.) water.

BALM MELISSA

One of my favourite tastes, I always associate it with my student days at old Heidelberg University (we did not spend all our time quaffing beer). It is a great help to all those who are studying seriously for examinations; it relieves headaches, nervous disorders, reduces feverishness, a lot of it may induce sweating; it prevents nightmares; and from the times of yore has been held a sovereign remedy against impotence. It is a wonderful tonic. Leaves used.

Recipe: 4 oz. (0·113 kg.) Balm Melissa leaves; 3 lb. (1·136 kg.) sugar; 1 gal. (4·5 l.) water.

A most fragrant and aromatic wine.

BARLEY
Rich in vitamin B (much of which will be lost when you make it into wine); it cools the blood and acts as a highly nutritious tonic.
Recipe: 1¼ lb. (0·5 kg.) barley; the juice of 3 oranges; 3 lb. (1·36 kg.) sugar; 1 gal. (4·5 l.) water.
The grain is used.

There is a very narrow gap between botanic medicine and dietetics, and as our knowledge of dietetics grows by studying the old herbals we must come to wonder at the amazing knowledge our forefathers had stored up. We are approaching knowledge from another angle, we classify things 'more scientifically' which is good, but we cannot avoid astonishment when we realise that our forefathers got the same results (often better).

BASIL
It has a delightful flavour. This is a great cleansing herb, a nerve-strengthening tonic with soothing properties. The leaves are used.

BERGAMOT
A soothing and gentle tonic.
Recipe: 4 oz. (0·113 kg.) bergamot leaves; 3 lb. (1·36 kg.) sugar; 1 gal. (4·5 l.) water.

It wasn't until Nicholas Culpeper (1616–54) produced his *Complete Herbal or English Physician* that herbal knowledge was given into the hands of any literate poor or middle-class reader; in spite of the quaint English it is still a valuable book if one takes time and patience to read it.

BILBERRY
Do not drink this if you are constipated. It is quite useful for diarrhoea and dysentery cases; it is helpful in several different nervous illnesses and tends to reduce feverishness. The berries are used fresh or dried.
Recipe: 3 lb. (1·36 kg.) bilberries; 3 lb. (1·36 kg.) sugar; 1 gal. (4·5 l.) water.

St. Teresa was born of a noble Castilian family, founded a religious order in Spain she won lasting fame for her goodness, became a mystic, died in 1582. She became the patron saint of Spain. She was a rare practical woman as well as a mystic and among her devotional writings is a short sentence which has challenged millions; it is worth remembering every minute of every day : *'You can never be too good-tempered.'*

BIRCH (SILVER)
A beautifully aromatic perfume, but a dry taste. Helpful in cases of catarrh, colds, influenza and fevers. This is also a diueretic, increasing urination.

I dealt at length with birch in my book *Herbal Teas for Health and Pleasure.*

BLACKBERRY

Good for anaemia because it is very rich in iron, and useful in many skin and nervous illnesses. A good tonic.

Recipe: The juice and boiled water in which five pounds of blackberries have been simmered into an almost liquid state (5 lb.=2·268 kg.); 3 lb. (1·36 kg.) sugar, 1 gal. (4·5 l.) water.

Blackberries, wild roses, dogwood and spindle trees are among the shrubs which are beginning to disappear from parts of the British countryside. This warning was given in reports by a number of research scientists to the Botanical Society of the British Isles only recently.

The tragedy is that the plants being destroyed contain far more mineral salts, vitamins, nutritional value and healing virtue than the crops which are replacing them.

BLACKCURRANT

This fruit contains some vitamin A, three of the vitamin B family and a very large amount of vitamin C. The fruit is most thirst-quenching and a great help in all cases of fever. The berries are used.

Recipe: Do *not* boil your blackcurrants, fast boiling will lessen their properties and effectiveness. Simmer them gently and slowly. Long process but worth it. 5 lb. (2·268 kg.) blackcurrants; 3 lb. (1·36 kg.) sugar; 1 gal. (4·5 l.) water.

That magnificent old giant of literature, the incomparable Thomas Mann, said at Chicago University, during a lecture : *'Time is a gift beyond price, given to us in order that we might become cleverer, better, more mature and more perfect within it.'*

BLUE MOUNTAIN

This is equally well-known as *Golden Rod* and grows in nearly every garden of Europe from Bosnia to Britain, and is found widely in America as well. It is a gentle stimulant, acts well to reduce fevers, and is a good tonic acting especially to better bladder, jaundice and kidney ailments. The leaves are used, and sometimes the flowers.

Standard recipe.

We must try to use both intellect and emotion to overcome the negative thinking that is, so often, behind the causes of disease.

I knew a lady who was terribly afflicted by rheumatism, she was full of the things she had lost in the Second World War, of the opportunities she had missed in life; of the great things which had gone wrong; friends who had abandoned her; of affliction which made it almost impossible for her to show her magnificent talents still. Yet this lady has a home which over sixty per cent of the world's population would find rich and luxurious, she does not have a lot of money, but she is surrounded by extremely beautiful things.

I made it my task to persuade her to think of something good and beautiful, to consider some past success, to anticipate some probable success instead of morose and pessimistic contemplation of failures past, present and probable.

'*Today is the tomorrow you worried about yesterday and it didn't happen.*' Joseph Millott-Severn.

BURDOCK

Many sufferers from sciatica and chronic rheumatic diseases have felt great relief from the use of Burdock.

Recipe: 4 oz. (0·113 kg.) burdock leaves or seed; juice of 2 oranges; 3 lb. (1·36 kg.) sugar; 1 gal. (4·5 l.) water.

Too often we assume that we know 'all there is to be knowed', like Kenneth Grahame's Mr. Toad, but hidden within the complex forms of simple herbs there are undoubtedly vitamins and mineral salts about which we as yet know little or nothing. I have a great respect for burdock.

BURNET

Culpeper, speaking of this herb, said : 'It preserves the body in health and the spirit in vigour.' It is a grand tonic, long held to be efficacious in staunching internal bleeding; it is recommended for all blood disorders and skin complaints.

Recipe: 6 oz. (0·169 kg.) burnet dried herb; 3 lb. (1·36 kg.) sugar; 1 gal. (4·5 l.) water.

You may go to see one of the superbly polished performances of an internationally known Spanish Ballet troupe, you will see a soloist do the *Zapateado*, you will clap; but I will tell you that to see the real soul and glory of the *Zapateado* (that most exhausting, tapping heel and toe exercise) you must go to one of the rougher parts of a big Spanish city, for example to the Barriochino of Barcelona, where at *La Bohemia* bar for example out of sheer joy, exultation and *joie de vivre* some vivacious amateur will jump up on the table and do a violent, dedicated *zapateado* which comes from the depths of the being; claps, shouts of '*olé*'—atmosphere !—Yes, that is the real thing ! Now do you see the lesson of that? It is this, we cannot all be shining experts in this world, but a really good, amateur performance in any single sphere may inspire people better, rejoice their hearts more, and give them more real atmosphere of living than any professionalism ever could.

CABBAGE

As well as supplying protein the Cabbage contains vitamins A, B and C; calcium, chlorine, fluorine, phosphorus, silicon and sulphur. Whereas in restaurant cooking nearly all the good is boiled out of the vegetable, when you make it into a wine you retain the goodness. Never cook it quickly. Simmer gently until there is a quart of juice (2·27 l.).

Recipe: A quart of cabbage juice (2·27 l.); 3 lb. (1·36 kg.) sugar; 6 pints (3·41 l.) water.

CAMOMILE

A fragrant wine which is most beneficial to those who suffer from easily becoming excited or upset, whose nerves are easily frayed. It is an excellent tonic which is most helpful for stomach disorders and particularly flatulence.

Recipe: 3 oz. (0·084 kg.) camomile flowers; 3 lb. (1·36 kg.) sugar; 1 gal. (4·5 l.) water.

This recipe can have either orange or lemon juice added. The wine tastes slightly bitter, and more sugar may be required, or ½ oz. ginger powder added (0·014 kg.).

CARDUUS-BENEDICTUS. *See* THISTLE WINE.

CARAWAY

Prof. Simonite declared that : 'Caraway ought to be grown in every garden.' Certainly many old herbalists recommended it for nearly every disease. As a tonic it helps gall-bladder and liver cases; it is moreover one of the finest treatments for indigestion. Use the seeds.

CARROT

These familiar vegetables contain large quantities of vitamin A; some vitamin C, and thiamine, riboflavine, and nicotinic acid from the B group. Sodium and sulphur are also present.

Recipe: Do not scrape your carrots, just brush them, chop with a knife, and put them into already boiling water, simmer gently until the roots are almost pulp. 5 lb. (2·268 kg.) carrots; 3 lb. (1·36 kg.) sugar; 1 gal. (4·5 l.) water.

One of the great fathers of herbal science, Galen, said your food should be your medicine and your medicine should nourish you, this means that the original idea of healing was allied all the time to dietetics. Dieticians have much to learn from botanic medicine and the herbalist has much to learn from studying dietetics.

CELERY

This is useful for people suffering from high blood pressure, stomach troubles generally, nervous disorders, and particularly esteemed for relieving rheumatic complaints.

Recipe: 5 lb. (2·268 kg.) celery. Shred the celery quickly into small pieces, simmer into a pulp; juice of 1 lemon; 3 lb. (1·36 kg.) sugar; 1 gal. (4·5 l.) water.

CHERRY

This is often found to be a wonderful remedy against a rasping or tickling cough.

Recipe: 7 lb. (3·175 kg.) cherries; 3½ lb. (1·588 kg.) sugar; 1 gal. (4·5 l.) water. Remove the stalks but allow the cherries to cook with their stones until pulped.

CINNAMON

Use the root *or* the powder. 2 dessertspoonfuls of powder being ample. This is one of the safest antiseptics known to man. It is a germicide in its own right. Use against colds, influenza, etc.

Recipe: Cinnamon as shown above; the juice of 1 lemon; 3 lb. (1·36 kg.) sugar; 1 gal. (4·5 l.) water.

Cinnamon and the following herbs have been in use for dietetic and medical uses for over 3,000 years : Anemone, Balm, Bryony, Burdock, Cabbage, Cloves, Elder, Fennel, Figs, Garlic, Heather, Ivy, Myrrh, Olive, Paeony, Quince, Rose, Sage, Sesame, Thyme, Violet and Willow bark.

Many of these are used today exactly the same as then, by herbalists and allopathic doctors.

It is true that the ancients wrote works which as far as we can understand contained errors; but Archdeacon Albert Christian said if modern Man with his superior techniques had thoroughly, fairly and efficiently tested these old remedies millions of pounds wasted on illogical and mostly fruitless research could have been spent on correct foods and decent housing for distressed areas, and millions of suffering people would have been healed.

CLARY

Once held to be an aphrodisiac! It has a pleasant taste, and is a tonic which seems to strengthen the kidneys. It is not recom—mended for women in pregnancy.

Use up to 4 oz., if you wish, but not more.

CLOVER (RED)

I often make clover wine myself, it has a very rich velvety taste, but seems to be remarkably rare. It was long considered helpful in case of cancer; it has a wonderfully calming effect on the nervous system, and for cases of hysteria. Some herbalists used it to restore sexual potency to those who have exhausted themselves by excesses, etc.

Recipe: The way I make it is as follows : Fill a 2-pint (1·14 l.) saucepan with clover heads, not pressed down, just loose. Simmer these gently in four pints of water (2·27 l.) until the water has a rich colour and the heads are pulp; this will take up at least a pint of water (0·57 l.) add five pints (2·84 l.) of water, and sugar 3 lb. (1·36 kg.) proceeding as usual.

CLOVES

This is a wine you are liable to make too strong for taste : beware ! Properly used, the wine will take away feelings of nausea, cleanse the stomach (cloves are both antiseptic and germicidal in effect); painful toothache can be allayed by clove wine.

Recipe: 12 cloves only; 3 lb. (1·36 kg.) sugar; 1 gal. (4·5 l.) water. Optional—juice of 2 lemons or 2 oranges.

Life is very much what you make of it. All men have two hands, time and opportunity; what have they done with it? Go to Urumchi —there is nothing; go to Florence—a town on the same latitude and there is the greatest triumphs of Humanity—the corridors of the *Uffizi* Palace, the *Santa Maria del Fiore* Cathedral, the Palatine Gallery, the *Pitti* Palace, the glorious *Piazza della Signoria*—enough beauty to glorify a whole nation—not just one city!

Coltsfoot

COLTSFOOT

For asthma, bronchitis, colds, coughs, all respiratory diseases there are few herbs so valuable as coltsfoot. Leaves or flowers are used.

Recipe: 4 oz. (0·113 kg.) coltsfoot; 3 lb. (1·36 kg.) sugar; 1 gal. (4·5 l.) water. If you like a wine with a lot of body you could increase the coltsfoot up to double the portion suggested.

'*The Law is the friend of the defenceless*' (Schiller).

COMFREY

A strengthening herb which sportsmen and bodybuilders might take note of, it improves muscle tone; it speeds up the mending of fractured bones (it is rich in silica and potassium).

Recipe: 4 oz. (0·113 kg.) comfrey leaves; 3 lb. (1·36 kg.) sugar; 1 gal. (4·5 l.) water.

'Kindness is the golden chain by which society is bound together' (Goethe).

CORIANDER

My wanderings in Greece and Macedonia have brought me into contact with this pleasant herb, for which it is claimed that it strengthens the muscles of the heart and the coronary system; certainly it corrects digestion.

Recipe: According to your own taste, use 1 oz. (0·028 kg.) coriander seeds; 3 lb. (1·36 kg.) sugar; 1 gal. (4·5 l.) water.

Allow for lengthy steeping of the seeds, to get the full flavour do not boil the seeds.

CORN

We all know the American folksongs about 'Ole Corn Liquor', well, now you can try the taste yourself. (This is 'Indian Corn' or maize.)

It is a good nerve tonic, benefits the skin, is low in protein and rich in starch; American herbalists report that it has a beneficial action on the endocrine glands.

Recipe: 2 lb. (0·907 kg.) bruised maize; 4 lb. (1·814 kg.) sugar; juice of any one citrus fruit; 1 gal. (4·5 l.) water. When making this soak the maize for 24 hours before you begin to simmer it!

Conquering an illness is just a step on the pathway to bigger and better life. There is a marvellous piece of wisdom in the seemingly foolish *Adventures of Baron Munchhausen* :

'But One is only truly lost *when* one gives up.' ('Aber man ist nur verloren, wenn man sich selbst aufgibt'.)

COWSLIP

One of the best-known country wines. Do make sure that you can distinguish the plant correctly if you collect it yourself. It can be used to benefit all nervous conditions from headache to epilepsy (not that a lot of alcohol is good for epileptics; they should consume it most sparingly).

Recipe: Enough loosely collected cowslip flowers to fill a 3-pint (1·70 l.) saucepan; 4 lb. (1·814 kg.) sugar; 1 gal. (4·5 l.) water.

If you allow leaves or stalks to be mixed in with the flowerheads this will make the taste more bitter, and you will have to use more sugar.

CURRANT (RED).—See *Black Currant*, the recipe is the same.

Its uses are for constipation and liver complaints.

How to Win Every Argument

(A) Don't argue about everything.

KNAPWEED

One of the famous vulnerary herbs—has been used for curing throat complaints and wounds.

(B) Search for Truth, never for supremacy.
(C) Keep calm. A hot temper never made anything true.
(D) Don't resent other opinions.
(E) Express yourself clearly and precisely.
(F) Be fair and patient at all time.

DANDELION

This is one of the finest wines and is smooth as velvet; you can get it crystal clear with a good *bouquet*, and a taste that one could only describe as delightful. It is a blessing for over-weight people who need to reduce; it is strengthening to healthy gland functions; it thoroughly cleanses the body.

It contains vitamin A and vitamin E, calcium, chlorine, magnesium, potassium and silicon.

Use the flowers, or failing that, the dried leaves.

Recipe: Take enough flowerheads as will go into a saucepan holding 6 pints (3·41 l.); cover them with 6 pints (2·27 l.) boiling water and leave three days long, after which add 3 lb. (1·36 kg.) sugar, yeast, etc., proceed as in general directions. If you use only the petals you will have a much clearer wine, but less *body*, the whole head has more medical value.

'Hate the sin but not the Sinner' (Pope John XXIII).

In my book *Herb growing for Health* I have shown that one of the most important reasons for growing your own herbs is that you can control the purity of conditions under which the herb is grown. How very few industrial, man-made pharmaceuticals are as fresh as newly-picked and dried herbs! Properly cultivated even the lowly dandelion is a wonderful and beautiful riot of radiant yellow at the edge of a flower bed.

DEWBERRY

The same recipe as for *Blackberry*, many people mistake one for the other when collecting berries. The properties are much the same : *The taste is different.*

DOG-ROSE. *See* ROSE.

ELDERBERRY

I never like to be without Elderberry wine. It is possible to get it to the colour and consistency of *Port!* Good against colds, constipation, many rheumatic and allied ills; I have used it for many respiratory cases, and find it excellent for sore-throats etc. Even using a little to gargle with !

Recipe: 3 lb. (1·36 kg.) fresh elderberries; 3 lb. (1·36 kg.) sugar; 1 gal. (4·5 l.) water. Increase up to 5 lb. (2·268 kg.) elderberries, according to how much *body* you like in a wine.

ELDERFLOWER

Excellent for colds, coughs and sneezes.

Recipe: As many sprays of elderflower as fill a pint saucepan (0·57 l.); 3 lb. (1·36 kg.) sugar; 1 gal. (4·5 l.) water. Citrus juice (orange, lemon or grapefruit optional, I prefer to omit it).

I counted 29 references to herbs in the Bible, among them St. Paul wrote : *'Another who is weak eateth herbs'* (Rom. 14. 2). Instead of letting God provide the cure and the healing, Mankind has, as typified by the hiding in the Garden of Eden, turned his back on God, fled into a wilderness of man-made remedies, vivisection and evil things which are not of God; no medicine sent by God would heal man of one disease and cause another. So many man-made drugs heal one illness and cause others that there are many universities with seats of iatrogenic medicine, exploring ways to heal sickness caused by taking man-made drugs to cure a totally different illness.

'Physic, for the most part, is nothing else but the substitute for exercise and temperance' (Addison).

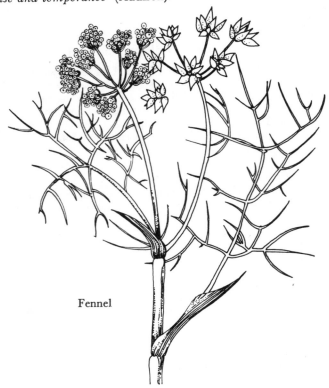

Fennel

FENNEL

This will greatly aid digestion, heart and nervous system, the taste is rather attractive.

Recipe: 3 oz. (0·84 kg.) fennel seeds; 3 lb. (1·36 kg.) sugar; 1 gal. (4·5 l.) water. Increase to six ounces fennel if you wish!

'*Only he who understands is sad*' (Arabic proverb).

FIG

Figs are aperient, they benefit skin and stomach.

Recipe: 2½ lb. (1·134 kg.) fresh or dried figs; 3 lb. (1·36 kg.) sugar; 1 gal. (4·5 l.) water.

A pinch of nutmeg or cinnamon will liven up the taste a bit, but put it in when fermentation has started and is well advanced.

'*Pitch a lucky man into the river Nile and when he comes out he'll have a fat fish in his mouth*' (Egyptian proverb).

GINGER

A cheering, strengthening and warming wine, very helpful against colds, indigestion, sore throats, diarrhoea and nausea.

Recipe: Use the root or the powdered root; 2 to 3 dessertspoonfuls of powder or three sticks of the root. 3 lb. (1·36 kg.) sugar; 1 gal. (4·5 l.) water. The addition of lemon or orange juice is optional.

In the British Museum there is bread which is 4,000 years old, dehydrated, mummified, but still unmistakably bread. From Egyptian records we know that in those days about two score varieties of bread were baked. In a German department store I once counted 96 different varieties of bread on sale. Bread is as old as civilisation itself, it is the key to civilisation because it represented a method of storing food. The time between preparation and consumption of bread enabled Man to develop civilised arts instead of spending all his existence hunting for or collecting foodstuffs. From Neanderthal times to those of Pompeii bread was used. The Bible makes over 200 references to bread, and a score more to loaf and loaves. The Roman conquest of Britain was chiefly motivated by the superior quality of the corn grown here—which was blended with that of Egypt to produce cheap and long-lasting bread.

Natural bread was normally made with many different grains— millet, rye and wheat, etc. The natural colour of bread is *brown*; the idea of bleaching bread to produce a white loaf is comparatively modern.

Try a wine and cheese party with homemade wines, various cheeses and whole grain breads of different taste—you'll be an instant success!

GOLDEN ROD. *See* BLUE MOUNTAIN WINE.

GOOSEBERRY

This attractive fruit contains iron, calcium, phosphorus and protein, making it a delightful tonic wine. The berries are used.

Recipe: 4 lb. (1·814 kg.) gooseberries; 3 lb. (1·36 kg.) sugar; 1 gal. (4·5 l.) water.

'Fire in the heart sends smoke into the head' (German proverb).

If you want to sparkle, to live Life with a capital L, you must have pure, natural bread, the brown, rough, wholemeal bread that made our forefathers the sort of men who could build cathedrals, cities, and the Parthenon and Pyramids with only their bare hands; men who sailed uncharted seas, invent Medicine, Poetry, Drama, Mathematics—the lot!

GROUND IVY. *See* ALEHOOF which is another name for this herb.

HAWTHORN

This is strengthening for the heart and circulatory system.

Recipe: Take enough of the flowers to fill two saucepans holding each a capacity of 2 pints (1·14 l.). 3 lb. (1·36 kg.) sugar; 1 gal. (4·5 l.) water.

HOPS

If a person has anaemia, general debility, nerve pains, or is over-excitable, hop wine is very suitable.

Recipe: 4 oz. (0·113 kg.) hops; 3 lb. (1·36 kg.) sugar; 1 gal. (4·5 l.) water.

Brown bread contains approximately 10% more vitamin B[1], 220% more vitamin B[2], 100% more iron and 8% more protein than does white bread.

Under Roman Law, bakers who adulterated bread were most severely punished for their anti-social crime. Writing a historical paper for a learned society some years ago on the Nika Riot in Constantinople (A.D. 532) I pointed out that one of the contributory factors was the literally poisonous bread being sold by that wily, unscrupulous politician—John of Cappadocia.

Insist upon wholemeal flour products, and, if you can get them, stoneground wholemeal flour and bread; do not worry at the rougher taste, there will be more flavour, and the gritty taste comes from the substances which contain all the natural vitamins and mineral salts you need so much.

HYSSOP

For nearly all respiratory diseases, nervous illnesses, and as a cleansing tonic.

Recipe: 4 oz. (0·113 kg.) hyssop leaves; 3 lb. (1·36 kg.) sugar; 1 gal. (4·5 l.) water.

My advice is 'Put away that garden-spray', do not start killing off the weeds around you until you at least have some idea what they can do for you. The plants you seek to preserve (because they are pretty) may be unusable and even toxic, but the lowly weeds destroyed to make room for them may well contain the medicine you and your family need. Consult *Herbgrowing for Health*.

LAVENDER   *

A good tonic for people with strained nerves, hysterical tendencies; very soothing and calmative. Good against worms, cleansing in jaundice cases.

Recipe: ½ oz. (0·014 kg.) or 1 oz. (0·028 kg.) lavender; 3 lb. (1·36 kg.) sugar; 1 gal. (4·5 l.) water.

In the Bible there is a clear injunction to worship God and not to worship man-made graven images.

I wonder how many people realise how much modern medicine has become a false god, a graven image, a man-made idol. Modern man has begun to worship 'Science' with a blind, unquestioning obedience; few people realising that this has become a technique of worshipping Man himself, and not thanking God for having created a world full of wonder, mystery and miracles.

LEMON

You can make this either with the pure juice or with the yellow peel (no pith). The lemon has so many medical virtues that it is impossible to list them in a work of this size. For all feverish conditions, for diarrhoea, for all liver conditions, skin and stomach conditions, lemons are most helpful.

Recipe: Add the juice of 10 lemons to sufficient liquid as to make 6 pints of water (3·41 l.); add 3 lb. (1·36 kg.) sugar. Then add yeast and follow the general procedure.

Sleeplessness is often due to a serious silicon deficiency, Mushrooms. Horsetail grass, Leeks and Comfrey are rich in silicon. Some types of liver disorders owe their origin to a deficiency of vitamin A. This is found in Okra pods, Parsley, Dandelions, etc. Other types of liver diseases are due to a serious lack of vitamin K which is found in Chestnut leaves and Alfalfa.

LEMON VERBENA

A cleansing and useful tonic.

Recipe: 3 oz. (0·084 kg.) lemon verbena leaves; 3 lb. (1·36 kg.) sugar; 1 gal. (4·5 l.) water.

A lack of vitamin D is often found at the root of thyroid disorders. This vitamin is found in Annatto-seeds, Wheatgerm, etc. Vitamin E is of great help in cases of muscular dystrophy, and Sesame, Bladderwrack, Dulse, and other plants are rich in E. Psoriasis and glaucoma both yield favourably to vitamin P found fairly abundantly in herbal sources, Buckwheat, Lemon-pith, etc.

Some very serious illnesses such as prostrate gland disorders, mongolism and the like all have in common a marked deficiency of vitamin F which is abundantly supplied by Sunflower-seeds, Peanuts, whole raw grains, etc.

LIQUORICE

Very helpful for all typically female complaints; beneficial in colds, coughs, sore throats, bronchial and ulcerated pulmonary conditions. A cleansing and most beneficial tonic. A slightly heavy taste.

Recipe: The easiest way is to get half a dozen sticks of liquorice from your sweetshop, chop them up very fine and pour on a pint of boiling water; if at the end of an hour they are not dissolved simmer them gently. Taste the resulting liquid, if you want more liquorice add some, if you are satisfied with the taste add 3 lb. (1·36 kg.) sugar, and enough water to make up 1 gal. (4·5 l.).

In the earliest medical records, liquorice was valued as a thirst-quenching substance. Theophrastus, pupil of Plato and Aristotle, and called the 'Father of Botany', claimed that the Scythians, living on liquorice and mare's milk cheese, were capable of going for up to 12 days without drinking. In old herbals liquorice is usually mentioned as beneficial for ulcers and stomach ailments, and it has long been a traditional ingredient of some indigestion mixtures.

Doctors at Glasgow University, writing in GUT, the journal of the British Society of Gastroenterology, reported a month's trial involving 33 gastric ulcer patients. Two capsules of powdered liquorice, taken three times daily, markedly reduced the size of the ulcer which in seven cases disappeared from X-rays view.

LOVAGE

This is, of course, a relative of Parsley, but it has a very attractive aroma; it is carminative, working gently and beneficially on the digestive tract; it is a mild stimulant.

Recipe: Enough lovage leaves as will fill a 2-pint (1·14 l.) saucepan; 4 lb. (1·814 kg.) sugar; 1 gal. (4·5 l.) water. Either citrus juice or some spice may be added if desired, but I think it is best on its own.

'*He who twice is Shipwrecked is unjust if he blames Neptune*' (Publius Syrus).

MAIZE. *See* CORN WINE.

MARIGOLD

This simple flowering plant is one of the best and safest internal antiseptics in the world; it is most helpful for all skin and nervous disorders; refer also to my book *Herbs for Cooking and Healing*.

Marigolds are very helpful to patients with a heart condition, they appear to strengthen tired arteries and the like.

'*Never mind the hunter's tears—watch his hands!*' (Arabic proverb).

Recipe: Take enough marigold heads to fill a 4-pint (2·27 l.) saucepan; 3 lb. (1·36 kg.) sugar; 1 gal. (4·5 l.) water.

No plant is useless; who are we to destroy plants that God has sent to our planet? If we were not so anxious to kill all the 'weeds' that grow amongst our crops we would find some insects would feed off them instead of off the crops. The ills that men suffer because they do not trust God or want to avoid a little work would fill a thick book.

'*This people honoureth Me with their lips, but their heart is far from Me* (St. Mark 7 : VI).

This is the crux of the matter, mankind is so obsessed with his own cleverness that he ceases to allow that God is cleverer, much more loving, and all-providing than we can conceive of.

There are diseases abroad now that our fathers never dreamed of, but there are always herbal cures which produce safe results. I know a case of erysipelas which failed to yield to all manner of antibiotic drugs, but which cleared up within 24 hours after a herbal decoction based on marigolds was taken !

MARJORAM

Soothing, kind to the nerves, a gentle tonic.

'*Impatience changes smoke to flame*' (Erasmus).   Standard recipe.

MARSHMALLOW

Very cleansing for the mouth, a soothing tonic; helpful in cases of bowel disorders, internal bleeding, for disorders of the genital organs, and the ordinary run of colds, coughs, etc.

Recipe: 4 oz. (0·113 kg.) marshmallow herb; 3 lb. (1·36 kg.) sugar; 1 gal. (4·5 l.) water.

'*Next to the originator of a good sentence is the first quoter of it*' (Emerson).

MEADOWSWEET   *

For diabetic people, and for disorders of blood, skin and stomach.

Recipe: 6 oz. (0·169 kg.) meadowsweet; 3 lb. (1·36 kg.) sugar; 1 gal. (4·5 l.) water.

'*Riches made more men covetous than covetness ever made men rich*' (Scots proverb).

MINT. *See* PEPPERMINT WINE.

MOUNTAIN ASH. *See* ROWAN WINE.

MULBERRY

Helpful against biliousness, a useful tonic.

Recipe: 3 lb. (1·36 kg.) mulberries; 3 lb. (1·36 kg.) sugar; 1 gal. (4·5 l.) water.

Nettle

NETTLES

For many illnesses, anaemia, blood disorders, bladder, kidney, lymphatic ills. It is one of the very best tonics, and a great favourite of mine. It contains calcium, chlorine, iron, potassium, silicon, sodium and sulphur.

Recipe: Take enough nettle tops as will fill a 4-pint (2·27 kg.) saucepan; 3 lb. (1·36 kg.) sugar; 1 gal. (4·5 l.) water. This is a herb which I heartily recommended in my book *How to Defeat Rheumatism and Arthritis.*

OATS

A highly nutritive tonic, excellent for blood and nervous system. Oats are rich in protein, phosphorus, potassium, iron, silicon, sodium, and magnesium.

Recipe: 1 lb. (0·454 kg.) oats; 3 lb. (1·36 kg.) sugar; 2 lb. (0·907 kg.) dried raisins; the juice of 1 lemon; 1 gal. (4·5 l.) water.

'All men honour love because it looks up—not down' (Emerson).

ORANGE

Oranges contain calcium, iron, phosphorus and protein; also vitamins A, B and C.

It is good against colds, and a fine tonic.

Recipe: The juice of 10 to 12 oranges added to 6 pints of water (3·41 l.); add 3 lb. (1·36 kg.) sugar; then add yeast and follow the general procedure.

'Avalanches teach men how to pray' (Swiss proverb).

PARSLEY *

A tonic for those who suffer from indigestion, bladder, kidney, liver and stomach disorders.

Parsley contains chlorine, iron, magnesium, potassium, silicon, vitamin A and vitamin C.

Recipe: Take enough parsley (fresh) to fill one 2-pint (1·14 kg.) saucepan; 3 lb. (1·36 kg.) sugar; 1 gal. (4·5 l.) water. Add the juice of one orange.

Vast sums of money have been spent upon cancer research throughout the world, but to my knowledge nobody has thoroughly and scientifically investigated some of the old herbal cures for cancer, among them Aloysius Browne's case—he had known cancer of the bowels cured by a prolonged course of dandelion juice; there is considerable evidence that some forms of cancer have been cured by prolonged eating of fresh violet leaves.

PARSNIP

A great favourite.

Recipe: Shred 4 lb. (1·814 kg.) of parsnips, use 4 lb. (1·814 kg.) of sugar, and take 1 oz. (0·028 kg.) of yeast per gal. (4·5 l.) of water. Strain before putting in winchesters.

It is very potent, increasing powerfully for one or two years. Never underestimate its kick!

PEPPERMINT

For indigestion, sickness, stomach pains, colds, and influenza. Peppermint contains magnesium and potassium.

Recipe: 4 oz. (0·113 kg.) peppermint; 3 lb. (1·36 kg.) sugar; 1 gal. (4·5 l.) water.

The Ancient Greeks warned all Mankind of the perils of *hubris*, pride against the face of Heaven. The decline of classical instruction, and its replacement by technological and scientific subjects in the curriculum may teach Man how to analyse things better, but clearly it does not teach him how to use his discoveries.

PLUM

A tasty and useful tonic which is very popular.

Recipe: 5 lb. (2·268 kg.) plums; 4 lb. (1·814 kg.) sugar; 1 gal. (4·5 l.) water.

According to your plums, so you may need more plums to acquire the satisfactory, velvety taste which is the hallmark of a good plum wine. If there are too few plums the wine will lack body and can be very insipid, so test it at every stage of its development.

White sugar, commonly eaten all over the civilised world, is a real menace to all of us.

It consumes oxygen at a most alarming rate, and I advise the reader to go without white sugar completely.

The sugar cane grows somewhat like the familiar bamboo. It

may grow as high as 15 feet; the extracted sugar is less than 20% of the weight of the cane which is smashed and sprayed with water. Allowing for impurities, the amount of sugar remaining for use is about one-eighth of the total.

The mixture is placed in spinners, so arranged that the chief essence, known as black molasses, is drained off; this is a highly beneficial substance, and it is pure, wholesome, very rich in mineral salts, specifically calcium, copper, manganese, potassium. Molasses contains phosphoric acid, an irreplaceable basic requirement for health of the nervous system, and all the vitamin B group (except B^1).

The trouble is that the product which is most commonly known is not the raw, powerful, healthy molasses but the *weakened* sugar, which as it gets weaker and weaker becomes paler and paler.

What do you, the consumer, get for all the expensive process of refining, other than a 'pretty' product? Is there any original vitamin B left in it? Is there any natural vitamin left in it at all? Is there any calcium, copper, manganese or potassium left in the product? You are paying more for a product containing less!

PRIMROSE

Few people today seem to know that the pretty Spring flowers they admire so well have valuable medical properties. Sufferers from sciatica, thrombosis, and gall-stones will benefit from primroses.

Recipe: Take as many flower heads and leaves as will fill a 2-pint (1·4 l.) saucepan; 3 lb. (1·36 kg.) sugar; 1 gal. (4·5 l.) water. The addition of lemon juice or orange juice is optional.

'The power of the Gods hardly equals the utility of wine,' proclaimed physician Asklepiades, a disciple of Hippocrates, while the latter, rightly known as the Father of Medicine, thought : *'Wine is wonderfully appropriate to man, in good health and in illness, and should be administered opportunely and with measure, according to individual constitution.'* This is certainly one of the most delightful epigrams on the virtue of wine, formulated twenty-five centuries ago.

QUINCE

This is such a bitter fruit that nobody can eat it if it be not cooked, made into a jam or a wine.

Nevertheless, the quince has many values, it cleanses the body very thoroughly, and can be taken for almost any skin or stomach disease including disturbance of sexual functions.

Recipe: If you use the pulp to make jam and the juice of 4 lb. quinces you will benefit both ways. 4 lb. (1·814 kg.) quinces; 4 lb. (1·814 kg.) sugar; 1 gal. (4·5 l.) water.

RAISIN

Raisins contain potassium, phosphorus, calcium and iron, and make a very nourishing tonic wine.

Recipe: 2 lb. dried raisins (0·907 kg.); 3 lb. (1·36 kg.) sugar; 1 gal. (4·5 l.) water.

Widely appreciated in all the provinces of Greece, wine had always been the object of important trade in spite of its high price. From the eighth to the sixth century B.C. the development of viticulture was most important. Cultivation was organised as in modern times. Wine plants were carefully lined up in parallel rows. The lopping was done in six different shapes according to the vine plant, the soil or the strength of the winds.

As to the number of vine plants, Virgil wrote that it would be easier to count the sand grains of the sea.

RASPBERRY

An energising tonic, especially beneficial to the nervous system, to anaemic cases and for many blood disorders. It is slightly aphrodisiac.

Recipe: 4 lb. (1·814 kg.) raspberry; 3 lb. (1·36 kg.) sugar; 1 gal. (4·5 l.) water.

'Mind unemployed is Mind unenjoyed' (Bovee).

RED CURRANT. *See* BLACKCURRANT WINE.

RHUBARB

When you use this familiar plant you are following in the steps of Tibetan and ancient Arabian herbalists who made known its virtues a thousand years ago. It is aperient, and suitable for cases of constipation, but strangely enough it will cure dysentery. I recommend it to sufferers from migraine or any other form of headache of nervous origin. It can awaken an appetite in convalescents. Only the reddish stems are used to make wine; *never use the leaves.*

Recipe: 5 lb. (2·268 kg.) rhubarb; 4 lb. (1·814 kg.) sugar; 1 gal. (4·5 l.) water.

The entire constituents of earth, air and water are formed from varying combinations of the 92 known mineral elements; and the advancing knowledge of dietetics shows that the human body is no exception. Each decade shows us that some peculiar trace mineral substance has a precise use within the body's functions; germanium has been shown to act beneficially upon bone marrow and the red blood corpuscles; gallium affects the health of the blood; zinc facilitates muscular control by the nervous system. All the time Mankind is slowly learning, and in many cases, as research among the classics shows us, re-learning what the Greeks and Romans (and others) knew and did not doubt.

ROSE-HIP

One of the major sources of vitamin C. The number of simple herbs which are very rich in vitamins and mineral salts is unending; it is increasingly clear that many of the old herbalists were basically dieticians, which is why herbal medicine is so safe. Vitamins A, B^1, B^2, C, E, K, and the rarer P are present in rose-hips; so are calcium, iron and phosphorus; to get these all together in artificial tablets at a chemist would be very expensive!

Let us take a look at vitamin C, which is essential for good, efficient nervous functioning. Any deficiency of it soon shows up in irritability, skin troubles, and similar nervous symptoms. It is not stored up by the body, and a fresh supply daily is most important to avoid deficiency. The richest supplies of this wonderful vitamin are found in herbs! The Norwegian rose-hips contain 6,000 milligrams C per 100 grams weight! English rose-hips contain at least 200 mg. per 100 grams. In addition the hips contain: 500 international units of vitamin A; vitamin B $(1)=0.10$ mg.; vitamin B $(2)=0.007$ mg.; vitamin $E=47$ mg.; vitamin $K=100$ units; vitamin P 240–680 units; also some niacin, iron, calcium and phosphorus.

Recipe: One good way is to put the rose-hips through a dry mincing machine, cut them up as fine as possible so that when you pour the hot water over them and leave them to steep (completely covered over) you will get the best extraction from them; *it is important not to use boiling water* which would destroy much of the vitamin value. 3 lb. (1·36 kg.) rose-hips; 3 lb. (1·36 kg.) sugar; 1 gal. (4·5 l.) water.

ROSEPETAL

> '*Gather the rosebuds while ye may*
> *Old Time is still a flying*
> *And this same flower that smiles today*
> *Tomorrow will be dying*'
>
> (Herrick)

In the Southern Balkans and throughout Greece the beautiful petals of roses are widely used for scent, for *attar of roses*, for jams and for wines.

There used to be one English regiment which on one day of the year celebrated in the officers' mess by the ritual eating of a rose! The rose petal is also rich in vitamins like the hips of its wild brother *Rosa canina*. The rose petals help against catarrh (however obstinate); they are beneficial for all nerve complaints. I have no experience of this but some authorities claim that the petal eaten fresh will prevent an anticipated miscarriage.

Rosepetal wine is slightly aperient, but a fine tonic.

Recipe: The disadvantage of this is that one should use the petals when they are at the height of their glory—which is all very well if you live in Persia, Catalonia or along the banks of the Maritza but not so good if you have half-a-dozen pretty bushes in your back garden. If you want a strong medicinal wine you need your largest saucepan full of petals; if you want only the flavour of roses and less medicinal properties take just a two-pint saucepan, and fill that loosely with rose petals. Also needed, 2 lb. (0·907 kg.) sugar and 1 gal. (4·5 l.) water. In this case *it is extremely important for you not to over-sweeten*; you can always add sugar but you cannot take it away; the taste and aroma must be preserved if you want to enjoy this wine.

I have dealt at length with very valuable medicinal uses of roses in my work *Herbgrowing for Health*.

'Who hath not known ill fortune never knew himself or his own virtue' (Mallet).

ROSEMARY

Rosemary is a gentle antiseptic which has been used for nearly 2,000 years. It is of tremendous value in all nervous conditions, in blood and stomach upsets. Many ladies who have trouble during periods would benefit by taking rosemary either as a wine or as a tea. 'It helps a weak memory and quickeneth the senses,' wrote Nicholas Culpeper (1616–54). In the words of Shakespeare's Ophelia : 'Rosemary, that's for remembrance.'

Recipe: ½ oz. (0·014 kg.) to 1 oz. (0·028 kg.) dried or fresh rosemary; 3 lb. (1·36 kg.) sugar; 1 gal. (4·5 l.) water.

If you want the best medicinal results don't add any other ingredient except yeast.

Rosemary is a great help for baldness and falling hair; recipes are given in my book *How to Keep your Hair on*.

SAGE

Either common Sage or Red Sage can be used. This is a tonic rich in iron content and helpful in cases of colds, coughs, influenza, sore throats, constipation, digestive disturbances; it is also calming for nervous conditions.

Recipe: Take as many sage leaves as will loosely fill a 2-pint (1·14 l.) saucepan; 3 lb. (1·36 kg.) sugar; 1 gal. (4·5 l.) water.

In the English language the medicinal property of the herb associated with wisdom has been used to convey the idea of sagacity : One often hears of the *Seven Sages of Greece*, they were :

Solon, who taught 'Know Thyself';
Chilo, who proclaimed : 'Seek a purpose in life';
Thales, Bias and Cleobulus;
Pittacos, who said : 'Make the best possible use of time'; and
Periander, who taught : 'Hard work can resolve most if not all things.'

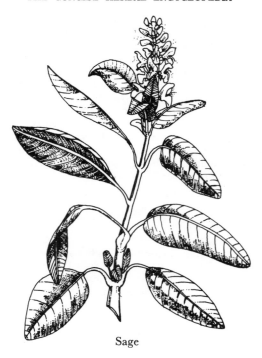

Sage

ROWANBERRY

This beautiful tree, sometimes called the Mountain Ash, produces berries wrongly considered 'poisonous' in my childhood days;
actually they have such strong acid content that the human stomach
cannot digest them *uncooked* (even when cooked they must be
diluted, e.g. 25% rowanberry + 75% apples). Be this as it may, a
good friend in Copenhagen taught me how to make wine and jam
from *Rønnebaer* as the Danes call them.

The berries are anti-scorbutic and astringent, very rich in vitamin
C; it is a health-giving tonic, and a remarkable wine in its own
right (I usually have to keep mine locked up with the Port!)
Recipe: 3½ lb. (1·588 kg.) rowanberries; 4 lb. (1·36 kg.) sugar; 1 gal.
    (4·5 l.) water.

Do not throw the cooked pulp away, use it to make jam or Apple
and Rowanberry pie in proportions given above.

'*A young idler makes an old beggar.*' (German proverb).

SAW PALMETTO   *

A very useful and universally applicable tonic, one that you
might employ fairly safely when you are not sure what is really
wrong with you, this like many lesser known botanic substances

contains some hitherto unidentified vitamin or other healing property.

Recipe: 4 oz. (0·113 kg.); saw palmetto powder or berries; 3 lb. (1·36 kg.) sugar; 1 gal. (4·5 l.) water.

'Men's best successes come after their disappointments' (Ward Beecher).

SILVER BIRCH. *See* BIRCH (SILVER) WINE.

SILVERWEED

One of the first herbal wines I ever made. The plant is quite ubiquitous, to be found at nearly every wayside, much neglected in spite of its virtues. I saw one family stop their car in a patch of Silverweed, they were sneezing and blowing their noses violently; crushed under the wheels of their car was the remedy which could have cured their terrible colds. For feverish chills Silverweed is highly recommended. It is also gently astringent and can be used to halt diarrhoea.

Recipe: 4 oz. (0·113 kg.) silverweed leaves; 3 lb. (1·36 kg.) sugar; 1 gal. (4·5 l.) water.

'He who has a thousand friends has not a friend to spare' (Ali Ben Abu Saleb).

SPEARMINT

Use the same recipe as for *Peppermint Wine.* The virtues of Spearmint are similar to those of Peppermint.

'I scorn the affection of seeming modesty to cover self-conceit' (Burns).

STICKLEWORT. *See* AGRIMONY WINE; this is another popular name for agrimony.

STRAWBERRY

The strawberry is fairly low in calories, it contains some protein and a little oxalic acid, it is slightly diuretic; 'it works by urine and is a remedy against jaundice,' wrote Prof. Simonite; many cases of bladder and kidney illness have benefited from taking strawberries.

Recipe: 4 lb. (1·814 kg.) strawberries; 3 lb. (1·36 kg.) sugar; 1 gal. (4·5 l.) water.

'Honesty is like an icicle, once it melts, that's the end of it.' (American settler proverb).

TANSY

Most useful for cases of blood and cardiac disorders and beneficial for many nervous conditions, a valuable tonic, but do not make too strong, otherwise the wine will be too bitter.

Recipe: 3 oz. (0·084 kg.) tansy; 3 lb. (1·36 kg.) sugar; 1 gal. (4·5 l.)
       water.

You might increase this to 4 oz. if you want a stronger taste and
more powerful medicinal effects.

Cottage gardens always had cultivated Tansy.

'Love is a debt which inclination always pays, obligation never'
(Pascal).

THISTLE

A friend of mine was quite incredulous when I told him that the
golden velvety liquid he had been drinking was not a medium
dry sherry but Thistle wine. It can be a delightful drink as well as
a tonic with diaphoretic properties (it makes you perspire); it can
be helpful in cases of migraine, for a feverish cold, it has long been
used against worms and other parasites that try to inhabit the
human body.

Recipe: Enough thistle tops as will fill a 2-pint (1·14 l.) saucepan;
       simmer these gently until they are pulped and the liquid
       well coloured; 3 lb. (1·36 kg.) sugar; 1 gal. (4·5 l.) water.

'Honour won't patch' (Scots proverb).

Thyme

THYME

Here is a most tasty wine, like the foregoing one it is powerfully effective against worms and body parasites; excellent for digestive troubles; it will help in cases of asthma, coughs, hysteria and nervous ills.

Recipe: Between ½ oz. (0·014 kg.) and 1 oz. (0·028 kg.) thyme; 3 lb. (1·36 kg.) sugar; 1 gal. (4·5 l.) water.

VERVAIN. *See* LEMON VERBENA WINE for the recipe.

The properties of vervain are helpful in respiratory and nervous disorders.

WHEAT

Wheat contains vitamins A, thiamin, riboflavin (B), E, protein, carbohydrate, oil, iron, manganese, copper and phosphorus. I recommend its use for all cases of exhaustion, nervous ills and many blood and stomach disorders.

Recipe: I usually take one whole packet of wheatgerm (e.g. *Bemax* or *Froment*); 3 lb. (1·36 kg.) sugar and 1 gal. (4·5 l.) water.

YARROW

It has been used for over 2,000 years to heal wounds and haemorrhages when applied as a fresh or dried herb. A wine from it can be used to help all colds and fevers, hysteria, nervous disorders, and many forms of rheumatic complaint (for this last I think the tea would be most effective).

Recipe: 4 oz. (0·113 kg.) yarrow; 3 lb. (1·36 kg.) sugar; 1 gal. (4·5 l.) water.

Some time ago I met a young medical student in the throes of a most terrible head cold, literally streaming with catarrh, as we talked he assured me that herbal medicine was 'old-fashioned rubbish'. He trod down a few stalks of yarrow on the wayside which I use to cure colds; with all his vaunted knowledge he had 'enjoyed' his cold for three weeks, and was no better. I have known herbal cures get rid of a cold in 48 hours!

If men insist on worshipping false gods they must not be surprised if their tin idols turn out to have feet of clay.

> 'To overcome evil with good is good,
> To overcome evil with evil is evil.'
> (Mahomet)

HERB BEERS

NETTLE

Take enough nettle tops to fill four pint saucepans loosely, wash them. Add one ounce of hops and ¾ lb. of malt. Boil all ingredients slowly in four pints of water. Stir frequently during the boiling process. Add a pinch of cinnamon or of ginger if fancied. Prepare a large, clean bucket with ½ lb. of brown sugar. Pour the boiling liquid on to this after half-hour's boiling and add ½ oz. yeast. Leave this, covered over by fly-proof muslin, for three days, after which the mixture should be ready for bottling.

N.B. Some people strain away the malt before putting the mixture on the sugar.

This is ready for drinking after a week or so. Alcoholic potency tends to increase after another week or two.

BURDOCK AND DANDELION

The same recipe as for nettle beer, but use three part burdock leaves to one part dandelion flowerheads.

An ounce of sarsaparilla root, finely powdered, can be added to this recipe.

GINGER

The same recipe as for nettle beer, except that only one ounce of shredded ginger is needed to one gallon of water. An ounce of cream of tartar and the juice of one or two lemons is advisable. Omit the cinnamon or ginger spices.

SAGE

The same recipe as for nettle beer, but half the quantity of sage is required for one gallon of water.

HEATHER AND HONEY

Enough heather flowers to fill one pint saucepan; only the flowers, *not* the twigs or the leaves; 1½ lb. of pure honey instead of sugar. Four pints of water. Same process as for nettle beer.

HOPS

This is the commonest and most widely enjoyed beer. Simmer 2 oz. of hops for three hours in 3 gallons of water to which 1 lb. of malt (varies according to taste) and 3 lb. of sugar have been mixed by slow stirring.

Add one ounce of yeast on toast as the mixture begins to cool.

4. How to Make Cosmetics from Herbs

Beauty is the pilot of the young soul, wrote Emerson. I believe that beauty is a natural birthright, not just a prerogative of the young. Beauty is you at your best. There are a thousand types of beauty, none of them true save it comes from good health rather than from chemists' potions; many man-made chemicals work disaster upon the skin. The great beauties of yesteryear had only lotions made from simple flowers from hedgerow and streamside—their fame lingers like the fragrance of immortal perfume. Natural beauty is a fragile possession; like a *Ting* vase or some *Sung* celadon, carelessness may destroy it for ever.

The following herbalists' advice will be of very considerable help to those who are tired of paying exorbitant prices for wares made from coal, petrol and various metallic and inorganic substances—some of which are considered by experts to be capable of causing cancer.

EYES

Apple juice has been found helpful for reddened eyes and against some forms of conjuctivitis.

Carrot juice makes a simple but effective eye tonic, applied with an ordinary eye bath.

Cucumber juice is excellent for strained eyes.

Elderflowers.—Drop a handful into a pint of boiling water; simmer them gently, and allow to cool—it makes a splendid lotion to strengthen eyes.

Eyebright.—Take some flowers and leaves, prepare as described for elderflowers. Very good for tired or weakened eyes.

Watercress juice makes another tonic eye lotion.

Witch-hazel tincture can be massaged around the eyes to ease strain, take away the dark rings, and tone up the loosened skin. Cut down on starchy foods, increase your protein intake, etc.

Eye make-up.

Ground almond shells can be burnt and mixed with olive oil and a little melted beeswax to produce the same black shade that Cleopatra, Dido of Carthage and Helen of Troy must have used for eyebrows, etc. By mixing powdered sage instead a green shading can be obtained. Dried powdered violets would give a purple shade.

Crowsfeet.

Massage in witch-hazel and lemon juice at night before retiring.

HAIR

Oil to brush on the hair (especially dry hair). 1 oz. of each of the following : Almond oil, sunflower oil, ½ oz. of the following : Rosemary oil, olive oil. Warm them up together, do not boil. Allow to cool and use as required.

Oil of lemon could be used or oil of bergamot instead of the oil of rosemary.

Help for greasy hair. Mix 4 oz. witch-hazel with 2 oz. pure lemon juice and 1 oz. rosemary water (decoction). Apply as required.

Dandruff. Mix 2 oz. eau de Cologne (or alcohol) with 4 oz. pine oil and 1 oz. decoction of comfrey. Massage in night and morning.

Shampoo. Mix one egg with the juice of one lemon and one teaspoonful of either rose water, lavender water, etc. Whip well together, apply to the hair, leave on for 10 minutes, then rinse off with two distinct rinses.

Fixative. Apply a   mixture of lemon juice and equal parts of water. With lemon juice you can apply either bay rum, oil of rosemary or oil of bergamot instead of water.

Colour rinses. Chamomile flowers for fair hair. Elderberries for black hair. Henna for reddish hair. Mix with water and apply, leave on for 30 minutes before rinsing off.

Greying hair. Indicative of lack of copper in diet and vitamin B deficiency. Correct diet and apply colour rinses. For other troubles of the hair consult my book *How to Keep your Hair on.*

TEETH
(1) Mix ½ oz. cinnamon with 1 oz. arrowroot. A very useful toothpowder is ready for use.
(2) Mix a cupful of dried rose petals with 2 oz. of powdered charcoal. Rinse the mouth out after using this powder.
(3) If either of these is mixed with witch-hazel it can be used as a paste.

LIPS
Dry or cracked lips.
Cover frequently with a smear of almond oil or olive oil.

Lipstick. Mix 1 oz. beeswax with 1 oz. almond oil, simmer them until they have melted, then add a herbal colouring material : *Archil* from the Canary Isles gives a mauvish tint; *Rubia tinctorium* gives pink to red shades, and *Calendula officinalis* flowers give an orange (marigold) shade.

MOUTHWASH
Witch-hazel. One teaspoonful with five teaspoonfuls water. Tincture of myrrh, ½ teaspoonful with five teaspoonfuls water. Eucalyptus and water can also be used in the same proportion.

SKIN CARE

Never use the same towel for your face as you use for hands and the body.

Dry skin. Due to a deficiency of vitamins A and D. Massage in almond oil and orange juice.

Greasy skin. Mix witch-hazel and rosewater in 4 to 1 ratio with a little cucumber juice.

Skin tonic. Mix the juice of one avocado pear with the juice of half a lemon—this also makes a very efficient *aftershave lotion.*

Aftershave lotion. In addition to the avocado and lemon formula one can try pure witch-hazel—this is also an antiseptic.

Skin cleanser. Equal parts of melon juice, coconut and almond oil. Adding ½ oz. of beeswax for each total of five ounces of other ingredients, makes a solidified cream (melt together and allow to cool).

GUMS

These need exercise which modern man-made and artificial substitute foods do not provide.

Try chewing one or two whole carrots every day, you've never seen a rabbit with bad teeth!

The value of sodium fluoride in keeping gums and teeth healthy is theoretical and by no means proven; keep it and all chemicals away from your mouth, use the simple herbal tooth powders, etc. An apple a day before you go to bed will help offset some of the damage that sweets and carbohydrate diets will do.

My father's father ate a hard, slightly sour, pear every evening as long as they were available, he kept his gums and his teeth very healthy . . . but do not try that unless you have a very strong digestion.

General note: Massage with inner pith of lemon peel.

NAILS

Finger and toe nails can be massaged with almond or olive oil. If any infection sets in (especially on the toes) apply oil of cloves and keep bandaged until healed to avoid further infection.

To remove stains from nails use pure pine turpentine; massage with oil after the stain has gone.

Avoid manicure instruments and do not put chemicals on what was intended to be a sensitive, informative part of your body. Do not cut the cuticles of nails.

Three teaspoonfuls of talcum powder mixed with two teaspoonfuls of rose water or witch-hazel will make a good cleansing and polishing agent for the nails.

A little chamois leather on a flat piece of wood is a better polisher than most you can buy in a store.

Damaged or weak finger nails are a sign of ill-health generally;

you must be short of mineral salts and vitamins; check the dietetic section of this book.

HANDS

Some of our preconceptions about health and beauty are without much factual foundation; the *pale hands I loved beside the Shalimar* is nice enough in a song (I used to sing it to a girl friend of mine when I was young) but no criterion of beauty at all.

Handcream. Mix I drachm of *astragalus gummifer* with 6 oz. rose water and 8 oz. witch-hazel, leave them for a week to soak (cover the dish against evaporations then add 1 oz. glycerine and 1 oz. eau-de-Cologne. A.g. is also known as gum tragacanth.

Chapped hands. Massage in olive oil in which groundsel has been soaked. Or apply a mixture of honey and cucumber juice.

GENERAL NOTES

Wrinkles. Boil two dessertspoonfuls of comfrey in water, strain well and add this to equal parts of witch-hazel. Shake each time before use, apply sparingly to the skin before night.

Cucumber juice and rose water mixed also help. Juice of avocado pears and lemons can be used.

Freckles. Wipe with dock juice (*Rumex aquaticus*) nightly. Cowslip juice (*Primula veris*) also helps.

Acne. Cabbage juice mixed with equal parts of witch-hazel, or equal parts of witch-hazel and apple cider vinegar.

Bathwater. Add juice of pine needles or birch leaves. Rose water, a few drops of oil of jasmin or oil of bergamot or lavender water are refreshing.

Biliousness. Try eating a few mulberries or try some apple cider vinegar.

Boils. Bandage a slice of fresh-cut onion on to the boil and leave on all night. Renew until cured. This method is very effective.

Burns. Apply juice of raw potato. Put a few drops of pure oil of peppermint on within minutes of the burn, this can prevent blistering and pain, but must be done quickly after the burn.

Corns. Apply the juice of sundew (*Drosera angelica*) but keep away from unaffected skin.

Frostbite. Smear lightly with honey.

Giddiness. Thyme tea. $\frac{1}{2}$ teaspoonful in a teapot, pour on a pint of boiling water.

Hairfall. Massage the scalp with juice of *Adiantum aureum*.

Headache. Invariably due to internal conditions. Clear up any constipation, clean the liver and kidneys out. This is a symptom, not a disease, do not be fooled into taking some chemicals to kill the pain, endure the pain, and then cure the cause.

Menstruation. To speed it up : nettle tea or tansy tea. I oz. to a pint of boiling water made in teapot. For *excessive* : a tea made of *vinca major.* ½ oz. to a pint of boiling water. *For painful* : sit over a small bowl of two gallons of water in which six or seven spoonfuls of feverfew (*chrysanthemum parthenium*) have been cooked.

Nervousness. Chamomile or valerian tea. 1 oz. to a pint.

Nose bleeding. Nettle juice or vervain juice, apply on small piece of cotton wool or kapok.

Nipples sore. Marigold juice.

Pimples. Due to internal ill-health. Check diet. Apply witch-hazel or marigold juice.

Pregnancy. For an easy delivery, a daily cup of raspberry leaf tea.

Sexual organs. Wash regularly, especially after intercourse. Add marigold juice or a little apple cider vinegar to the water.

Sleeplessness. My favourite remedy is to add a dessertspoonful of honey to a cup of hot (but not boiled) milk; add a pinch of cinnamon.

Stings. Rub on juice of onion or juice of yarrow.

Strains and sprains. Apply a poultice made of comfrey leaves.

Toothache. Rinse the mouth with tincture of myrrh (1 part) and warm water (3 parts). Then apply oil of cloves on cotton wool to the troubled area.

Warts. Apply dandelion juice.

5. *Herbs for Diets*

Mankind has long been aware that the food he consumed has a direct relationship to his health and energy. In the process of sophistication Man has learnt to make a fine distinction between 'food' and 'nutrition', and within this concept has accepted that health is primarily conditioned by nutritive elements contained within his foodstuffs; it has been a long process, and there is an uneasy awareness that the process of learning about nutrition is far from complete, relevant to this latter point.

In my thesis: *'Diet as a Factor in Improved Cerebral Functioning'* I wrote:

'Any man with a car or a boat is obliged to spend much of his time cleaning and repairing it, in order to maintain its functions at their peak performance, to prolong its utility and its life; few people give to their bodies as much time and care as they bestow upon mechanical appliances.' This is a fact which brings a feeling of guilt to all of us. Most human beings eat with a carelessness that shocks the dietician, particularly when we regard this as a prerequisite of disease, for there was never a cause of disease yet where the body was not clogged up with waste matter, impurities, toxins and suffered from a lowered vitality and loss of elimination efficiency before the disease *began to manifest itself*. Illness is the faulty functioning of the body as a whole; a fact clearly indicated in the writings of Hippocrates and Galen but generally neglected for many centuries; in my monograph *'The Cause and Cure of Disease'* I wrote: 'Identical symptoms may often appear for different diseases; again, symptoms may change. . . .'

The indications are that germs may well be little more than scavengers, part of whose functions is to force out into the open the accumulated debris of many years of unwholesome living, unbalanced diet and uneliminated toxins.

As a dietician I believe that we simply haven't finished our studies; allow me to quote an example. It is assumed, as a result of the work of Ross and other scientists, that the mosquito carries the disease of malaria, for certainly when bitten by malarial-mosquitoes people go down with malaria. As a dietician with some knowledge of logic I say that it is more likely that the injected substances from the mosquito *destroy* hitherto unidentified substances in the human bloodstream, and that it would be easier, cheaper and more effective to learn what deficiency it induced than to go all over the world trying to kill off mosquitoes; in any case, from a homoeopathic point of view the substance to restore it might be found either in the mosquito or in some botanic substance upon which it relies. This type of investigation should be widely explored.

I perceive a significant closing of the gap between the frontiers of Dietetics and Botanic Medicine. The practitioner of botanic medicine need a thorough grounding in dietetics in order to aid diagnosis; I append three simple examples :—(i) Sleeplessness is often due to serious silicon and calcium deficiencies. (ii) Many cases of skin disease are solely due to deficiency of the vitamin B complex. (iii) Some cases of asthma are readily traceable to vitamin E deficiency. On the other hand the dietician should make it his business to look into the botanic sources of both mineral salts and vitamins, for these are the purest and most natural sources. Hereinafter I shall attach a list of these sources; some plants even contain hormones we need !

There is an ancient Chinese proverb : 'Man who drinks medicine but eats badly wastes doctors' knowledge.'

The dietician and the practitioner of botanic medicine have both to diagnose the real cause of disease; to educate the patient into healthy living; to prescribe according to knowledge and experience such measures which will facilitate the body's exertion of its own natural recuperative powers and induce a return to normal healthy functioning of the body. As long ago as the 1820s George Combe was teaching that *Health is the natural state of affairs and sickness is not!*

Regrettably certain interests foster the fallacies of germ-theory and wonder-cure; their motive is clearly to capitalise illness for financial gain, to exercise power through the weapon of monopolised knowledge.

Wonder-pills, injections and cure-without-effort on the part of the patient are illusory, inefficient and illogical. *The disappearance of symptoms does not mean that the cause is completely removed and the disease healed; nothing hinders healing so much as the instantaneous abandonment of diet and medicine when the original symptoms have disappeared.*

A complete cure is present only when the patient feels permanently 'on top of the world'; the sober reflection that few people ever feel that way emphasises how universal are sickness and ill-health in civilised society. Youth is fundamentally good health; the excesses and follies of youth and the adherence to traditional cultural patterns e.g. drinking habits, tobacco, sexual gluttony, etc., often so undermine the body's constitution that the *joie de vivre* of early years never returns; sickness follows sickness over the years and finally death ensues. James Hilton in 'Lost Horizon' inferred that most human beings commit suicide. There is another saying : 'Men dig their own graves with their teeth.'

It comes as a shock to some to find that many simple and despised herbs are sources amazingly rich in vitamins and mineral salts, and that cultivated plants are often less rich in such properties than wild ones. Roughly speaking, the wealth of vitamins and mineral salts depends upon the health and condition of the plant and its soil.

Prof. Barry Commoner of St. Louis University, Missouri, said that Man is more dependent on Nature than ever before because technology cannot replace the full dietetic nutriments of natural food (1969). As it is Nature is on the brink of a cataclysmic collapse. Every time you use a herbicide spray you may be destroying a plant you will need in a few years' time—either for diet or medicine. Less than 1% of insect life is known to be pests to human enterprise.

Human bodies need regular, balanced supplies of mineral salts. Here is a list of herbs which contain mineral salts.

Potassium

Birch bark, blackberries, borage, carrageen, carrot, leaves, chamomile flowers, coltsfoot, coconut, comfrey, cress, dandelion, eyebright, fennel, figs, lentils, lettuce, mint, mullein, nettle, oak bark, parsley, plantain, primrose-flowers, walnut leaves, watercress, yarrow, calamus, mistletoe, peppermint, sanicle, summer savory.

This mineral salt promotes health of heart, muscle and nerve tissue. Deficiency of potassium is found with constipation, catarrh, gallstones, high blood pressure.

Do not take sodium if you have a potassium deficiency.

Iron

Asparagus, barley, bran, burdock, root, devil's bit, hydrocotyle, asiatica, lentils, lettuce, meadowsweet, mullein, nettles, parsley, rest harrow, rye, silverweed, spinach, strawberry (leaves also), toadflax, watercress, wheat, yellow dock.

Iron deficiency brings coldness in hands and feet; flabby skin; poor metabolism and muscle tone, anaemia and lack of strength.

Chlorine

All plants contain chlorine but beets, cabbage, coconuts, figs, olives, radishes and sea-greens are most rich in it.

Deficiency facilitates build-up of toxins in the body; poor digestion, loss of hair, muscle tone, sexual vitality and vitamin E.

Superfluity of chlorine robs the body of iodine, and obesity may result.

Sodium

Carrageen, carrots, celery, chives, cleavers, devil's bit, fennel, lentils, meadowsweet, nettle, okra pods, rest harrow, shepherd's purse, sorrel, spinach, strawberries, watercress, willow, mistletoe.

Necessary for keeping calcium in solution. Deficiency results in cramp, slow-to-heal cuts, and constipation.

Excess may lead to stomach ulcers.

Phosphorus

Almonds, barley, cabbage, chickweed, lentils, marigold flowers, meadowsweet, oats, okra pods, peas, rye, sesame, sorrel, wheat, watercress, calemus, carraway seeds, garlic, liquorice root.

Essential for brain, nervous system, bones and lungs, which cannot be well without it. Needed for healthy gland functions. Deficiency leads to muscular inefficiency, poor memorisation, loss of vitality, the *always-tired* feeling.

Iodine

Agar-agar (Malayan seaweed), artichokes, bladderwrack, dulse, garlic, Icelandic moss, Irish moss, kelp, mushroom, runner beans.

Iodine enables the body to resist disease, keeps the glands healthy, and it lowers nervous tension well. Excessive iodine is toxic.

Calcium

Arrowroot, bran, cabbage, carrageen, chamomile, chives, cleavers, coltsfoot, dandelion root, flax seed, horsetail grass, lemons, lettuce, limes, meadowsweet, mistletoe, nettle, onions, oranges, pimpernel, plantain, rest harrow, rhubarb, shepherds purse, silverweed, sorrel, spinach, toad flax, okra pods.

Needed for bone health, cell vitality, recuperation, convalescence, teeth strength, blood clotting and heart efficiency. Deficiency facilitates hysteria, rickets, pseudo-rheumatic pains and typical illnesses of old age.

Sulphur

Broom tops, cabbage, carrageen, cauliflower, chestnuts, coltsfoot, eyebright, fennel, figs, garlic, horseradish, meadowsweet, mullein, okra, onions, oranges, pimpernel, plantain leaves, potatoes, rest harrow, shepherd's purse, silverweed, watercress.

This prevents premature senility, and is good for the brain and nervous system. Deficiency : Bronchial, digestive, optical and skin troubles.

Magnesium

Almonds, barley, beans, bladderwrack, black willow bark, broom tops, carrot leaves, chestnuts, citrus fruits, devil's bit, dulse, dandelion, hydrocotyle-asiastica, kale, kelp, meadowsweet, mistletoe, mullein, okra, parsley, peppermint, primrose, prunes, rest harrow, silverweed, toadflax, walnut leaves, watercress, wintergreen.

Very needful to relax brain, muscles, nerves and promote healthy sleep. Purifies the body, slightly laxative. Deficiency : Constipation, sleeplessness, obesity and extreme blood acidity.

Silicon

Horsetail grass (probably the richest source of silicon in the world); asparagus, artichokes, barley, cabbage, celery, comfrey, dandelion, leeks, oats, radishes, spinach, strawberries, sunflower-seeds, tomatoes, turnips, also in most mushrooms.

A powerful aid for teeth enamel, hair, eyesight, nerve efficiency, complexion, muscle tone, etc.

Deficiency leads to nervous and muscular exhaustion, baldness and skin diseases.

A chronic absence of silica has been recorded in epilepsy and cancer cases, also in some forms of obesity and rheumatism.

Fluorine

Very different to the man-made *sodium fluoride* which form of industrial aluminium waste is pressed upon a gullible public as a substitute for natural fluorine. Garlic and watercress are the main sources. Cabbage and spinach have some fluorine.

Excess is dangerous to the spinal cord.

Deficiency facilitates anaemia, headaches, poor teeth, and skin ailments.

Manganese

Almonds, endive, mint, nasturtium flowers, olives, parsley, peanuts, potatoes, walnuts, watercress, wheatgerm.

Deficiency leads to a damaged pituitary gland. Manganese is probably helpful to some drug addicts. A brain and nerve tonic. Antiseptic and germicidal.

Vanadium

Found in kelp. Strengthens blood phagocytes. Deficiency leads to premature ageing.

Zinc

Found in nuts, wheatgerm and green leaves. Essential for efficient muscular control—also digestion.

Deficiency may be a factor in diabetes, and starved sex glands.

Sources of hormones and physiologically related compounds

Alder leaves, clover, elder flowers, lime flowers, nettles, pussy-willow and wheatgerm.

Aletris farinosa, alfalfa, garlic, liquorice, sarsaparilla and yams.

(For further details on the hormones in plants refer to M. Kreig's book *Green Medicine*).

In these lists I have given native English sources first and foreign sources afterwards.

Vitamins, mineral salts and hormones are all easier to absorb when administered in botanical forms; the sick body will often react violently to these substances when of fish, animal or synthetic origin.

Most of us learn early on in life how important OXYGEN is to the health of the body; oxygen must be absorbed internally as well as through the breathing.

Horseradish, mint, onions, parsley, peppermint, potatoes, radishes, rhubarb and tomatoes all give us oxygen.

Our bodies also need carbon, hydrogen and nitrogen.

CARBON is found in apples, beans, cereals, dates, grains, grapes, lentils and potatoes.

HYDROGEN is found in nearly all berries, fruits and vegetables.

NITROGEN is found in almonds, beans, peas, peanuts and walnuts.

VITAMINS

A: Alfalfa, apricots (dried), carrots, dandelion, okra pods, paprika, parsley, watercress.

Needed for eyes and skin efficiency.

Excellent for digestive organs, respiratory, glandular, and excretory functions.

Deficiency : Hay fever, slow reactions, accident proneness, damage to bone growth.

B: 1. (Thiamine, Aneurin). Asparagus, barley, beans (dried), bladderwrack, dulse, fenugreek, okra pods, wheatgerm.
2. (Riboflavin, Niacin [nicotinic acid], Folic acid). Bladder-bladder wrack, dulse, fenugreek, okra pods, wheatgerm.
3. (Pantothenic acid). Black molasses, peanuts, whole wheat grains.
6. (Pyridoxin). Cereals, whole meal.
12. (Cyanocobalamin). Alfalfa, black molasses, bladderwrack, kelp, wheatgerm.

The B group is related to brain, nerve, digestion, and eye health. It is related to metabolism.

Deficiencies show up in gum disorders, skin diseases, hair falling out, diarrhoea, headaches, nose and throat troubles, insomnia etc.

C: Acerola, blackcurrant, broccoli, burdock, cabbage, cantaloupe, melon, capsicum, chervil, coltsfoot, citrus fruits, elderberries, kale, marigold, mustard-and-cress, paprika, parsley, rose hips, tomatoes, turnip tops, watercress.

Essential for the proper absorption of protein, for connective tissues, muscles, glandular tissues, sex organs etc. Deficiency shows up in frequent colds, eye troubles, inability to absorb calcium etc. Inability to resist infections.

D: Watercress and wheatgerm (Fish oils are the best sources).

Vital for balance of calcium and phosphorus, for heart efficiency, muscle tone, and nervous stability.

Deficiency leads to bone troubles, heart and muscle flaccidity, poor skin reaction etc.

E: Alfalfa, bladderwrack, brown rice, dandelion leaves, dulse, kelp, lettuce, linseed, sesame, sunflower seeds, watercress, wheatgerm.

Needed for heart, liver and glandular efficiency. Deficiency leads to lack of oxygen in tissues, muscular and glandular troubles.

F: Peanuts, wheatgerm and whole grains.
Blood and heart efficiency.

K: Alfalfa, chestnuts, peanuts, shepherd's purse, soya beans.
Essential for proper clotting of the blood.
Deficiency : believed to be a factor in jaundice.

M: Asparagus, beans, beets, broccoli, cabbage, cauliflower, celery, cucumbers, kale, mustard, parsley, spinach, tangerines, turnip, watercress.

Essential for formation of redblood cells, protein metabolism, etc.

Deficiency links with anaemia, glossitis, sprue, cirrhosis and endocrine disturbances.

P: Buckwheat, citrus fruits, grapes, paprika, plums, rosehips. Tones up the arteries—gum health.

PROTEINS

Proteins must be absorbed in an acid medium; botanic sources provide this most adequately; soya beans, peanuts and nuts generally, also vegetables, contain more protein grams per ounce than animal sources.

CARBOHYDRATES

Abundantly present in nearly all fruit and vegetables. Of the sugars, glucose is present (*inter alia*) in fruits, plant juices, onions, sweet corn and unripe potatoes; fructose is present in fruit, plant juices and cane sugar; sucrose is found in carrots, beet sugar, cane sugar and many sweet fruits and roots.

Starch is abundantly present in beets, carrots, cereal grains, parsnips, pumpkins and turnips. It is rather low in the following : asparagus, beans, cabbage, cauliflower, celery, dandelion leaves, endive, green corn, green peas, lettuce, radishes and spinach.

Fats are found also in botanic sources : Nuts (almonds, brazils, peanuts, etc). Seeds (sunflower seeds) olives, wheatgerm.

I cannot do better here than quote Dr. Bruce Copen, Ph.D., D.Sc., etc. : *Proper diet is just about the most important factor to be taken into consideration in the treatment of chronic diseases. . . . Nearly all chronic diseases are associated in some way or another with wrong eating, and no individual can expect a cure unless the diet is taken into consideration.*

For weight reduction, eat proportionately large amounts of proteins, meat, fish, eggs and cheese, and reduce the foods with a high caloric count, such as cream and butter, cakes, chocolate. The calorie is the measurement that indicates the amount of heat or energy released by given food.

Foods with *low calorie content* : Raw apple, broccoli, cabbage, cherries, endive, figs, grapefruit, kale, lemon, baked potato, artichoke, brussels sprouts, celery, chicory, kohlrabi, lettuce, mushrooms, parsnips, radishes, asparagus, cauliflower, cucumbers, fresh fruit, sauerkraut, peppers, rhubarb, spinach, tomatoes, leeks, onions, fresh pineapple, brown rice, turnips, vegetable juice, watercress.

High calorie foods: Alcohol, avocado, bass beans, beef (fatty), biscuits, butter cakes, chickpeas, creamed chicken, chicken pie, codfish cakes, cookies, cooking fat, corn, doughnuts, duck, éclair, fish sticks, fudge, goose, hamburger, ham, herring, cheese, lamb, macaroni and cheese, mackerel, muffins, meat loaf, nuts, perch, peanut butter, pies, pizza, pork, fried potato, sweet potato, raisins, rice pudding, salmon, sausage, spaghetti sauce, tuna, waffles, welsh rabbit. (Avoid these if slimming).

Cholesterol is fat deposit which collects inside blood vessels and clogs, causing hardening of arteries. The body synthesizes cholesterol from animal fats. *Cut the fat from meat before* you eat it and *avoid cooking oils made from animal fat,* such as lard.

Olive oils, soya bean, corn and cottonseed oil contain unsaturated fatty acids, and form no cholesterol.

Tonic Diets

Examine the lists of foods given under mineral salts, vitamins, etc. Choose those most closely answering to your needs and let some of these predominate in each meal every day until your health is better.

6. *Herbs in Cooking*

The housewife who has heard of *cordon bleu* cooking may well envy the subtle distinctions of taste which are the secrets of the world's best chefs. This section will help the cook to achieve some new and exciting tastes which may well approach the charm of well-thought-out foods served in the best restaurants.

JAMS

Apples can be mixed with blackberries, cranberries, cherries (remove the stones), damsons, loganberries, ginger, plums, raspberries, rhubarb, lemon juice, rowanberries, and also spiced if wished; use the apples alone, then with cinnamon, cloves (very sparingly, four or five cloves for 2 lb. jam), mint, nutmeg, tansy or thyme.

Blackberries can be mixed with apples, lemon juice or pears. As can *Blackcurrants*.

Blueberries can be mixed with apple in equal parts.

Cherries. Mix with apples, pears, shredded walnuts or a little ginger.

Damsons. Mix with apples, ginger, rhubarb.

Gooseberries. Mix with apples, red or white currants, sultanas, rhubarb or ginger (small amount only).

Ginger mixes with apples, pears, rhubarb, oranges or lemons. The daring cook may try a little with grapefruit or lime marmalade.

Pineapple makes a delightful jam; as the taste is rather subtle it is not advisable to add any other taste to it.

Plums provide a strong taste, and can be mixed with apples, pears, rhubarb, and a few apricots.

Pears are somewhat neglected in jam-making. I believe the most popular jam I ever made was pear and ginger jam; do mix the ginger with the sugar first!

Raspberries appear to have a sharper flavour if some lemon or red currants are added; try them with pears.

Rhubarb and Ginger, my dear mother's favourite jam! Try also rhubarb with lemon, oranges or grapefruit.

Strawberries. I advise against adding anything to this jam, the taste is rich—a little lemon juice suffices.

Try your hand with less well-known fruits such as greengages, mulberries, whortleberries, dewberries, etc. Also try mixing a few limes or quinces with your marmalade recipes.

OMELETTES

My mother, a superlative and gifted cook, always allowed my father to make the omelettes. The results were surprising, delightful and rarely duplicated. My father had a remarkable knack of inventiveness and a capacity to blend ingredients which defied competition. Some of his secrets I know; many more I never learned, alas!

ADDITIVES

Almonds, finely chopped, put in just before the omelette is ready to serve and is still slightly liquid.

Angelica, grated into thin strips, sprinkled on before the omelette is served.

Grated apple, put in when the eggs and butter are mixed.

Asparagus. Fix a few heads in the omelette as served on the plate, one or two cherries may also be added.

Balm Melissa, the dried herb, is mixed with the eggs, etc.

Basil is a delightful ingredient to sprinkle on an omelette when it is lying in the pan as frying starts.

Bay leaves are too strong to be used entirely, you may put one or two in the pan before the omelette is placed in it, but having heated them and extracted a little oil from the leaves remove them.

Betony is a pleasant-tasting herb. Try a sprinkling of it.

Brandy, by no means a herb, but of distant botanic origins; a few drops of brandy on an omelette before it is served add a surprise taste to what may appear to be a plain dish.

Caraway seeds were used sometimes by my father in his expert omelette making.

Carrot. Grated, raw carrot is a pretty and tasteful addition.

Cayenne pepper in small doses.

Celery seeds. Recommended.

Chervil, a rare and interesting taste, use sparingly.

Chives. Finely sliced, must be tried.

Cinnamon. Truly recommended, but not too much.

Coriander seeds. An exotic taste, slightly sweetening the dish.

Dill. When I lived in Sweden this was a favourite additive; it has a most pleasant taste.

Fennel seeds and *Fenugreek.* Use sparingly, add to mixture as it goes into the pan.

Garlic. Do not add to the omelette, just wipe the interior of the pan well with a clove of garlic before putting the mixture in.

Horse-radish. Fresh, shredded and added before frying begins.

Hyssop. The fresh, dried leaves are very aromatic and powerful, use sparingly, add one minute before removing the omelette from the heat.

Lemon peel. Add a little freshly grated on to the omelette before serving. Alternatively a little lemon juice.

Lemon thyme. Much neglected, but sprinkle some leaves into your omelette before frying. Use sparingly.

Marjoram. Mix before frying.

Mint. Mix during frying.

Nasturtium. Mix a chopped leaf into the mix while frying.

Nutmeg. Sprinkle a little on the dish before serving.

Orange peel can be sprinkled over an omelette before serving.

Oregano. Mix before frying.

Paprika. Sprinkle in during frying.

Parsley. Delightful, but use sparingly, some people cannot stomach too much parsley.

Peppers. According to taste, do not overdo.

Raisins. We liked them in omelettes, have you tried them?

Rosemary. Add with original mixture before frying.

Sage. Use to mix before cooking the omelette.

Tansy. A sprinkling of powdered leaf and buds, a favourite taste of earlier generations.

Tarragon. My favourite omelettes are made with this herb.

Thyme. Use sparingly, a delightful taste. Add during cooking.

BISCUITS AND BUNS

Basil, caraway, coriander seeds, cinnamon, cocoa, ginger, lemon juice or peel, nutmeg, tarragon, and tansy.

FISH

Basil, bay leaf, capers, cassia, celery seeds, chives, coriander seeds, dill, fennel, lemon-thyme, mint, paprika, parsley, rosemary and thyme. Try grilling salmon with juniper berries.

SALADS

Almost any herb can be added to salads—nasturtium leaves, tarragon and watercress should be tried. Mix citrus fruit pieces or juices to a salad.

BREAD

Cinnamon, coriander, currants, sultanas, raisins, various ground nuts, caraway seeds, saffron, thyme and candied fruit peel may be added to bread and rolls.

SOUPS

Almost any herb mentioned in this section may be added individually or in mixture to soups. But do make sure you taste the herbs first and know what flavours they will produce. Do not use spices, only green herbs.

STEWS

Parsley, sage, rosemary and thyme are the usual herbs. Try oregano, tarragon, chives, or marjoram.

MEAT AND GAME

Apricots or pineapple with greasy roast meats; stew the fruit very lightly, and add to the dish at the time of serving.

With grilled hearts or liver, try rosemary or tarragon. Chillis, paprika, mustard (many sorts available).

Mint sauce is a favourite with lamb, but try marjoram or lemon-thyme one day.

Beef is wonderful with horseradish, but coriander, rosemary or tarragon should be tried. Venison goes well with juniper berries.

SPAGHETTI AND PASTA DISHES

Allspice, basil, capers, chervil, chives, garlic, mint, oregano, paprika, parsley, rosemary, sage, saffron, thyme, turmeric.

GUIDE TO LESSER-KNOWN SPICES AND HERBS

Allspice. Attractive taste, suitable for biscuits, buns, cakes, fruit compotes, meat dishes (cold) and pasta.

Borage. 'I, borage, bring alwaies courage' ran the old English saw. It also brings pleasure when sprinkled on vegetable salads.

Calamus. Aids digestion, a delicate fragrance. Pastas or salads benefit most.

Capers. Best with mutton, boiled chicken and in stews.

Cardamon. Added to cakes and fruit salads mostly.

Cloves. Added very begrudgingly to *Lebkuchen* cakes.

Coriander. A herb whose seeds are gaining in popularity. Used with buns, cakes, meats and much else. A beautiful perfume to the nostrils and taste buds.

Marigold flowers. Decorative, nutritious and healthy. Salads, soups and sweets.

Nasturtium. The leaves make a good salad additive. Often the seeds are used too, but I think they are too bitter to be used liberally.

Nigella seeds. Can be used on cakes and bread.

Poppy seeds. Sprinkle a few dried seeds on your bread before it comes out of the oven.

Sesame. These seeds are used with blanc-manges, soups, cheese dishes and pastry.

Tarragon. Not so well-known as it deserves. Try a steak grilled with tarragon, and served with a red wine covering. Its uses are many and very varied, do try it!

7. *Herbs for Veterinary Purposes*

Animals left in their wild state have a quite remarkable instinct for finding herbs which will heal them of all manner of illnesses, showing recuperative powers when they are wounded or sick that amaze us.

BIRDS

A caged bird is particularly helpless, not only in being caged and unable to seek its own medicine, but often because it has been bred of a line of caged birds which have never seen what birds living in freedom eat when the plants are available.

Asthma. Provide fennel seeds, chopped fresh watercress, and some capsicum seeds. Alternatively, liquid extracts of the herbs could be used to saturate some sugar and provided once a day.

Colds. Fennel, chickweed (fresh), and one or two drops of aqua camphor in the drinking water. Check the room for draughts! Provide more fresh green food daily.

Birds with a cold may lack iron in their food so check against list of herbs containing iron (dietetic section).

Digestive disorders. Constipation: Fresh green grasses, buds from the *fraxinus ornus* (manna tree-flowering ash), fennel seed or fennel water on sugar. Senna pod water on sugar may also be used— a few drops at a time on a piece of sugar.

Diarrhoea. Seeds or fresh leaves of buckshorn. Plantain (*plantago coronopus*) caraway seeds, a pinhead of arrowroot powder (use very sparingly).

Ulcers/Worms. Plantain juice (*plantago major*), a few drops of sugar, once daily.

Tonic. Capsicum powder 10 grains/powdered gentian 30 grains mixed with honey. As much as a cherry stone put into the cage daily.

Winter tonic. 30 grains tincture of quinine 1 oz. of water, in which 30 grains of caraway seeds have soaked for two nights. 2 or 3 drops on a piece of sugar, daily.

Wash. Boil 4 drachms of cinnamon in a pint of water. When it is cool add half a cupful to the bird's bath water.

Angina/Diphtheria. Treat as for colds, one drop of eucalyptus in a dessertspoonful of water, soak sugar in this and offer to the bird. Keep the cage spotlessly clean with antiseptic washes. People in poor health may develop the same diphtheria condition, every care should be taken.

Parrots. Often suffer from infectious psittacosis which humans may take. Keep the bird and yourself spotlessly clean. Disinfect the parrot's cage, stand and surroundings daily. Capsicum, cinnamon, fennel, or juniper berries and slippery elm paste made with honey have been recommended for such conditions in the bird.

General Note: Many birds like fresh dandelion leaves, comfrey, chickweed and grasses.

CATS AND DOGS

Doses given are for dogs : usually for cats you should reduce the dose by half.

Worms. Ground areca nuts 60 grains powdered. Small dogs as for cats. Two doses should be enough. Clean the animal's sleeping quarters thoroughly.

Digestive disturbances. A teaspoonful of slippery elm powder mixed with milk and a little honey into a paste. Once daily. Increase fresh food, greens, etc. Clean out drinking bowls and food plates, sleeping quarters. Chickweed, comfrey and dandelion leaves can be mixed with the food or otherwise administered.

Sores, Cuts, Wounds. Apply a paste of slippery elm and honey, bandage it on so that the animal cannot remove the covering.

Mange: See under CATTLE AND HORSES.

In general, use the same herbal remedies for your animals as you would for yourself, but QUARTER STRENGTH *and* use only twice daily, morning and night.

Do get your animal out to the grass where it may seek its own remedies. NEVER *give a sick animal tinned food* or patent biscuits.

Rabies: See LIVERWORT.

CATTLE AND HORSES
General Notes

For all cattle and horses add a little apple cider vinegar to the feed and they will tend to keep free of infection.

Doses for Calves and Colts. 1 month, $\frac{1}{20}$ full dose; 3 months, $\frac{1}{10}$ full dose; 6 months, $\frac{1}{6}$ full dose; 1 year, $\frac{1}{3}$ full dose; 3 years, $\frac{1}{2}$ full dose.

Blistering. Mix $\frac{1}{2}$ oz. oil of camphor with 1 oz. tincture of mustard oil, rub into the affected part as often as required.

Conditioners. Horses seem to thrive on aniseed. Such mixtures as the following will be found very effective : 2 oz. fenugreek, 2 oz. capsicum, 2 oz. serpentaria, 4 oz. ginger, 4 oz. gentian, 1 lb. flaxseed meal.

Mix powdered ingredients together and give two dessertspoonfuls daily with feed.

Constipation. Owing to their diet these animals rarely if ever suffer from this, but a return to fresh grass will put them right.

Coughs. Mix 4 oz. creosote liquid extract with 8 oz. fennel seed water. A dessertspoonful every three hours. Liquorice may be added, some horses like it.

Cuts, sores and wounds. Apply slippery elm, honey and ½ oz. tincture of myrrh mixed. If painful, add a few dried poppy seeds to the mixture.

Diarrhoea. 4 dr. of oil of peppermint, 4 oz. of chopped plantain mixed with linseed and oats or hay. Clean out the stables, etc., very thoroughly and disinfect them.

Embrocation. 15 oz. acetic acid, 18 oz. alcohol, 1 oz. camphor, 6 eggs, 45 oz. distilled witch-hazel, 51 oz. oil turpentine.

Eye troubles. Wash with equal parts of quince juice, witch-hazel water.

Foot sores. Mix equal parts of creosote, beeswax, linseed oil and cinnamon powder (half part). Apply daily to affected limbs well above and below the actual area of hurt as well as on it.

Heaves. 1 oz. balsam copaiba, 12 oz. apple cider vinegar, 2 dessert-spoonfuls twice daily.

Hide-bound pains. 2 oz. elecampane, 2 oz. liquorice root, 2 oz. fenugreek, 2 oz. rosin, ½ oz. copperas, 2 dr. ginger, 1 dr. gentian, 1 dr. valerian, 3 oz. linseed meal.

Influenza. ½ oz. camphor, 2 oz. liquorice powder, 1 oz. creosote water, ½ lb. black molasses, 2 oz. slippery elm powder. Mix 2 dessert-spoonfuls twice a day.

Mange. Soak all harness and blankets in *creosote*. Apply a paste of sulphur and creosote to affected areas.

Sheep Dip. 1 lb. soap; 20 fluid oz. oil of cloves; 50 gallons of water. Add the cloves to boiling soapy water.

Udder inflammation.

I—40 gr. salicylic acid, 1 oz. mercurial ointment, 3¼ oz. liniment of camphor. Apply and rub the udder carefully twice a day.

II—1 dr. belladonna root, 1 oz. oil turpentine, 1 dr. camphor, 6 oz. solution green soap, q.s. Mix and make a liniment. Bathe the udder several times with hot water. Dry and apply above liniment.

Urine, to increase: ½ drachm of oil of juniper with some flaxseed meal (about 1 oz.) added to the feed.

Commonly used herbs in veterinary work: Aloes, Areca nut, Buchu, Camphor, Capsicum, Catechu, Cinchona bark, Creosote, Fennel seed, Fenugreek, Gentian, Ginger, Ipecacuanha, Juniper berries, Mustard, Quinine, Rhubarb, Tobacco. *Sulphur, Vinegar and Whisky are often also added.*

8. *Dyes from Vegetable Substances*

Until about a century ago most of the colours and dyes used in the world were of vegetable origin. The range of colours from herbs is quite remarkable, and all the more attractive because of the richness of the colours. While many of them do not stay so strong over the years, they have the advantage of not being poisonous, like some of the inorganic dyes that can seep into an uncovered cut or wound and cause septicaemia.

There is just one essential ingredient to get these attractive dyes . . . pure water—this means rain-water or water from an unpolluted spring or well. Tap water in towns is invariably impermeated by chemicals which destroy the hue and life of the dye.

Large pans are required in which the cloth or garment can be spread out in the mixture without touching another garment. Later in the process it is possible to crease cloth or clothes and tie them in such a way that the dyed and undyed areas form an interesting pattern—from such simple tricks are fashions born ! Fibreglass containers can be used for pans.

The cloth to be dyed must be clean and free from dust and grease. The cloth is lowered into the dye and totally immersed in it. The dye must NEVER be added to the pan when the cloth is in it.

Vegetable dyes vary slightly according to the mineral salts in the soil from which the plants were taken. To obtain a good match for a dye try to take the plants from the same area. If a plant grows naturally on clay or chalk try to collect that, rather than specimens growing on other types of soil.

Fixatives are essential to give the dye better lasting power. Take 1 lb. alum to 4 oz. cream of tartar, dissolve both in enough hot water to cover them in a dish. Add rain water, about 8 gallons. Heat up slowly while the cloth or garment is in the tub. Use rubber gloves while handling the object to be *fixed* or dyed. After one hour in the hot fixative, remove cloth to dry, squeeze gently, and hang it. In olden days this was done in a barn or outhouse—and daylight was usually excluded.

Dyes are simple to make : one collects the herbs (the amount controlling the depth of the colour of the dye); tie them up in muslin or any old clean piece of cotton, then just boil them slowly in the water which is going to be used to dye the cloth. The time the herbs boil controls the colour of the cloth.

When a sufficient quantity of coloured liquid has been obtained, the cloth, already treated by fixative, is lowered into the vat, and very slowly brought by simmering to the boil. Allow the finished product to hang over a clothes line, preferably not in full daylight. One gallon of dye does 8 oz. wool. Wool is the best cloth for a beginner to work with.

LIST OF DYES

It is true that almost every herb yields some dye substance, but many of them are useless from a really practical point of view.

When you experiment keep a notebook and jot down the details of the following facts : Plant used; Amount of weight used; Month (affecting plant) in which the plant was collected; results noted. Some garden plants such as dahlias, which are not usually used in medicine, can be used for dyes. When dyes are being made or used or experimented with keep your hands covered with heavy-duty rubber gloves, and avoid splashing your skin with them.

Remember that the use of a substance such as copper or alum in the dye will alter the hue entirely.

Alder bark yields brown or black, according to quantity used.

Birch. The bark can be boiled for a delightful brown colour.

Cornflowers yield a charming blue colour.

Dahlias a bright orange.

Dogwood bark produces bright red colours.

Golden rod. The flowers produce a yellowish hue.

Green colours can be produced by dipping cloth previously dyed yellow into a mixture which shows up blue.

Guaiacum chips produce a reddish colour, and variations can be obtained by adding tin dust, alum or tartar.

Purple colours. Dye the cloth blue and then dip in red dye.

Sassafras yields a reddish orange colour.

Walnut shells and nuts can be boiled down to produce a fascinating brownish colour.

Woad (Isatis Tinctoria) produces wonderful shades of blue, according to the amount used and cloth dyed.

Yellow dock roots give a sightly dark yellow.

9. Herbs in Magic and Witchcraft

One of the most difficult things about this book has been deciding which materials to omit. The competition for inclusion was tremendous, but I did not want to produce some weighty volume which would be too heavy for any reader to carry around.

I decided not to include herbs which were used in witchcraft but which would be totally unsafe to be used for any normal medical purpose by an untrained layman. Some herbs such as parsley have very useful medical effects (kidneys, etc.) but are comparatively devoid of anecdote, myth or magic. The common potato is frequently carried around when freshly dug up from the earth to ward off rheumatism. I know of two cases where rheumatic cases did carry a potato with them and their ailment disappeared. Psalm CXXXVII mentions that the ancient Hebrews hung their harps on the willow trees, but there are some problems about a layman's use of the willow. Tansy, favourite of many gypsies, was used in some country parts to flavour buns and cakes up until about 1900. It was held to be a symbol of immortality; the herb is good for high blood pressure and cardiac pains. It also seems to have been used by some witches, but they didn't keep very good scientific notes, and they probably used it for little more than the effect it has in curative properties. Many of the old ladies tersely called witches were from families who had come down in the world, had little but their knowledge to sell, and were more feared than thanked when they did cure people. In view of the way in which they were threatened, bullied and burnt it is not surprising if some of them did turn a bit nasty and drop something lethal in the cattle fodder now and then. That they knew how to use a little psychology is quite evident; it was about the only weapon they had to preserve their lives in a crude age—long before old age pensions and a welfare state had been visualised.

Fortunes were probably told from herbal teas long before the oriental drink came to Britain. Southernwood was used as an aphrodisiac, but why go to all that trouble when a dietician can give you a few vitamin pills which will be more efficacious? I think we should realise that in such lore, whether we believe it partly, wholly or not at all, facts and observations can be hidden, stored up in the folk-memories, and what to us is strange or useless may have priceless significance to later generations.

'When found make a note of,' said Dickens' Captain Cuttle. This tendency has been with me from very early years, and most of the old couplets and stories quoted in this book came from my grandparents, and from old people with whom I have talked some time or another. Much of the information included in this work is unique and will form a mine of information of interest to young and old.

Several herbs are mentioned in connection with love-philtres, and, speaking as a qualified psychologist, I must explain that much of the efficacy of such drinks depends upon the psychosomatic condition of the patient; if a person believes a drink is an aphrodisiac even something such as fennel tea would act like it—for that one individual (Shakespeare did think that herb possessed such power) the trouble comes when the true believer recommends the same cure or aid to his/her friends—it doesn't work in too many cases. Very often the worst thing a physician of any persuasion can do is to say to a patient : *'There's absolutely nothing the matter with you that a good night's sleep won't cure'*; the patient often *wants* to feel there is something wrong that only some hocus pocus can heal. We cannot go around blaming gnarled old crones or gaffers for doing exactly the same as many doctors and psychologists are doing today —selling comfort rather than cures.

Admittedly, many of the professional and amateur warlocks and witches did not know too much about the herbs they used. They often prescribed the wrong herb; but a list of all the herbs used to produce magic charms would be rather embarrassing; most of them are herbs used to cure constipation, indigestion or relieve an alcohol-flooded liver.

Like the priests of the ancient Mayas, some wizards and wise women used drugs which were dangerously hallucinogenic, narcotic and habit-forming. The horrible visions, the 'darkness made visible' which results from any drugs of addiction, explain fully not only the things claimed to have been seen but also the sheer inconsistency of the varying reports. In other cases it is clear that covens used hypnotic drugs to facilitate a condition of hypnosis (mass hypnosis is sometimes easier than individual hypnosis); what happens when the victims reach a condition of narcolepsy depends upon the ulterior reasons behind the ritual. It has often been perverted sexual instincts. I once asked Dr. Thomas, one of the most learned men I have ever known, what witchcraft is; his reply is significant : 'It is the desire to enjoy all the benefits of a religion without any moral responsibility either to God or to fellow humans.' There are some witches' covens today where a semblance of worship is followed quite sincerely—usually to Demeter or one of the old Graeco-Roman deities, and it would be wrong to say that these are anything but genuine attempts to find a religious way of life, but why in a permissive society they need to be exclusive or secretive bodies is not logically explained. I follow the thinking of that splendid Scottish thinker George Combe who taught that it is natural and logical to do good but neither logical nor worth while to do evil. The reader who is not acquainted with the law of Karma, the ancient doctrine of the Wheel of the Law, should study it. Karma applies to nations as well as to individual men and women. Nothing good is ever left unrewarded, and nothing evil (the absence of Goodness) is ultimately ever left unpunished, because it is we ourselves who establish a personal magnetism which draws ourselves towards the ends we have chosen. The exploiters become exploited : the robbers become robbed. Death itself is no escape, for by reincarnation we must come back again to learn the lessons we failed to master before.

There are many claims in witchcraft that certain people can call up spirits, control them (Prof. Alexandre David Neal has a wry comment on this in her *With Mystics and Magicians in Tibet*), make use of occult powers to harm others and so on. In all the cases examined somewhere along the line the participants take some herbal concoction; in each case it is made from herbs which are dangerous hallucinogenic drugs or are drunk in a quantity calculated to make responses of the human nervous system untrustworthy. I have specialised in the field of Mind and Brain and Nervous System; my works, *Treatment of the Diseases of the Nervous System, Diet as a Factor in Improved Cerebral Functioning* and the *Influence of Herbs in Psychosomatic Medicine* (original in German) are technical papers not written for the edification of the layman, but I will assure any reader that the harm done by taking these drugs is incalculable, and often, as far as medical knowledge goes, *irreparable*. One of the drugs which witches took in order to be able to fly was prepared from ergot of rye, which is a source of the dangerous, addictive drug LSD, currently used by far too many university students—one of the commonest symptoms is an overwhelming conviction that one is flying or able to fly. Several deaths among addicts have been recorded. Wasn't it Pope who said : *'Presume not then the heavens to scan, the greatest study of Mankind is Man'*? If somebody doesn't return the love you offer, ask yourself first whether you are such a 'catch' for them as you fancy? A little self-improvement might be far more attractive than all the love potions in the world. If it is fear of impotency which drives you to search for aphrodisiacs, do not neglect to try some vitamin E if you are male or vitamin C if female before you experiment with any philtres. Many herbs given here do contain vitamins and nutritive minerals salts, and if used as advised no ill-effects should be experienced.

If you want to contact the spirits of the departed go to a good spiritualist's medium, preferably one who does it for love, not for money. Do not assume that this is a hunting ground for any amateurs.

If you are superstitious do not let that worry you at all. Our general interest in superstitions shows an alert mind, a person who is determined to do the right things in life, and make the best out of available circumstances. Never scoff at another's superstitions, however much you doubt them yourself—that person may be educationally programmed so that he/she cannot live without them. How far anybody can ever influence you with their beliefs and superstitions depends upon individual willingness to be convinced; that superlative writer Prosper Merimée in his *'Carmen'* quotes a proverb of the Spanish gypsies : *'No fly enters a closed mouth.'*

We can lie to others but ultimately we can never lie to ourselves, deep down inside there is always the nagging knowledge that things do not happen just because we wish them to (if wishes were horses beggars would ride), like the little girl who was overheard to pray : 'Dear God, please make Lisbon the Capital of Spain, 'cause that's what I put down on my exam paper.'

In the 'Holy Rimes' there is a phrase in which God expresses sheer amusement at Man's belief or disbelief because neither can alter the basic reality of spiritual life. There are truths about the deep spiritual life of Man, but if we try to force them we will lose them and ourselves. Somewhere, as Shakespeare put it, 'there is a divinity that shapes our ends'; in the classic words of Emerson's poem 'Brahma' :

> *'They reckon ill who leave me out,*
> *When me they fly I am the wings,*
> *I am the doubter and the doubt,*
> *And I the hymn the Brahmin sings.'*

As to there being a God I can quote only an amusing anecdote : Once upon a time there were two fleas on an elephant's back, and the one said to the other 'I don't believe in elephants, do you?' Life here on earth is a schooling, let none of us insist that he already knows *all* the answers, but let each of us devote ourselves to the search for Truth, the search for Goodness, and the search for Beauty, for where these meet in harmony there lies true Wisdom.

ASTROLOGY AND PLANTS

The plants quoted are said to be most valuable to the people born under the appropriate sign of the Zodiac. I have no confirmation to give on this point, but I think it is useful and relevant to include the list.

Capricorn 31st December–19th January
Comfrey, fumitory, horsetail grass, shepherd's purse, wintergreen.

Aquarius 20th January–18th February
Marigold, snakeroot, southernwood, valerian, walnut.

Pisces 19th February–19th March
Chamomile, Irish moss, liverwort, mint, verbena, wormwood.

Aries 20th March–20th April
Garlic, hops, nettles.

Taurus 21st April–20th May
Coltsfoot, sage, tansy, thyme.

Gemini 21st May–20th June
Caraway, lily-of-the-valley, parsley.

Cancer 21st June–20th July
Chickweed, honeysuckle, lettuce.

Leo 21st July–21st August
Eyebright, marigold, mistletoe, St. John's wort, walnut.

Virgo 22nd August–22nd September
Fennel, liquorice.

Libra 23rd September–22 October
Feverfew, pennyroyal (a mint), thyme, violet.

Scorpio 23rd October–22 November
Blackberry, hoarhound, horseradish, wormwood.

Sagittarius 23rd November–20th December
Agrimony, clover, dandelion, oak.

One of my friends is the nephew of Gustav Holst (1874–1934) whose 'Planets Suite' is very interesting because he showed the planets in a different mood to most people interested in mysticism and astrology :
Mars—Bringer of War.
Venus—Bringer of Peace.
Mercury—The winged messenger.
Jupiter—The Bringer of Jollity.
Saturn—Bringer of Old Age.
Uranus—The Magician.
Neptune—The Mystic.

NUMEROLOGY

Many students of the mystical things around us are well acquainted with the meaning of numbers, the art of *adding* vowel values and then consonant values, etc.

It might be an interesting line of research for them to make notes of the popular usual names of herbs, and compare the results for different patients and different diseases; such a work might possibly open a whole new line of research. For the benefit of the enterprising I am adding here the usual table of numbers based on the English alphabet.

1	A	J	S
2	B	K	T
3	C	L	U
4	D	M	V
5	E	N	W
6	F	O	X
7	G	P	Y
8	H	Q	Z
9	I	R	

The theory is tied up with the vibrations of personality rates for each different person and thing in the country where the language is normally spoken.

If, say, a Malaysian plant were investigated, the investigator would have to use a different chart based on the alphabet of the language. I simply do not know what to do about picturegram languages such as Chinese, Japanese, etc. Let us be thankful for the work of Cadmus, the Greek, who is supposed to have invented our alphabet.

COLOURS

The science of the study of Colour, Coloronic Therapy and the use of colour as a significant factor of psychological behaviour is well advanced now. This is something to start the reader thinking about some interesting facets of colour.

1. Nearly all herbs used have fairly light colours. Many herbs which are toxic to Man and inadvisable to use have very dark shades (Yew, etc.).
2. Some colours appear to be particularly suited to some people; cannot some research be done as to whether they are best healed by herbs with coloured flowers matching them?
3. It is probably more than a coincidence that several of the best herbs which relieve eye ailments have flowers light blue in colour, and often correspondingly small in size. (Eyebright, speedwell, etc.).

Now a rapid guide to predominating characteristics of Colour in personality.

Red. Full of force, energy, humane instincts, often reforming instincts.

Orange. Sportive, humorous, indulgent, sunny temperament.

Yellow. A good mixer, rather philosophical at heart.

Green. Practical, intelligent, constructive outlook.

Blue. Loyal conservative nature but liable to sudden changes.

Indigo. A true servant of Humanity, trusting nature, faithful.

Violet. Administrative talent, a leader, talkative.

These are the seven primary colours; there are tints and shades of them which make up literally thousands of distinctions. When you feel very ill at ease or bad-tempered, change the colour of the clothing you are wearing, and see what a difference it may make.

LOVE-POTIONS

There are a few herbal substances which affect the muscular system and glandular processes of the loins in both sexes, or more rarely in one. In days when better results can be gained by a correct use of vitamins the matter is more academic than practical, but for the record I would like to mention that the following plants have been used :

PLANT	NOTES
Almond	Nutritional properties (*prunus communis*).
Asparagus	Nutritional properties (*asparagus officinalis*).

Beans	Once at least a psychosomatic aphrodisiac. Aristotle and his contemporaries considered them a source of lust.
Cabbage	Nutritional properties. Certainly in its cooked form it is hardly likely to have any value as a love-potion.
Carrots	Nutritional properties.
Cardamons	These seeds are popular in cooking—perhaps their value connects with the wise saw: 'The way to a man's heart is through his stomach.'
Celery	Nutritional properties.
Damiana	A tonic to the nervous system, suitable for sexual neurasthenia. Mildly aphrodisiac (*Turnera diffusa*).
Garlic	In spite of the claims made for garlic as an aphrodisiac, as a North European I cannot think of any odour more suitable to act as a passion killer than that of garlic. Its medicinal virtues are not only unquestioned but unrivalled.
Lentils	A good source of protein, but some dieticians maintain that a high protein diet may in some cases lessen desire.
Pansy	See the main text of this book.
Quebracho	Very good for healing some forms of asthma and lung complaints (*aspidosperma quebracho*).
Saw Palmetto	This is one of the nearest substances to a true aphrodisiac. It has a strengthening effect upon many cases of debilitated sexual glands, distinctly of a tonic nature. The powdered berries are used (*serenoa serrulata*).
Walnut	Nutritional properties.
Yohimbe	Strengthens muscles and glandular secretions of the loins generally. Commonly used as an aphrodisiac. It is unadvisable to exceed the prescribed dose. Available only upon prescription usually (*pausinystalia yohimbe*).

The phrase 'nutritional properties' refers to the presence of essential mineral salts and vitamins.

IN THE MAIN TEXT VARIOUS REFERENCES ARE MADE TO LOVE-PHILTRES, POTIONS AND APHRODISIACS, e.g. Marjoram.

WITCHES WHO FLEW WITHOUT WINGS

In England, Southern and the warmer parts of Central Europe most of the recipes or spells for flying without wings begin with the suggestive phrase 'Take all your clothes off', and some advocates of the black arts insist that nudity is essential if the spell (or any spell) is to succeed; it is, they say, a general law of the craft. Strangely enough, some other forms of wizardry—e.g. Shamanistic rites of Lappland, Tibetan lamaism, etc.—do not mention this supposed condition. All colder climates are less frivolous. NONE OF THE UNDERMENTIONED PLANTS SHOULD BE TAKEN.

These are some of the plants which witches used to rub on their bodies in order to fly; drinks were also made from them—often with fatal results.

PLANT	EFFECTS
Aconite	A poison, no perfect antidote is known; different amounts affect different people in various ways, some tolerate more than others. Once used to poison rats and wolves. Hallucinations induced in some cases before heart collapse (*aconitum napellus*).
Cowbane	Too powerful and toxic for any layman to use. Fatalities have been recorded from its use, in some cases hallucinations occur before death (*cicuta virosa*).
Ergot of Rye	Very commonly used in ancient witchcraft ceremonies. A dangerous abortifacient often causing death. Hallucinations are common in most cases when this has been taken. Antidotes to the poison are uncertain. This is the substance from which lysergic acid diethylamide (LSD) a very dangerous hallucinogen derives. One of the symptoms of LSD addiction is the firm conviction that one can 'fly'; deaths have been recorded of addicts suffering from this delusion. LSD is known to produce irreversible chromosome changes and occasionally sterility; when children are born to LSD addicts they are sometimes born addicts and show withdrawal symptoms from birth (*slaviceps purpurea*).
Hemlock	Produces paralysis and death of a painful nature. Highly toxic, can produce hallucinations (*conium maculatum*).

Other references in the main text.

ONE LAST THOUGHT FOR WOULD-BE WARLOCKS. . . .

Why go to all that trouble when airline tickets are so cheap?

10. *Herbal Tobaccos*

It is not widely known that the smoking mixtures used by North American Indians, from whom the habit spread throughout the world, were herbal.

Tobacco smoking had a quasi-religious significance for most tribes, and acquired a ritualistic, almost liturgical, value among several of them. Ancient Aztecs used tubes to inhale smoke through their nostrils, and the Redskin pipes of peace testify to the solemnity surrounding the ceremonies.

In 1559 Hernandez de Toledo introduced the tobacco plant to Europe. Sir John Hawkins introduced it to England in 1565, but Sir Walter Raleigh was the first man to popularise the use of it in England. King James I initiated his own anti-pollution campaign and persecuted smokers. The medical profession, so often today accused of encouraging some forms of drug addiction, was responsible in the eighteenth century for recommending smoking as a kind of internal antiseptic and germ-killer, a view for which there is little support now.

Although the tobacco plant of the genus *Nicotiana* is used almost exclusively now, the Redskins of America seldom used this herb alone. Many of them used *Lobelia Inflata* whose leaves have a remarkably beneficial effect upon bronchial catarrh, and which clears accumulated collections of mucus. *Most herbal tobaccos are based upon coltsfoot*, with chopped betony, chamomile, rosemary or lavender or thyme being added for flavouring.

Mullein and Sage also make good mixtures. Liquorice is a very good flavouring substance for home-made smoking mixtures.

Those who like a milder flavour might try using *uva ursi* (bearberry) as a basic herb, mix this with a small quantity of eyebright or bog myrtle (*menyanthes trifoliata*).

A beginner might do worse than mix ½ oz. red rose petals with 1 oz. coltsfoot and ½ oz. ordinary tobacco.

Nicotiana Tabacum is a most dangerous herb to take internally. Nearly a century ago the herbalist, Mathew Robinson, was warning his readers that it could produce lung diseases, serious digestive disorders and nervous illnesses if taken internally or chewed. It is safer to use other herbs for smoking, although the *N.tabacum* is a valuable herb for all external poultices, having been prized against rattlesnake bite or the bite of a mad dog : One takes the leaves, bruises them so that the juice begins to run, and then binds them on the wound with a clean bandage or handkerchief. It has been used in an enema to relieve constriction of the bowels. In America the Indians made smoking mixtures of such herbs as dittany (*dicta-*

mus albus), origanum, sassafras bark and mountain balm (*eriodic-tyon californicum*) in addition to the herbs noted above.

A GOOD TOBACCO FOR HEAVY SMOKERS
    4 oz. Coltsfoot.
    2 oz. Mullein.
    2 oz. Rose leaves.
    2 oz. Virginia tobacco.
    4 oz. Yarrow herb.
Cut finely, mix well, use in pipe or in cigarettes.

SMOKING—To give it up
    Each cigarette destroys approximately 25 mg. vitamin C in the body. A rich intake of this vitamin is essential to anybody who on health grounds wishes to give up smoking. Additional vitamin B complex will be required because any effort to break a habit involves a strong nervous-mental strain, this consumes more of the B complex than is usually realised.
    To distract the attention, as it were, from the absence of cigarettes such herbals products as sassafras bark, comfrey leaves, or gentian roots can be chewed.
    Very often a habit such as smoking is a psychological escape-route or a substitute for something else (e.g. to disguise the fact that the person hates his job), and a full analysis of one's life helps un-cover the mental motivation; this facilitates giving up the habit).

11. *Tropical and Overseas Herbs*

Those whose business interests clash with the freedom of herbal remedies often neglect to mention that many of the famous cures used by doctors throughout the world are made from herbs—curare, quinine, cocaine, oje, etc.

This section contains a guide to some of the known and lesser-known jungle medicine and other herbs which are available from importers rather than from our native heaths.

HERB; PROPERTIES; ORIGIN; TYPICAL SINGLE DOSE

Acacia arabica. Ulcerated gums. Bark chewed. Ethiopia and E. Africa. Gum used for dysentery. 20 grains in boiling water, cool, and drink slowly.

Ajo silvestre. External application for headaches and migraine. Found in Brazil.

Aloe peryi. Menstrual suppression. Purges lower bowels. Zanzibar. $\frac{1}{2}$ grain powder to $\frac{1}{2}$ pint water. 1 or 2 teaspoonfuls.

Alstonia constricta. For tropical fevers and tropical types of rheumatism. Australia. 2 grains in $\frac{1}{2}$ pint water. $\frac{1}{2}$ cupful.

Angostura. Stimulant. Tropical fevers and dysentery. Venezuela. 5 grains powdered bark. 1 pint of water. $\frac{1}{2}$ cupful.

Areca catechu. Tapeworms and internal parasites. Nuts chewed, but not swallowed. East Indies.

Arrowroot: See MARANTA.

Asarabaca. A pinch of the powdered herb sniffed up the nose clears mucus and headaches of nervous or catarrhal origin. Siberia, Europe and America.

Assacu. Leprosy sores, applied in plasters. Brazil. Extremely effective.

Boldea frangrans. Also called Boldo. Slimming, torpor of liver, catarrhal conditions of the bladder, mildly antiseptic. Chile. 10–15 grains.

Barosma betulina or *Buchu.* Extraordinary beneficial effects on bladder and kidneys, especially in case of fevers, inflammations of the same. S. Africa. 10 leaves to 1 pint.

Cacahuillo. Indians use it for spear or arrow wounds. Brazil. Dose unknown, usually external poultice.

Calatropis. Elephantiasis, leprosy, tropical skin diseases. India. Bark in powdered form bandaged on affected parts.

Camphora officinalis. Apart from its known uses in Europe this is widely used for venereal conditions (other than syphilis and gonorrhoea).

Cetico. A Brazilian herb, not clearly identified by botanists. The inner lining of the bark cures various eye infections when applied as a poultice. Dr. Leonard Clark's sight was saved probably by this herb after snake venom had entered his eyes.

Chaulmoogra. Leprosy and psoriasis, stiffening joints. Assam and Malaya. Minute doses of the oil by mouth or by application to the sores.

Cineraria maritima. Cataract of the eye. West Indies. A few drops in the eye once or twice a day.

Copaifera (also called Copaiba). Bladder and some venereal infections. S. American jungle plant.

Damiana. See TURNERA DIFFUSA.

Dorema ammoniacum (Gum ammoniac). Expectorant for very severe respiratory and bronchial infections. Persia. 5 grains powdered gum in ½ pint water.

Echinacea augustifolia. Internal and external application against gangrene and dangerous skin conditions. Western U.S.A.

Epigaea repens. Severe bladder and kidney diseases. America. 1 oz. to a pint.

Erythroxylon catauba. Used by native witch doctors to heal cancer. Amazonian basin. Dosage unknown.

Eucalyptus globulus. Apart from the uses in bronchial and respiratory diseases the aborigines of Australia applied it thickly to several forms of cancerous growths. Opinions vary as to the size of the dose.

Ginseng. See PANAX QUINQUEFOLIUM.

Goa araboba andira. Skin diseases and internal parasites. Brazil. Applied externally in powder form. Opinions differ as to internal doses. Use sparingly.

Gossypium herbaceum. Considered to be an abortifacient. East Mediterranean countries. ½ fluid ounce in ½ pint water.

Guaiacum officinale. Used with sarsaparilla for some venereal conditions and for all blood purifying tonics. Central and South America. ½ fluid oz. in ½ pint water.

Guarana paullinia cupana. Used for women's complaints. Brazil. 15–30 grains powdered, baked seeds, in ½ pint water.

Guarea rusby. Tuberculosis was treated with this by the Indians of the Argentine. A single dose of the powdered herb should not usually exceed 10 grains.

Guayaba. Conjunctivitis and tropical eye sores. Brazil and Guyana. External application.

Henna (lawsonia alba). Apart from dyeing ladies' hair for over

4,000 years the antiseptic properties of the leaves were used against smallpox and many severe skin complaints. On certain feasts the Muslim tint their hands and faces with henna. All Middle-Eastern lands.

Hura crepitans. Jungle snake bites, leprosy, causes some tropical poisons to subside. Amazonian basin. External application recommended. Internal doses unknown.

Hydrocotyle asiatica (major/minor). Claimed to be a decisive factor in promoting longevity; a good herb for elderly people with stomach, bladder or bowel trouble. The *minor* is much more difficult to obtain, but was held to be more efficacious by the Chinese authorities who wrote about it.

Ipecacuanha. A remarkable medicine used by *brujos* of *Xingu* territory and elsewhere in the Amazon watershed for a large number of illnesses. It sweats out many fevers, producing copious sweating. It brings severe vomiting. The shredded or powdered root is used. Leave the herb in boiling water to infuse one or two days. 1 oz. to a pint. Drink half a cupful as required : CHILDREN SHOULD HAVE ONLY A TEASPOONFUL DOSE.

Ishpanga. Unidentified by botanists. Brazil. Used to cure amoebic dysentery. Discovered by Dr. L. Clark, whose work for medical knowledge deserves better fame and rewards.

Jaborandi pilocarpus microphyllos. Owing to the violent properties of this herb it is classified as a poison. This is not definitely so, only occasionally when carelessly used do its alarming properties to produce and expectoration come to the fore. It is a hair tonic without rival, and among Campas, Jivaros and Aguarunas was used as a cure for diabetes. The leaves ½ oz. to one pint of boiling water, left to simmer for five minutes. Strain. Drink when cool. Two dessertspoonfuls at a time. External application in greater strength. If using a strong lotion for growing hair wear gloves, or hair may grow too freely on the backs of your hands !

Jambolana. Diabetes mellitus. ½ oz. seeds to 2 pints water. A wineglassful at a time, two or three times a day. Australia.

Kava kava. Muscular weakness, tonic etc. South Pacific Islands. Shredded roots. 1 oz. to 2 pints. ½ cupful as required.

Liatris spicata. Bright's Disease. Menstruation difficulties. U.S.A. 1 oz. to 1 pint water. ½ cupful after meals. 3 daily.

Liquorice. Used in the time of Hippocrates for coughs, tubercular and similar conditions. The Moors used it for ulcers and similar upsets. In any form, but the prepared root is best.

Lobelia inflata. An exceptional herb from Eastern U.S.A. It clears respiratory tract of poisons and mucus most thoroughly and powerfully. Woodland Indians used it for a vast range of illnesses, as did early colonists. Do not exceed 1 oz. to a pint of boiling water. 4 teaspoonfuls at a time should suffice. Cleanses the liver, etc.

Logwood haemotoxlyon campechianum. Used by Indians in Central America to prevent bleeding from the womb, lungs and tropical dysentery. It has no constipating effects. 1 oz. shredded bark to a pint of water. One wineglassful. Stronger in emergencies.

Maranta arundinacea (Arrowroot). Dysentery and diarrhoea. Powder usually used. Also leaves for rheumatic pains. Jamaica. The crushed, bleeding root was put on arrow wounds by Indians, hence its name. A teaspoonful in milk or water.

Morapirama. Dr. Clark reported that the Chamas used this to cure some forms of paralysis. Brazil, Peruvian jungles, etc. Colombia.

Matica (artanthe elongata). Stops all kinds of bleeding internal or external. Guyana. 1 oz. to a pint of water. ½ cupful.

Myrrh (balsamodendron myrrha). One of the world's oldest medicines. A safe internal antiseptic. Sore gums, throats, Vincent's angina, some skin complaints e.g. thrush. Mixed with three parts of eucalyptus it makes a wonderful mouthwash. There is a reference in Genesis to the Ishmaelites taking myrrh on their camels to Egypt.

Nushumbi. Prevents teeth decay. Peruvian jungles. Chew leaves.

Panax quinquefolium (ginseng). Tonic. The Chinese herbalists claimed it would cure everything, and promote healthy old age. China. Opinions vary as to the size of the dose.

Pareira brava. Urinary and some venereal conditions. Brazil and Upper Amazon lands. 1 oz. shredded root to 1 pint boiling water. ½ cupful.

Polemonium reptans. A Scandinavian favourite for very severe lung diseases. 1 oz. to a pint. ½ cupful.

Polymnia uvedalia. Beneficial influence on glands. N. America.

Pomegranate. Chewed to strengthen gums, and for ulcers of the mouth and throat. Hill country throughout Asia. Fruit.

Populus candicans (Balm of Gilead). Tonic. Kidney diseases and many skin complaints. Western Saudi Arabia. 5 grains of dried buds in ½ pint of boiling water, simmer 5 minutes. Cool and drink. Apply fresh buds to skin.

Quassia amara. Kills worms and several internal parasites. Chronic diseases of stomach, etc. West Indies. 1 oz. wood chips to one pint.

Quebracho. Respiratory diseases. Used by Ranquele Indians for disorders of women's periods. Argentine. Bark used. 1 oz. to one pint.

Quinine. This was the original bark of the Jesuits. It is really only effective when the original Indian powdered bark is used. *Chemists use sulphuric acid to extract its power—a method which destroys some of its properties.* By such stupidity are miraculous herbs 'discredited'. Reduces all types of fevers, including malaria and intermittent fevers. Tonic. Do not exceed dose. *Cinchona officinalis.* Grows in Colombia and the Andean Mountains. 5–10 grains is the average dose of the powdered bark.

Sacha curarine. Snakebite of tropical snakes : In enema form. Brazil. Rolled bruised leaves.

Sanguinaria canadensis. A Canadian herb which has a fine reputation for relieving chronic respiratory diseases in an advanced condition. Records are available that tumours have subsided after use of this herb. Canada. 10 grains powdered root per one pint of water.

Santalum album (Sandalwood). Internal antiseptic. Inflammation of the bladder and conditions such as arise from serious skin or venereal diseases. Malaysia. A few drops of the oil of the wood in a ½ pint of water, taken one or two teaspoonfuls at a time. In weaker solution to clean the teeth. Mouthwash.

Sarsaparilla (smilax ornata). The original red S. which the conquistadores learned from the Aztecs to use against syphilis. Today it is frequently mixed with Guaiacum chips. Like other famed herbs it has been subjected to chemicalisation to extract is properties artificially, and under such false conditions found less effective. Herbs must be used naturally to get the traditional and best results. C. America.

Sassafras varifolium. Said by Indians and early settlers to prevent some types of blindness from developing. Use as a wash for optical disorders. Often mixed with sarsaparilla against venereal and similar conditions. Steep 1 oz. shredded bark in hot water, leave 24 hours or more. Strain and use. Half a cupful is the average dose required. N. America.

Serenoa serrulata (saw palmetto). Discovered by the Delaware and other forest Indians. A remarkable tonic for glandular and hormonal disorders, restoring atrophied sexual organs and wasted muscles to strength and vigour. The powdered berries are given in doses ranging from 5 to 10 grains.

Sesamum indicum. Ophthalmia, eye diseases, skin diseases and some nervous cases. India. Generally two or three leaves are boiled in 2 or 3 cupfuls of water for internal doses, but the crushed leaves are applied directly for eye and skin cases.

Squaw vine. North American Indian women used it for most female complaints. 1 oz. to half pint boiling water.

Styrax benzoin. Respiratory infections and bronchial ills common to tropical rain forests. East Indies. 1 grain in a little water, applied externally.

Sumach-rhus aromatica. To restore continence of urine. Diabetes. U.S.A. 1 oz. shredded bark to a pint.

Topa. Natives use it in Brazil to heal gunshot wounds. Powerful antiseptic. Leaves applied externally.

Toluifera balsamum. Tropical and other skin diseases. Severe respiratory illnesses. Peru and High Andes. 5 grains of resin powdered. Also *toluifera pereirae.*

Turnera diffusa. Restorer of sexual organs' efficiency. Central and South America. 5 grains in another medium, e.g. *ulmus fulva.*

Ucho sanango. Jivaro *brujos* boil the leaves. The patient chews the boiled leaves, and broken bones and fractures mend well and naturally within a week or two. Brazil.

Ulmus fulva. I have used slippery elm to cure so many diseases that I could write a book about this one herb. The powdered inner bark is used. Bladder, bronchial, cutaneous, hepatic, stomachic, and rheumatic conditions can be treated with this. All wounds, cuts, ulcers and sores can be treated with slippery elm and honey mixed and applied, covered with a bandage. It is mixed with milk or water, and usually a little honey and eaten or applied without further trouble. American settlers learned to use it from the Indians.

Vinca rosea. Remarkable cures for diabetes have been reported after the use of this herb. South Africa. 1 oz. to a pint. Several diabetics I have known to take this experienced much relief within a short time.

12. *Herbs and Health*

HOW TO PREPARE HERBAL MEDICINES

Can you prepare a simple cup of tea? Yes? Then you know how to make up a herbal medicine. Tea is a herb, you have probably been using it for years. All herbal medicines can be prepared by putting from half an ounce to one full ounce into the teapot, pouring on them one pint of boiling water, letting the mixture stand until it is cool (15 minutes at least) then drinking it.

HOW MUCH SHALL I TAKE?

For general conditions take a wineglassful three times a day, that is roughly about every four hours. Don't wake up at night to take any, get a good night's sleep if you are feeling unwell.

WHICH PART TO USE?

Always use the dried leaves, unless you are especially advised to use the dried flowers or the powdered bark (the bark is usually bought powdered, so there is no problem). If you prepare a drink from the bark it is exactly the same as making an instant coffee; add sugar if you like, but do not add milk.

HOW MUCH TO USE?

Let us get one thing clear; you cannot get better by doubling the amounts recommended; if in the text you are told to use only half the usual amount then do not exceed half an ounce of dried herb for the one pint of boiling water. Give your body a fair chance.

WHAT IS A DECOCTION OR A LOTION?

Exactly the same thing as above, but the decoction is made with the herb being boiled in the water in a saucepan (literally a 'boiling'). Lotions are usually employed to be rubbed on to the body externally.

FOR EXTERNAL USE ONLY

Never take inwardly any herb which is recommended for external use only, it won't help you half so much inside.

Pay attention to these points:

1. DO NOT USE ALL THE REMEDIES AND RECIPES OFFERED AT ONCE. They are alternatives, many being given on the understanding that the ingredients for one may not be available.
2. ACQUAINT YOURSELF WITH THE TECHNIQUES OF ARTIFICIAL RESPIRATION; they are more difficult to apply if you are using them for the first time.

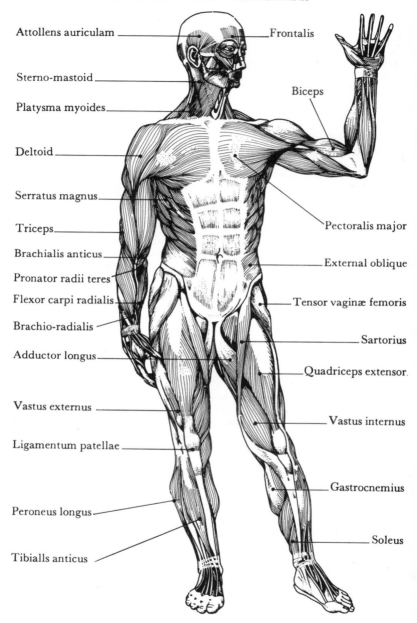

Attollens auriculam

Frontalis

Sterno-mastoid

Platysma myoides

Biceps

Deltoid

Serratus magnus

Triceps

Brachialis anticus

Pronator radii teres

Flexor carpi radialis

Brachio-radialis

Adductor longus

Vastus externus

Ligamentum patellae

Peroneus longus

Tibialls anticus

Pectoralis major

External oblique

Tensor vaginæ femoris

Sartorius

Quadriceps extensor.

Vastus internus

Gastrocnemius

Soleus

MUSCLES AND TENDONS FRONT VIEW

3. DOSES ARE QUOTED; DO NOT THINK A PATIENT WILL GET BETTER TWICE AS QUICKLY IF YOU DOUBLE THE DOSE. A sick person cannot stand strong doses as easily as smaller doses. *If in doubt halve the doses quoted*; better a slow recovery than no recovery. You know your patients, do use your judgment, and realise that no physician can ever know your patients as well as does the wife and mother of the patients.

4. HERBAL TEAS are simply made in a teapot; you take the recommended amount and pour on the amount of boiling water specified, then allow the mixture to draw as you do with ordinary Indian tea, and pour when you judge it cool enough to drink.

5. IF YOU ARE USING HERBS NEW TO YOU take up to three teaspoonfuls first and make them into a weak tea, and taste that.

6. WHEN ORDERING HERBS FROM A SUPPLIER PLEASE GIVE THE LATIN OR SCIENTIFIC NAME TO MAKE SURE YOU GET THE RIGHT ONE.

7. TREATING SERIOUS DISEASES **yourself is a heavy responsibility for you to bear, and you are advised to treat them yourself only when no medical help is available; in most cases the dietetic advice can be followed whatever course of treatment is pursued.**

8. UNDERSTAND THE THEORY OF HEALING WHICH RUNS THROUGHOUT THIS BOOK. Basically there is no disease; only a sick person who displays some symptoms resembling more or less symptoms classified according to our imperfect experience. Our primary goal is to strengthen the patient's bodily functions so that they may follow their natural course and rid the body of whatever bacteria, virus, etc., is present during the illness. When we use medicines which 'kill' germs we can never be too sure that they will not kill some useful and valuable little organisms in the body which are, so to speak, on our side. When we cultivate the body's natural defences we cannot go wrong. The whole classification of diseases into a collection of specific symptoms is open to question; hardly any patient shows all the symptoms of any one specific illness! Never panic over a fever, it is the body's defence mechanism coming into front-line action to repel the invading organisms.

9. PSYCHOSOMATIC MEDICINE is a new name for the relationship of body and mind in sickness and in health. A happy, cheerful patient will fight his way back from death's door; a depressed, negative-thinking person can die from an attack of the hiccoughs—or something similar.

10. IN EXTREMELY DESPERATE CASES do not neglect seeking Spiritual Healing and prayer. Only a very inexperienced person or a knave would deny the miraculous cures which every practitioner of any form of medicine has seen resulting from these methods.

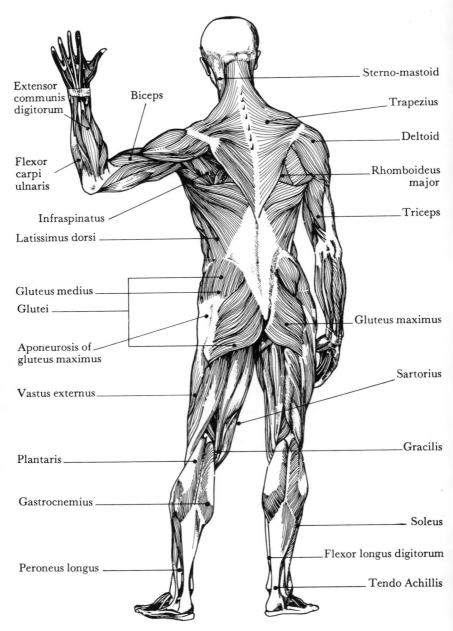

Extensor communis digitorum

Biceps

Sterno-mastoid

Trapezius

Deltoid

Flexor carpi ulnaris

Rhomboideus major

Infraspinatus

Triceps

Latissimus dorsi

Gluteus medius

Glutei

Gluteus maximus

Aponeurosis of gluteus maximus

Sartorius

Vastus externus

Gracilis

Plantaris

Gastrocnemius

Soleus

Flexor longus digitorum

Peroneus longus

Tendo Achillis

MUSCLES AND TENDONS BACK VIEW

ABSCESS

The white matter which fills an abscess represents the dead leucocytes of the body which have swallowed up bacteria invading the body and died; they also form a little wall, blocking off the diseased area from other parts of the body to prevent the infection from spreading. Do not be too anxious to cut or open any abscess unless you are quite positive that you can afterwards keep it absolutely germfree (very difficult). The treatment in all cases must begin not from the point of attack but by building up the body's resistance.

Sunlight is an excellent aid, and if possible expose as much of the body to the sun as practical. Otherwise ultra-violet light will help. If you or friends or neighbours have an ultra-violet lamp use it. Don't forget to cover the eyes with dark glasses, and keep about four to eight feet away from the lamp, depending upon its strength.

Halibut liver oil or cod liver oil (cheaper) should be taken every day; it is rich in vitamins A and D which are much needed at this time.

Silica foods such as cabbage (raw), cucumber, lettuce, oatmeal. strawberries should be increased.

Sulphur-containing foods such as figs, onions, oranges and radishes should be consumed regularly, especially the onions—raw if possible. If it is considered to be absolutely necessary to foment the abscess, use *marshmallow and ragwort* leaves soak in hot water for a few minutes and applied directly to the place; a poultice of *slippery elm* can then be applied, just mix the powdered herb with warm water in which a few drops of eucalyptus oil have been sprinkled.

Comfrey and marshmallow leaves can also be used in the same way : many houses lying near a stream, brook or pond have comfrey growing there. *Nasturtium seeds* can be crushed and applied, covered by lint dipped in hot water, to an abscess.

Plantain leaves are very good, dipped in hot water and applied to the abscess; many lawns are full of one form of plantain or another.

Raspberry leaves can be soaked in a like manner and applied, they have many therapeutic properties.

Agrimony tea is advisable, it is a tonic for the run-down condition which makes abscesses possible. Take ½ oz. dried herb, put it in a teapot, and cover it with one pint of boiling water, allow to draw ten minutes, sweeten only with a little honey, drink as much as you like.

Chickweed is my own favourite remedy. A tea can be made, exactly the same way as described under agrimony (above). Fresh, washed leaves of this tiny valuable medicinal herb can be placed straight on to any abscess and sore, they draw out a lot of toxic matter. Renew the dressing every six hours; keep covered with clean, firm—but not tight—bandage.

Chickweed

Fruit and salads should figure prominently in the patient's diet. *When an abscess begins* to heal apply fresh, cold comfrey leaves or marshmallow leaves.

ACIDITY

Like many of the simpler named illnesses this can be a terribly discomforting and painful occasion for the sufferer; naturally we want to bring relief at the earliest possible moment.

Apple cider vinegar is my first stand-by, hardly a household in the land should be without this marvellous substance (have you read Dr. Jarvis' book *Folk Medicine*? He recommends apple cider vinegar without fear or favour). One teaspoonful in half a cupful of warm water, taken every 15 minutes will bring speedy relief.

Lemon juice, a teaspoonful either taken neat or with half a cupful of warm water.

Potato juice or the water in which new scraped potatoes have been boiled is another good remedy for acidity.

Turnip-tops. In the old days when the depression and the slump had merged to make people's life a nightmare many families found that the turnip-tops boiled as greens were even more nutritious than the turnip-roots. The water in which they are boiled is a good tonic, and can be used for many cases of acidity.

Never forget that the loss of health in every case is due to an infringement of one or more of Nature's laws. There is an old Cantonese proverb : *Beat a snake on the head, don't beat it on the tail* (da say tau but iu da say may). Remember that acidity is a symptom that something is wrong inside, it is not the end-result itself. The moment that it becomes clear that acidity is becoming regular examine the diet carefully, see whether you are getting enough sleep or enough relaxation during the 24 hours of the day— all work and no play makes Jack a sick boy, not a dull one such as our old wise saw suggested.

ACNE

One of the most distressing and unsightly ills that can befall a busy family's mother is to see the children break out in acne. Firstly, let us look at the lines of a poem by the old American herbalist who reminds us that inside our bodies there is a skin which is a continuation of our outside bodily skin, and the health of the outside one reflects what is going on inside of us :

> '*If all goes well with the outside skin*
> *You may feel pretty sure all's right within;*
> *But if anything puts the inner skin out*
> *It is sure to trouble the skin without.*'

Antonette Matteson wrote those lines nearly a century ago, she was a well-loved herbalist and a noted clairvoyante; they are as true today as the lines were then.

Devil's bit juice is used to wash the skin.

Lemon juice is mixed with equal quantity of water to wash the skin.

Herbal remedy: 2 oz. clover flowers (red are best), 2 oz. nettle tops, 2 oz. boneset. Mix herbs and put into half a gallon boiling water, then simmer until only a quart remains. One wineglassful every three hours. Some herbalists would add to the mixture when it was cool a little quinine, cayenne pepper or ginger, and usually some melted honey.

Nettle tea is a simple and effective remedy, to be drunk over one or two weeks.

Liquorice is one of the best sweets that acne patients can eat.

ANAEMIA

Although this illness doesn't just 'happen' like many home accidents there are days when the patient feels definitely the worse for wear, and instant help is required.

Basically the cause of the disease is linked with the disturbance of the copper and iron intake of the body; if there is not enough copper in the diet the iron absorbed cannot do its job, being mostly wasted; when the iron intake of food is not fully employed the body's blood supply begins to suffer from a lack of oxygen which accounts for many of the unpleasant symptoms of anaemia—weakness, giddiness, rapid breathing (to compensate for the lack of oxygen); inflammation of the tongue is often present.

Nettle tea contains many mineral salts, being particularly rich in iron; administered with honey for sweetening this makes a very good restorative for anaemic patients : my *Herbal Teas for Health and Pleasure* gives a good many details about nettles.

Honey and lemon juice is a very good thing for the young girl who is suffering from anaemia. The juice of half a lemon with a full tablespoonful of honey given every three hours is a good relief.

Parsley eaten raw or taken as a tea (half an ounce to one pint of boiling water should suffice).

Watercress should form part of the daily diet while it is in season, it is of tremendous value to anaemia patients because of high mineral salt content.

Pumpkins are a beneficial item of diet for anaemic patients, and can be eaten as often as desired.

Purslane eaten as a salad, or a tea made of the seeds.

Catnep tea, refreshing and valuable.

Chickweed tea is a favourite standby, there is hardly a garden in the country where some chickweed cannot be found.

Dandelion is better than coffee for anaemic patients; generally speaking, chicory is not thought to be advisable. Many fine dandelion coffee substitutes are marketed—and are very tasty.

Apple cider vinegar administered in honey and warm water, well-mixed, is another instant help which patients will appreciate.

Raw oats for breakfast is a recommendable breakfast item for all patients of this condition.

APOPLEXY

While I hope no reader of mine may be involved in treating an apopleptic patient, hoping is no substitute for a word of timely advice.

This is basically due to a clotting of blood vessels, or the rupture of a blood vessel in the brain, it may come on after stooping, bending, heavy exertion, violent emotional excitement, over-exposure to the sun or heat, etc. The patient may collapse and fall asleep. Be careful not to confuse this with the appearance of alcoholic stupor.

The bowels of a patient, or of a person likely to suffer from it, must be kept moving, constipation must be avoided. Heavy meat and alcoholic consumption must be avoided. Medical advice must be sought after an attack, even if not available during one.

Place the patient's feet in hot water with a couple of dessert-spoonfuls of *mustard powder*.

Cayenne pepper, a level teaspoonful to one cup of luke-warm water, was a favourite remedy of old herbalists.

Herbal tea made up of the following : 2 oz. balmony, 2 oz. bayberry bark, 1 oz. ginger root, 1 oz. liquorice root, 2 oz. poplar bark, can be added to one half-gallon of boiling water, which is then simmered until about one quart remains. When it is cool administer one wineglassful every 3 hours.

ARTHRITIS

This is an extensive range of illnesses covered by the same name. I have dealt at length with Rheumatism and associated ills in my work *How to Defeat Rheumatism and Arthritis*, and any sufferer is advised to get a copy of that work.

Camphorated oil can be massaged into affected parts; if this is not possible *eucalyptus oil* can be liberally applied. Either of these will greatly alleviate the hurt of the pains during an attack, also use *oil of cloves*, this is stronger, much more expensive, but preferable to the first two; it is very strong. Dilute with 10 parts olive oil.

Garlic should be chewed (yes, it is burning hot, but a good medicine) or, if available, capsules of garlic oil taken.

Catnep tea brings some relief in early stages.

Celery seeds are a standard remedy. Plenty of celery should be taken in the diet, the rough leafy tops are especially valuable.

Olive oil should be massaged into the limbs every night. My father, a very famous and capable masseur, invariably used Olive Oil in preference to all others for these cases.

Special herbal tea made of the following : 2 oz. agrimony, 2 oz. bogbean, 2 oz. burdock, 2 oz. yarrow, $\frac{1}{2}$ oz. raspberry leaves, $\frac{1}{2}$ oz. powdered guaiacum. Place the mixed herbs in $\frac{1}{2}$ gallon boiling water, simmer slowly until only a quart is left. Cool. Drink a wineglassful every three hours.

Primrose leaves shredded up can be added to the salads of all arthritic patients.

Honeysuckle flowers. One loosely-filled cupful can be used for a tea made with one pint of boiling water. One wineglassful every three hours is recommended.

Mustard baths to which a pinch of cayenne pepper has been added are very helpful in relieving pain. Alternate hot and cold bowls of water help patients to recover in many cases.

Nettle and sage tea is one of the best standby remedies, and the mineral salt and vitamin content of the herbs is most useful.

ARTIFICIAL RESPIRATION

Do this properly, don't be half-hearted about it if you want your patient to be wholly alive, not half so.

1st method:

(1) Make sure the patient's mouth is not blocked, if it is put your finger in and clear the patient's mouth of vomit or anything blocking it.

(2) The patient should be lying on his/her back, the head tilted right back, stretching the throat.

(3) Kneel by the side of the patient. Place your hand firmly over the nose, closing it, then blow air down the patient's

6

open mouth—and throat. Do not be violent, but be firm and deliberate.

(4) Turn your head away quickly, because after the first blow the patient may vomit. If so, clear away the vomit, wipe the patient's mouth and resume blowing; if there is prolonged vomiting, turn the patient's head on the side so that the vomit cannot choke the patient.

(5) Look to see whether the patient's chest rises and falls during this blowing.

(6) Blow down the patient's throat about 12 times a minute, this is roughly how fast you breathe in and out yourself, not too difficult.

(7) Alternatively you can blow air down the nose and put a hand over the patient's mouth.

Do not use so much force on women or young children as you would instinctively use for a full-grown man.

2nd method:

This was invented by a Danish Lieutenant-Colonel, Holger Nielsen, and is the method which I favour most myself. The main advantage is that the patient's tongue can never fall back into the mouth and choke him. It is more hygienic for the rescuer than the other method.

(1) Place the patient face down in the prone position, fold the patient's arms so that the backs of the hands come in front of his head, and then the head can be rested sideways on them.

(2) Clear the patient's mouth of vomit or any obstruction with your finger. Kneel on one knee at the head end of the patient, so that you look down the length of the outstretched body. The bent knee comes near the head of the patient, the rescuer's other foot is placed by the patient's ear.

(3) Place the heels of your hands between the shoulder-blades of the patient. Keep the arms straight; swing forwards, balancing on knee and foot, pressing gently downwards on the area covered by the hands, then quickly withdraw the hands along the line of the patient's arms, grasp the patient's arms just above the elbow and lift them forward and upwards gently until you feel the body's natural resistance, then return to the first position; repeat 12 times a minute. Reduce pressure for women and children.

ASTHMA

Few things can be so worrying to a housewife as to find that one of her nearest and dearest or a favourite neighbour is in the grip of an asthmatical attack. The patient feels tightness across the chest, breathing becomes rapid, wheezing is very audible, the patient cannot recline but must sit up or walk to breathe at all, often needing an open window—however cold the weather outside. There is usually heavy sweating.

Agrimony tea is very helpful in many cases. Use one ounce to one pint measurement. Apart from having several valuable medicinal properties this herb can give a delightful flavour to any pot of ordinary Indian tea if you add just one spoonful, and it is a valuable addition to your kitchen herbs.

Lemon juice administered a spoonful at a time every 15 minutes will greatly aid asthma sufferers. Remember that the simple lemon was used for healing up to a score of different illnesses, it is very rich in vitamin C, and contains the rare vitamin P. No kitchen should ever be without lemons.

Hot cloths applied to the spine of the sufferer relieve much of the discomfort. (**Never** force an asthmatic to lie down, you may kill him).

Coffee taken very strong—preferably on an empty stomach— is one aid, but not always so efficacious as the others.

Hot water baths can be given to the hands or feet of the patient.

Massage of the spine is often a source of relief. Circle upwards.

Herbal tobacco is to be recommended, and a very good formula is : 2 oz. coltsfoot, 2 oz. rosemary, 4 oz. stramonium (*Datura stramonium* thorn apple or Jamestown weed), 2 oz. mullein. Shred the mixture up finely and smoke in a pipe or rolled up in cigarette papers.

Remarkably enough, it is reckoned by many medical authorities that the calming effects of smoking often outweigh any other consideration for asthmatics : only herbal tobacco should be used.

Most asthmatics have some deep-rooted psychosomatic cause for their illness, a few hours of listening to them and trying to help them may do more to relieve the illness than much other medication.

BACTERICIDES
Experiments have shown that buttercup juice can destroy anthrax germs, pneumococci, staphylococci and streptococci. A report says that it will also kill tuberculi. It is unsuitable for internal use. I have no personal experience of its use.

BALDNESS
It is distressing for a housewife to face the fact that the man she loves is going bald. The subject of baldness is an immense one, and I have dealt with it at length in my book *How to Keep Your Hair On* explaining every detail known about the subject and listing all the known and safe remedies.

Beetroot juice massaged into the scalp every night helps certain types of baldness.

Nettle juice can also be massaged into the scalp every 12 hours; there are many reports of the success of this remedy.

Rosemary oil can be used to massage the scalp, but if the scalp is already greasy try to get a spiritous preparation of Rosemary and use that instead.

Yarrow is a most useful herb and this should be both drunk as a tea once a day and a little of the cold tea rubbed into the scalp. The dietetic treatment outlined in my book is essential.

Bay rum preparations can be had almost everywhere and these are very useful against several types of scalp diseases.

Camomile makes a good lotion and shampoo for fair hair.

Elderberry juice is more suitable for dark-haired people and restores colour to dark-haired people who have a touch of grey appearing at the temples.

Maidenhair fern and willow leaves can be mixed together, chopped up finely and placed immediately into some warmed-up olive oil; simmer this over the slowest possible heat, apply a pinch of cinnamon, cayenne or clove powder as you take the saucepan from the heat, stir vigorously; use the oil for massage sparingly every night.

BEDWETTING

This is often a sign of insecurity on the part of the offender, but it can be a sign of a weakened bladder or worms.

Mullein tea is helpful.

Marjoram eaten in salads or made as a tea is an established remedy because of its effects as a nervine.

Thyme eaten as one teaspoonful of herb to three teaspoonfuls of pure honey, is excellent when worms are considered the cause.

Thyme tea can also be made, one flat teaspoonful to one teapot full is adequate—this is roughly one pint of water.

Asparagus is an important item of diet for enuresis—bedwetting.

Horsetail grass tea is very rich in silicon and calcium which are usually deficient in patients who wet the bed, or have no retention power over their urine.

Golden rod tea is very useful for these patients, and is very widely grown in most gardens of the country.

BILHARZIA

An unpleasant, parasitic illness causing bood in the urine faeces. The life-form breeds in snails in Egypt, West and South-East Africa, and is carried by impure drinking water. Dr. J. C. Clatworthy of Ugheli, Nigeria, did research on Coriander o heal bilharzia. Dr. Akilu Lemma of Ethiopia has used the berries of *phytolacca dodecandra* to kill the snails in which the bilharzia parasites breed; he hopes that by killing the snails the infection of the water supply will be stopped.

BITES

Firstly, don't panic! Remember Goldsmith's dog that 'for some private ends went mad and bit a man. The man recovered from the bite, the dog it was that died'.

Parsley juice squeezed on to insect bites is very effective.

Witch-hazel is a very good standby, a powerful antiseptic. I have experience of its usefulness for *wasp* stings.

Onion slices freshly cut and applied to any insect bite or even to the bite of a dog are excellent germicides; bind on with a bandage : Spanish onions are best.

Fennel seed made in double strength tea (2 oz. to 1 pint) is good after dog bites, snakes or other serious bites; a poultice of the seeds put on to the bite externally draws out the poison.

Basil crushed and applied directly to the bite of scorpions, snakes, and other dangerous insects.

Snake bites. Suck out the poison, apply potassium permanganate crystals or solution one part to 100 parts warm water. Calm the patient down; fear does a lot of harm after any bite. In the case of children remember the old Punjabi proverb : '*A saucerful of water to an ant is a river.*' Don't dismiss their complaint too easily, it robs them of confidence. In doubt apply raw onions.

Also see SNAKE.

Garlic may be used where no onions are available.

BLADDER DISORDERS

This covers a wide range of ailments but usually birch leaf tea, made with five or six birch leaves to a teapot of one pint of boiling water, drunk cold, one wineglassful at a time, will aid the sufferer.

Asparagus should be eaten fairly frequently.

Horsetail grass, that remarkable plant looking like a horse's tail, one of the oldest living plants in the world (it dates from carboniferous times), contains medicinal properties which are most useful. Make a tea as described above.

Old recipe: $\frac{1}{2}$ oz. basil, 1 oz. betony, 1 oz. golden rod, $\frac{1}{2}$ oz. tansy. Mix the herbs; put them into two pints of boiling water; allow it to simmer for 15 minutes; when cool give the patient one wineglassful every three hours.

Bladder patients should give up (temporarily at least) alcohol, strong tea and coffee, sauces, condiments, mayonnaise, curries, etc.

See also the entries under KIDNEY COMPLAINTS.

BLOOD-POISONING

This may occur with or without abscesses; if bacteria collects in certain parts of the body (pyaemia) it is more serious; the form known as sapraemia is accompanied by marked fever and a general malaise owing to the absorption of poisonous matter from the bowels or wounds etc. There is usually a high temperature and if not attended to efficiently death may follow.

Garlic is essential and the patient should chew up one clove every hour for the first three hours, and then one every three hours for the next day, but not during the night.

Onions may be used if no garlic is available. Some herbalists insist that they are better—but this applies to big onions, not to little spring onions.

Echinacea is a very powerful substance and is used for all such serious conditions as this. Usually available from herbal suppliers as a liquid extract; half a teaspoonful being taken in a half-cupful of warm water every hour for the first six hours, and thereafter once every three hours. It may also be found in homoeopathic pills; directions would be given on the box when these are bought.

Sarsaparilla and sassafras powder can be mixed together to make a most nutritious and cleansing tea; a little honey makes it more palatable.

BLOODSTAINS
In the excitement of healing a cut or staunching a flow of blood the younger members of a family are inclined to care little whether they use the best tablecloth or your best dress to staunch the blood.

If the stain is not dry take the nearest clean handkerchief, stuff it into your mouth until it is covered with *saliva*, then wash the blood off with that; human saliva washes off blood very efficiently.

Silk, nylons, delicate cloths, can usually be cleaned of bloodstaining by applying a thick paste of starch and water, applying it to the stain, leaving it until dry and then brushing it off.

Salt water, or rather water to which a very generous allowance of salt has been added, is very useful; soak the cloth for an hour in the saline mixture, then rinse in warm water and a soft soap (not a detergent); the bloodstains should disappear easily and without trace.

BLOOD TRANSFUSIONS, ETC.
Many people feel moved to refuse a transfusion on religious grounds. The idea contravenes the laws given in Leviticus and Acts XV. It is not my wish to comment either way on the matter, but Dr. J. J. Coffey of Blackpool, Lancashire, England, reported that a patient given up for lost by his doctors was fed largely on spinach for two days and made a really astonishing recovery without a transfusion.

There is one danger about being a blood donor. The maximum amount which any donor is allowed to give under most legal systems is four pints. Some people may not be able to give so much. Blood carries mineral salts and a good deal of other nutritive elements such as oxygen; these are not replaced easily by all donors. In view of the fact that some bodies conducting transfusions are using chemicals made from the snails' eggs of *Helix astera* (Dr. Tovey,

Brighton Symposium, 1967) it is possible that those who object to the process may well be right.

A French court fined a doctor £15,000 for a transfusion in which a healthy, well-built policeman died. (1966).

BOWELS, INFLAMMATION OF

Diarrhoea is the most usual symptom, but if only the small intestine is concerned there may be constipation (no passage for 48 hours or more). Pain comes and goes. There is usually a high temperature.

Bed rest is essential.

Fasting will often benefit the patient; in any case, the intake of food must be lessened, and nothing constipating may be given. Warm drinks of various kinds can be given.

Slippery elm and honey. Take a dessertspoonful of slippery elm and another of pure honey, mix them together with warm water and administer every hour.

Flannels soaked in warm water may be applied to the abdomen.

Herbal remedy: 1 oz. mint, 1 oz. queen of the meadow, 1 oz. St. John's Wort, calamus root (sweet sedge). Mixed into $\frac{1}{2}$ gallon of boiling water which is then simmered slowly until only one quart remains. Honey and cinnamon or ginger can be added. Drink one wineglassful every hour.

BRAIN FATIGUE

Apart from the brainy children of the family coming home and studying for their examinations, such a condition is by no means uncommon among harassed housewives themselves.

Sassafras makes a much more nutritious drink than does coffee, and is far better suited; it is a delicious and refreshing tea. The herb had best be boiled in the water rather than just dropped in a pot; only by lightly boiling it can you extract the value from the bark.

Sarsaparilla makes another delightful drink, and this too is better boiled or put into the coffee-percolator.

Special herbal remedy: 1 oz. marjoram, 1 oz. pennyroyal, 1 oz. rosemary, 1 oz. sage, 1 oz. wood betony. Mix and add to $\frac{1}{2}$ gallon boiling water. Simmer down to one quart. When cool drink one wineglassful every hour on the first day and one every four hours on succeeding days.

Rose petal tea is very helpful, it is an age-old remedy going back to the Roman times.

Oat porridge is very advisable, the Scotch thrive on it; use the roughest oats obtainable, the mineral salt content is very high.

Deep breathing exercises should be done as often as possible before an open window or on the lawn, just a few minutes here and there will make a very appreciable difference after a few days.

BREASTS, HARDNESS OF

Herbal remedy: 1 oz. camomile flowers, 1 oz. marshmallow flowers. Add the mixed flowers to two pints of boiling water, simmer gently down to one pint. Apply the still warm flowers in a poultice to the breasts, and then drink one wineglassful of the drink every three hours.

Beans can be used to make a poultice, mix with a little olive oil : this applies only to any type of fresh beans, not to tinned beans.

BRONCHITIS

Heavy catarrh, feverishness, general malaise, raw feelings in the throat, tight sensation across the chest, coughing, and a heavy expectoration are symptoms of the disease; frequently a marked wheezing is audible.

Liquorice and honey can be mixed in hot water; taking a stick of liquorice and adding three or four dessertspoonfuls of honey, drinking a wineglassful whenever desired.

Raw lemon juice can be administered, with or without honey, every hour.

Brown paper soaked in vinegar (sometimes also sprinkled with cayenne pepper) used to be applied to the chest of the patient; I have no experience of this method, but I remember older relatives swearing by its efficacy.

Herbal remedy: 1 oz. coltsfoot, 1 oz. elder flowers, 1 oz. elecampane, 1 oz. horehound. Mix the herbs into one quart of boiling water, simmer slowly down to one pint.
When cool add a half-teaspoonful of cinnamon, mix well; drink one wineglassful every three hours. Any of the above ingredients could be used to make a simple tea at the rate of one ounce to one pint.

Mullein tea is a great help.

Inhaling steam from any of the specified herbs above can help clear the passages when they feel very stuffy; also a half-teaspoonful of eucalyptus oil dropped into a pudding basin of boiling water, the head is then covered over with a towel and slow, steady inhalation is carried on for a few minutes at a time—do not over-exert the patient by forcing too long inhalation.
Place cut onions round the head of the patient every day.

Onions or garlic can be chewed raw and as often as the patient can take them. They are slightly unpleasant but bring speedy relief.

Mustard baths for the feet are recommended.

Slippery elm mixed with cayenne pepper and honey and a little warm water can be taken once in the morning and once at night.

Diet. Plenty of salad and fruit is recommended.

Smoking is allowed, provided that the patient keeps to herbal tobacco; shred up and mix : 2 oz. coltsfoot, 2 oz. rosemary, 2 oz. betony (wood), 1 oz. lavender, 1 oz. mullein, 1 oz. sage. This can be used in a pipe or rolled into cigarettes.

BRUISES

Don't fret; apply one or more of the following remedies.

Witch-hazel. Very good for all sorts of bruises and sprains.

Hyssop leaves bruised until the juice runs placed on the hurt part.

Comfrey—my own favourite remedy for bruises—one applies the crushed leaves directly on to the bruise.

Solomon's seal—the powdered root helps heal bruises quickly.

BUNIONS

Your shoes probably do not fit properly, check them. Apply any of the remedies listed under Corns (q.v.).

BURNS

I never would have thought once this could work but it does :

Peppermint oil applied directly to the burn as soon as possible after the accident has happened. Make sure you use oil of peppermint; essence of, or extract of, does not work. Most chemists stock the pure oil. It lessens the sting almost at once.

Raw potato put straight on to a burn takes a lot of the pain out of it.

Marigold flowers are an old-fashioned remedy, bind lightly on to the injured part.

It is better to keep the burn dry and not to wash it.

Cold tea leaves relieve burns—Indian tea.

Charcoal powder can take a lot of the pain out of a burn.

Elder flowers can be used.

St. John's Wort is also useful, either as an ointment or as fresh herb.

CANCER   You must seek professional advice.

SELF-TREATMENT IS NOT ADVISED BECAUSE OF THE MENTAL STRAIN IT PLACES ON THE PATIENT. IF PROFESSIONAL HELP IS NOT AVAILABLE, TRY THE FOLLOWING :

Probably no disease strikes so much terror into the heart of a patient as this, but while not suggesting that there is an instant cure, I will give a few words of calm, encouraging thinking.

No growth is possible, as every gardener knows, unless the soil is favourable. The same applies with the human body. At some time, something happened in the body of a cancer patient to make it possible for useless and malignant cells (they destroy other useful cells) to grow and grow and grow, *absorbing nutrition*, and robbing other cells of it. If the soil becomes inhospitable the plant dies, and if the body changes its nutritional intake the cancer cells find it harder, if not impossible, to survive.

Salt is strictly out of the diet, cut it out completely.

White sugar and white bread are to be replaced by black molasses for a sweetener—or pure honey; and only brown, wholemeal bread should be eaten.

Black molasses is an essential necessity in the diet of cancer sufferers, its high mineral salt content is often hostile to the growth of cells of a malignant nature. At least three dessertspoonfuls a day should be taken.

Psychosomatic causes are present in every cancer patient. A leading Harley Street specialist remarked that he had never known any cancer patient without some deep-rooted psychological problem. Visit an analyst at the earliest possible opportunity.

Chemical additives to food and drinks must be avoided like the plague, they can only make the patient worse. Insist upon clean, fresh salads and fruit (I wash my salad food in lukewarm water with a teaspoonful of apple cider vinegar added).

Operations may only weaken the system. Hippocrates said, 2,000 years ago, that a cancer that is cut never heals completely. The patient must think carefully about this. A professional herbalist, naturopath or dietician may most likely produce better results. There are many homes run on naturopathic and herbal treatment, and these are widely advertised in some of the health magazines on sale.

Herbal treatment was often eminently successful, and some of the following herbs were used :

Violet leaves eaten daily, accompanied by strict dietetic treatment.

Nettle juice drunk daily; it contains a powerful combination of vitamins and mineral salts. Half a wineglassful every three hours.

Yellow dock leaves used as a strong tea (2 oz. to 1 pint of water); they appear to contain some unidentified substance.

Red clover flowers again made up as a strong tea (2 oz. to 1 pint of water). Half a wineglassful every three hours.

It must be understood, since every type of cancer has something quite individual and specific about it, that I can promise no unqualified success or cure for the use of any substance mentioned here, only that relief and healing were claimed after the use of them.

Milk. Some French experts discovered that cancer patients placed solely on a milk diet for several days at a time made a remarkable recovery from some forms of cancer, but this is not a universal cure.

Sage tea should replace ordinary Indian or China tea for most meals, using one ounce to a pint of boiling water.

Parsley should be eaten daily, as much as the patient can take comfortably.

Figs simmered in fresh milk should be eaten frequently; and if there is a visible growth on the surface of the body the same can be applied as a poultice to the place; cures have been known from this treatment, but nobody can guarantee that it is universally applicable, because there are so many types of cancer, but it is worth trying.

Oatmeal porridge is the best breakfast item for sufferers of this condition.

Walnuts should also be included in the diet very frequently.

Constipation must be avoided at all costs, a sufficiency of herbs and salads in the diet will usually prevent this, but if there is some severe constipation which will not easily be moved I recommend :

Slippery elm mixed with equal parts of honey and warm milk, drunk last thing at night and first thing in the morning, and followed by a hot drink. I have never known this to fail.

The general dietetic precautions exclude meat, eggs and fish from the menu; avoid foods strong in sulphur content, but take plenty of beet, cabbage, celery and parsley.

The juice of one lemon mixed with warm water is a daily drink recommended by some.

Signs to watch out for :

1. A sore throat that will not heal.
2. Unexplained bleeding and discharges.
3. A lump thickening on the breast, occasionally elsewhere.
4. Unusual bladder or bowel behaviour—bleeding, etc.
5. Changes in moles or warts.
6. Cough that will not heal.
7. Persistent indigestion. Pain in swallowing food.

Further notes on cancer:

The American biochemist Arthur Grollman reported in 1967 that an extract of ipecacuanha prevents the growth of abnormal cells in cancerous conditions.

Dr. Theodor Puck of Columbia University Medical Centre demonstrated that cancer is *a reversible process* : using two chemicals found naturally in the human body he returned malignant growths back to normal, healthy activity in hamsters within the hour! Finnish scientists of Helsinki University showed that leukaemia can be checked by the use of Chalones (found in the body naturally) to prevent cell growth : this is their normal function. Dr. U. Mohr in Germany believes that cancer cells lack their normal quota of Chalones and thus grow unhampered. Eight of his test mice survived healthily for 10 months after cherry-sized growths subsided following Chalone treatment.

Dr. Issels of the Ringberg Clinic, Rottach-Egern, Bavaria, has had success in treating terminal cases (given up as hopeless) and uses several herbal teas as part of his treatment.

The earliest cervical smear tests were carried out by an English herbalist Henry Rowsell of Minehead, Somerset, some 30 years before the idea was adopted by the medical profession.

Cancer of the tongue was once treated by strong decoctions of Black Haw roots, applied continuously during the day. Dr. Hugh Hogle reported that an 85-year-old cancer patient showed recovery after drinking tea made from Creosote bush (Chaparral). This has been researched at Utah University and reduction in the size of tumours has been recorded in several cases. It was used for cancer, tuberculosis and for leprosy by Mexican Indians. I have used it for severe respiratory illnesses and found liquid extract of creosote very effective indeed.

Dutch, German and Canadian scientists have explored the role of artificial foodstuffs and hormones in carcinogenic formations (McGill University, Canada). British Small Animals Veterinary Association Congress showed that 41% of cats die from cancer. Such data indicate that soil deficiencies and artificial foods may link with Chalone deficiencies.

In the psychosomatic field Dr. J. G. Bennette, in 1968, told a New York medical conference that some patients may develop cancer as an alternative to having a mental breakdown, the internally directed violence affecting hormones, nerves and cell growth.

CATARRH

Due to too much starchy food (carbohydrates) and sugary substances in cold weather, and several psychological reasons—e.g. stress.

Raw onions chewed before going to bed work wonders.

Garlic is the rapid cure; chewing raw garlic however does not endear one to other members of the family unless they also take a little bit, thereafter they cannot smell it any more.

Milk and onions boiled up together makes a lovely evening 'going to bed' dish, and is very good against early cases of catarrh.

Elder flowers mixed with equal parts of peppermint and yarrow made into a tea (one ounce of mixed herbs to one pint of boiling water); this is the first remedy I recommend when catarrh strikes the family.

Cinnamon and lemon juice makes one of the most effective gargles against catarrh. A little of the mixture can also be drunk in warm water every three hours—very helpful.

Liquorice and honey mixed together is very good against all catarrhal conditions.

Salt water can be used as a gargle and as a nasal douche, sniffing the water up one nostril at a time, and expectorating it through the mouth.

St. John's Wort made into a tea at the usual strength is helpful.

Eucalyptus steam. Place a teaspoonful of the oil in a basin of hot water, put a cloth over the head and breathe the rising steam; this clears the passages quickly.

Birch leaves can be used instead of eucalyptus, about six or eight leaves (dried or fresh) suffice.

Lemon juice and honey should be taken as often as desired.

Sage tea served with lemon juice instead of milk, and sweetened with a little honey, is a marvellous drink; that it helps relieve catarrh is quite beside the point.

Grapefruit peel that has been thoroughly washed can be used to give sage tea a unique and attractive taste.

Agrimony tea is popular and can be used instead of ordinary tea.

Mustard baths for the feet are a standard relief, if no mustard try

Pine needles in a bowl of water as hot as your feet can stand it.

Liquorice and honey are the only forms of sweet which a younger patient can take without making the cold worse.

Herbal remedy: ½ oz. coltsfoot, 1 oz. mullein, 1 oz. sage, ½ oz. thyme, 2 oz. yarrow. Mix the herbs and put them into one quart of boiling water, simmer this until only about one pint remains. One wineglassful every hour for the first day, and every three hours on succeeding days until cold is over.

Cakes and pastries must be cut down to a minimum, potatoes and all farinaceous foods (spaghetti, etc.) are to be vigorously reduced.

Salads and fruit with a reasonable amount of lightly boiled fish, chicken and light meat should form the basis of the diet.

Fresh air is essential for patients with catarrh. Artificial heating is dangerous for catarrh sufferers; central heating is deadly. If the weather is cold I recommend 'Scotch Central Heating'—this is a hot-water-bottle to the feet and a thick blanket wrapped round the waist and the feet; do not wrap up the chest, this hinders breathing. Except if the weather is foggy keep a window open all night long. A little walk every day will help cure the condition.

Herbal tobacco recommended: 1 oz. coltsfoot, 1 oz. eyebright, 2 oz. rose petals, 1 oz. mullein. Chop the mixed herbs up finely and use in a pipe or rolled up in cigarette papers.

Herbal snuff, made of powdered bayberry bark, can be used.

CHAPS

The treatment is much the same for chilblains (q.v.).

Marshmallow ointment may be used. It is prepared by simmering the leaves of marshmallow in coconut fat or lard.

CHICKEN POX

This is a contagious disease and precautions must be taken. There is feverishness, slight shivering at times, sometimes vomiting, often pains in the back and the legs. If professional help is not available, try the following :

Little pustules of fluid form, mostly on the face, and often on the back and the chest; within a few days they burst and brown crusts form over them. The fluid and the crust carry infection. If possible use paper sheets and paper pillow covers and burn them each night.

Witch-hazel should be used to wash the skin and remove the fluid and brown crusts. If there is a very heavy outbreak of pustules cover the skin with cloth soaked in witch-hazel, changing it every 24 hours.

Herbal recipe: ½ oz. basil, 1 oz. boneset, 1 oz. pennyroyal, 1 oz. skullcap. Mix the herbs and put them into one quart of boiling water; simmer until about a little more than a pint is left. When cool add a pinch of cinnamon and honey to taste. Give one wineglassful every three hours.

Figs form an essential item of diet for sufferers of this illness.

Rhubarb should be given; sweetened with a little honey, is a good pudding to give your patients.

Lemonade made from pure lemons with a little honey or raw brown sugar can be given as often as the patient will drink it. *Constipation* must be avoided at all costs.

Scratching of the pustules is the quickest way to spread the disease; if necessary the patient's hands must be bandaged up, if it is not possible to cover the itching parts as suggested above (witch-hazel).

Biscuit, cakes, pastry, pies and all carbohydrate foods must be rigorously cut down to the lowest minimum. The patient can eat as much fruit as he/she likes. Salads, boiled fish, a little chicken, and lean meat—including heart, kidneys, liver and tripe—can be given.

Tripe is a very good food for invalids, with the aid of mint, parsley, fennel, fenugreek, cardomon seeds etc. it can have some wonderful tastes, with chopped carrots and cauliflower you can make delightful dishes.

In Heidelberg when I was studying there I learnt from my dear, kind landlady that one could use the water in which *peas* had been boiled to wash the sores of chicken pox or other pustules; this *Erbsenwasser* is very rich in mineral salts, and I do not doubt that it is useful.

Another herbal tea: 1 oz. marigold flowers, 1 oz. pennyroyal leaves, 1 oz. raspberry leaves. Add the mixed herbs to one quart of boiling water, simmer this until about a quareer of the mixture has evaporated. When cool, give a wineglassful every three hours.

Parsley and black molasses should be eaten daily.

CHILBLAINS

This is an inflamed condition of the extremities, ears suffering as well as hands and feet. The skin becomes purple and itches badly; yellow fluid forms in transparent blisters which later break open and ulceration often follows making the healing very difficult. They are also painful.

Calcium deficiency is nearly always found. Often there is a *Silicon* deficiency as well, and foods containing these items must be increased in intake. *Cabbages* (raw, chopped), cheese, lemons, *lettuce*, milk, oranges and *spinach* contain calcium; those italicised also contain silicon which is also richly present in barley, figs, oats and strawberries.

Nettle juice can be painted over chilblains. *Nettle tea* is beneficial.

Herbal remedy: 1 fluid oz. of camphor, $\frac{1}{2}$ fluid oz. turpentine, 2 oz. lard or coconut fat. Melt the lard then stir in the other ingredients, simmer for a few minutes, remove from the heat and allow to cool. Paint on to the chilblains. My own favourite remedy is the simplest—nettle juice.

Garlic juice can be painted on to broken chilblains.

Onions can be used to help cure chilblains. One covers one side a slice of onion with salt, then puts the fresh side straight on to of the chilblain and covers it with a clean bandage, this is a very old country cure.

Snowdrop bulbs were cut open in the North of England and the freshly cut bulb applied direct to the chilblain; I have no experience of this cure.

Salt and hot water were used to soak feet when chilblains were present.

Friar's balsam was painted on to unbroken chilblains, many claimed that this was infallible.

Salt was occasionally massaged into the hands in cold weather to *prevent* chilblains from forming.

CHILDBIRTH

If you are expecting a happy event I recommend that you should from three months before the expected event drink regularly *raspberry tea* which has been used by herbalists for countless centuries to ensure an easy delivery—1 oz. to one pint of boiling water and take just as you would drink ordinary tea.

It is said to enrich the mother's milk, and is often continued after parturition. Many herbalists insist that this will prevent a miscarriage and prevent any uterine haemorrhage. Aloysius Browne, one of the great herbalists of the turn of this century, quoted an old nurse who had attended over 2,000 births, and who had used only raspberry leaf tea for each of them—she claimed she had never lost a child in any case.

Linseed tea was a favourite medium for easy pregnancy among the gypsies.

CHLOROSIS
This is a form of anaemia (q.v.) in which the skin takes on a slightly greenish tinge.

Herbal recipe: 1 oz. tansy, 1 oz. motherwort. Add the herbs to one quart of boiling water. Simmer gently until about a pint or more is left. Drink a wineglassful every three hours.

Catnip juice can also be taken.

CHOLERA
This is a terrible plague, but nothing is so disastrous as fear. There is the story of a Mohammedan who was walking along the road and met Cholera walking towards the city. Cholera promised the man he would kill only 1,000 people. After the plague it was found that 10,000 had died. The faithful man met Cholera and berated him severely for breaking his promise. 'Alas,' said Cholera, 'I did kill only 1,000 people, all the others died from fear.' **Never panic!**

Vomiting, diarrhoea, cramps of arms and legs, and violent abdominal pain bring the patient to the point of complete exhaustion. The body becomes severely cold, the pulse faint and weakness ensues. Death has been known to follow in 48 hours. **Keep the patient reclining in bed.**

IF PROFESSIONAL AID IS NOT READILY TO HAND try any of the following :

Catechu, *actually* Black Catechu (*acacia catechu*), should be given in doses of five to ten grains.

A herbal tea which has been used by herbalists for many centuries: 1 oz. bayberry bark, powdered, $\frac{1}{4}$ oz. cayenne pepper, 1 oz. cransbill root, powdered, 1 oz. tormentil root, powdered. Mix the herbs and place them in three pints of boiling water, simmer this until only a little more than half remains. Add 1$\frac{1}{2}$ oz. tincture of myrrh, and administer one wineglassful every 30 minutes for the first three hours, then one glassful every hour.

Garlic should be chopped and given to the patient to swallow hourly.

Raw onions can be used if garlic is not available. Hourly. Again, raw freshly-cut-open onions should be placed around the patient to kill off infection. I may add that the Russian scientists of Tomsk university investigated onions and were full of praise for their antiseptic, disinfectant and curative properties.

Herbal recipes: (a) 1 oz. bistort, 1 oz. peppermint, 1 oz. purple loosestrife. (b) 1 oz. angelica, 1 oz. balm melissa, 1 oz. sage, 1 oz. yarrow. In either case mix the herbs, add them to one quart of boiling water, simmer this until about a quarter of it has evaporated. When cool administer one wineglassful every hour.

Peppermint and sage tea mixed together in equal parts and given cold to the patient will help.

Seaweed tablets if available will help replace the loss of mineral salts.

Cinnamon and cayenne may be given, separately, as best the patient can absorb them.

COFFEE SUBSTITUTE

What's that? You've run out of coffee, the shops are shut and you have guests coming? Well, don't worry, there is help at hand.

Parsnips sliced thinly and roasted in the oven can be ground up and mixed with your coffee, they'll make it go further.

Dandelion coffee can be mixed with or used instead of real coffee : this is distinctly better for liver cases.

COLDS.   *See* the entry under CATARRH.

COLIC

This is a pain which can attack not only the youngest members of the family. It is basically a spasmodic contraction of the muscular parts of the intestines, and very discomforting it can be. It may come about from walking through damp streets, snow, or as the end product of prolonged constipation. Take care that the condition is not more symptomatic of a peptic ulcer or appendicitis.

Chamomile tea is one of the best first-aid remedies.

Peppermint tea and honey is a very suitable drink for the patient.

Linseed poultices can be applied to the stomach.

Meat and starchy foods should be avoided. Salads and fruit should form the basis of the patient's diet.

Wholemeal bread or crisp bread can be used, but very little butter.

Thyme tea is a very valuable drink in this condition.

CONSTIPATION

Is one of the most dangerous conditions, it means that the body's 'drains' are blocked, and we all know what drains can do to a house !

Honey and hot water every morning before breakfast. One teaspoonful to one cup of hot water, drink as hot as possible.

Slippery elm mixed with equal parts of warm water and honey can also be used before breakfast and before going to bed at night, it is a very effective curative agent.

Dandelion coffee should replace ordinary coffee.

Elder bark powdered and drunk in warm water is a good aperient.

Icelandic moss can be lightly boiled and the water helps cure constipation.

Liquorice is the only sweet to be allowed to constipated patients.

Rhubarb sweetened with honey or black molasses is one of the best things to give the sufferers.

Watercress or parsley should be eaten every day.

Apricots mashed with a little honey are very beneficial.

Purgatives should be avoided. Use more roughage with food (bran, etc.).

Plenty of walks and more exercise (e.g. swimming) is indicated.

CORNS

Don't neglect them, they are painful and won't go away without a determined 'push' on your part.

Dandelion juice put fresh on to the corn every night has been found very effective.

Lemon juice placed neat on the corn night and morning has produced very satisfactory results.

Turpentine was an old-fashioned remedy, it was painted on and covered over with a bandage, renewed every 24 hours.

Celandine juice is a time-honoured remedy. These pretty yellow plants grow, often to the gardener's despair, on many lawns.

Swede hollowed out, filled with salt; soak 24 hours, bathe the corn with the liquid, night and morning.

COUGHS. *See* ASTHMA and BRONCHITIS, the remedies can be used for most coughs and chest troubles.

CRAMP

This is a spasm of the muscles, and very painful indeed.

Clove oil diluted with olive oil can be massaged into the muscle.

Myrrh, tincture of, can be massaged on to the affected muscles.

Black molasses should be taken; cramp is often due to a serious imbalance of mineral salts.

Calcium and silicon foods should be given. *See* the entry CHIL-BLAINS, where these foods are listed.

Calamint leaves can be crushed and massaged on to the muscles.

CROUP

A cough which involves a blocking of the throat. Sweating is very heavy, the skin goes pale, the coughing is harsh and comes in violent fits. Put the patient into a hot bath in which both *cayenne and mustard* have been mixed. Dry the child with warm towels. It may be better for the child patient to be allowed to sit up rather than recline, breathing may be easier this way. *Vapour* is essential; put into a basin of hot water one of the following : *Pine needles, eucalyptus, birch leaves.* Place a towel over the patient's head and get him/her to inhale the steam, this usually shifts the blocking pus or phlegm; do not make children do this for more than a few minutes at a time. **Keep the patient calm,** explain that it is something which can be healed in a little time. Provided that steps are taken it is very rare that death occurs (do not tell the patient this).

Creosote oil is an excellent additive to a vapour bath. Creosote tablets can often be bought from a chemist.

Fruit and salad diet is advisable. Milk should rarely be given. No carbohydrates for the first day or two. Orange and lemon juice as much as lhe patient can take.

Constipation must be avoided. *See* the entry CONSTIPATION.

CUTS AND WOUNDS

Cleanse the wound first, as a general rule.

Witch-hazel is one of the best substances with which to wash a wound, and one I usually prefer.

Honey slapped straight on to a deep wound and bandaged firmly on invariably prevents infection because it absorbs moisture, and very few bacteria can live without moisture; be generous with the honey.

Crushed apple was an old-fashioned country remedy, owing to the high mineral and vitamin content of apples this is a logical approach.

Parsley, either crushed or the juice thereof, can be applied to many cuts and will produce healing, especially if dirt or foreign bodies have penetrated deeply into the wound, it encourages the formation of pus quickly.

Marigold flowers can be boiled lightly into a strong tea, when cold some should be drunk and the rest applied on to the wound, which is covered by a piece of lint soaked in the tea, and bandaged up.

Cream. Take a little fresh cream, cover a piece of lint with it and apply it to the wound or cut, this draws out the bacteria which find the cream a much easier medium to breed in than the human flesh where antibodies are fighting them. The top of the milk will do if you have no cream; renew every two hours, burn the old dressing.

A tourniquet must be applied if there is constant bleeding which cannot be staunched; tie a label to the tourniquet with the exact time at which it was applied, it must be released and then re-tied after a pause about *every 12 minutes* to prevent damage by lack of blood to the affected parts : professional advice must be sought in such cases.

Golden rod, which grows in most gardens, is a good wound herb; wash the leaves in slightly warm water, then crush and apply directly to the wound.

Daises grow all over the lawn; if you haven't persuaded your husband to destroy them all (you'd have only yourself to blame) use the crushed leaves and apply directly to any cut or wound, after a light washing of the same leaves; this remedy has worked wonders since the days of the Anglo-Saxons who called the plant 'day's eyes'.

Yarrow is the plant which the Greek hero Achilles was taught to use by the Thracian Centaur (horseman) Chiron; I have often used the juice of this marvellous herb myself when roaming in the wilds alone. I have never known it fail.

St. John's Wort is another famed herb for cuts and wounds, the juice or the crushed leaves (after a light wash) are applied direct, and bandaged on to the hurt.

Herbal ointment: 2 oz. dandelion, 2 oz. plantain, 2 oz. yellow dock leaves. Mix and put into $\frac{1}{4}$ gallon boiling water, simmer until one and a half pints remain, add coconut butter or lard until the liquid melts into the fat. Add 2 oz. beeswax and a little cayenne pepper (teaspoonful).

Allow to cool. When solid put in a jar and apply when needed.

DANDRUFF

Consult my work *How to Keep Your Hair On*; this is quite indispensable for all problems concerning the health of scalp and hair. For first aid, however, try the following :

Eucalyptus and clove oil mixed, three parts to one (cloves) massaged into the scalp every night; don't forget to cover the pillow with layers of paper or an old towel.

Greasy heads can be massaged with a mixture of equal parts of *rose-water, witch-hazel and eau de Cologne*, any of the ingredients can be tried individually if the others are not to hand.

Diet is the main factor behind dandruff, consult the book referred to for full details on this subject. As a broadly based rule, *carbohydrates* must be cut down and more protein and salad eaten.

Scabious flowers are often grown in gardens as well as found wild in the hedgerows; pick a few flowers and boil them in one pint of water for ten minutes; rub a little of the liquid into the scalp every night before going to bed.

Beetroot juice was said to be a cure for this condition, but I have no personal experience of using it directly, it is worth giving a try.

DEAFNESS

Deafness which is of catarrhal causation can usually be cured. *See* under CATARRH. Warm olive oil is useful, drop it slowly into the ears, a few drops of onion juice can be added; or else tincture of myrrh, again a few drops (up to five) should suffice.

DEBILITY

Usually due to loss mineral salts and vitamins.

Black molasses should be taken two or three times a day.

Honey must be used in place of sugar.

Fresh green salads and fruit must accompany increased protein diet.

Lemonade made from fresh lemons and sweetened with honey is highly advisable, try it with a pinch of nutmeg or cinnamon.

This is often a sign of anaemia (q.v.).

DEPRESSION

Basically mental in origin, if not dealt with it may cause serious illnesses to develop because of the close relationship of mind and body in health and sickness.

Apple cider vinegar and honey in warm water helps a lot. *Breakfast* should consist of yoghurt and birchermuesli or rough oat flakes; give up the cup of tea and a cigarette! Orange juice is excellent for breakfast.

Warm baths help. **Brisk walk before breakfast** is often very curative.

Milton said :

> *'The Mind is of itself its own place*
> *It can make a hell of heaven and a heaven of hell.'*

DIABETES

Symptoms : Increased thinness, increased thirst, increased urine output. The mouth and skin become dry and constipation is present.

A herb has been discovered in Argentina which is said to cure this illness even in advanced stages; the herb is *phyllanthus sellowianus* and I first mentioned it in my book for gardeners *Herbgrowing for Health*; it is not easy to acquire up to the time of writing. If professional aid is not available, try the following :

Herbal remedy which has been used for many generations : 1 oz. agrimony, 1 oz. clivers, 1 oz. dandelion root, 1 oz. juniper berries, 1 oz. parsley piert. Mix the herbs and place them in a half gallon of boiling water; simmer this until one quart remains. A wineglassful is drunk every two hours.

Carrots eaten raw should be included in the daily diet.

Dandelion coffee should replace ordinary coffee.

Herbal teas made of the following, either individually or mixed, can be used in the ratio one ounce of herb(s) to one pint of boiling water : Dandelion, golden seal (a half teaspoonful of powdered herb would suffice for one pint); in the ratio half an ounce to one pint—

the following lady's mantle, meadowsweet, Queen of the Meadow. Also bistort flowers and leaves.

Another herbal remedy long recommended : 2 oz. agrimony, 2 oz. bistort root, 2 oz. meadow fern berries, 2 oz. prickly ash berries. Mix the herbs and put into a half-gallon boiling water; simmer down to one quart. Before removing from the heat throw in ¼ oz. cayenne pepper. One wineglassful every three hours.

Almonds should form part of the daily diet for diabetics.

Honey should replace sugar, or black molasses can be used. *Constipation* must be avoided, see the entry in this book. *Sun and fresh air* are essential to the diabetic. *White bread and white sugar* are tabu. Only wholemeal, stone ground bread and molasses or honey can be used.

Sauna baths are helpful, but do not stay in the heat more than five minutes at a time; several entries into the heat can be made during one visit to the sauna, and a cold shower for a few seconds after each visit to the hot room is essential. Dietetic and herbal treatment by a professional are indicated. **Do not attempt to treat the condition without advice.**

Dogwood has been used by some herbalists with some success. All cases are individual and none of the substances recommended here will necessarily prove infallible for any individual patient.

Proteins, fruit and salads can be taken freely, carbohydrates must be restricted. Consult a dietician.

DIARRHOEA
An exhausting condition which often robs the body of much needed mineral salts and vitamins.

Often caused by a lack of iron in the body.

Nettle juice taken neat or in cold water.

Raspberry leaf tea drunk cool or cold.

Arrowroot powder administered with a spoon, unpleasant to taste but very speedily effective.

Herbal remedy: 1 oz. bayberry, ½ oz. peppermint, 1 oz. raspberry leaves. Mix herbs and put into one quart of boiling water; allow about a quarter of this to simmer away. When cool drink a wineglassful every three hours.

Blackberries can be eaten freely by the patient.

Spinach is a good item of diet.

Knapweed flowers can be chewed.

Mint sprigs can be chewed, fresh from the garden.

DIGESTIVE TROUBLES
Watch that diet !

Cinnamon and hot milk with honey helps relieve this.

Peppermint tea is very useful.

Golden rod tea is a great help.

Fennel or sage tea can be used with excellent results.
Never, never use bicarbonate of soda.

DIPHTHERIA
SEEK OUT PROFESSIONAL ADVICE, BUT IF YOU CANNOT GET ANY TRY THE FOLLOWING RECIPES. No guarantee can be given, because nobody can foresee the condition or severity of any individual attack. Symptoms, difficult to diagnose. Depression, general malaise, feeling of heavy catarrh, especially in the throat; vomiting and a little diarrhoea may set in. Stiffness at the back of the neck, terrible, often painful inflammation of the throat, tonsils swell, glands round the jaw feel tender, greyish flecks develop in the mouth and throat, then a thick, yellow membrane forms, there is a lot of mucous deposit; breath is very offensive and foul-smelling. The temperature rises rapidly to about 103° Fahrenheit. Death may occur within three to four days. **Do seek professional advice.**

Garlic. One clove must be chewed by the patient every hour for the first day.

Raw onions may be used if no garlic is available. Again onions should be placed around the patient, their germicidal properties are remarkable.

Gargling with milk is advisable, this picks up a lot of foul matter which should be burnt.

Lemonade and pure lemon juice should be given as often as the patient can endure it, mix with pure honey.

An old herbal recipe was : 1 oz. cinnamon, 1 oz. cayenne, 1 oz. gum myrrh. Simmered in one and a half pints of water for 10 minutes; add three dessertspoonfuls of apple cider vinegar when it has cooled down. Administer a tablespoonful every hour.

White oak bark can be used to make a gargle; the bark is powdered, and a teaspoonful is used to half a pint of warm water.

Sage tea is one of the best teas to give, it is rich in mineral salts (Red Sage is held to be the best for this illness) : one wineglassful every hour is to be administered.

Tansy tea (2 oz. to 1 pint) can be used both as a drink and as a very powerful gargle. The gypsies used it exclusively for this disease.

Feet must be kept warm, but **cold compresses to throat** often bring a great deal of relief.

Salt-water gargles are still used in some parts of Turkey for this illness. **All gargles** should be repeated at half-hourly intervals.

Infection spreads easily; remember to keep plenty of freshly-cut onions around the house, using them to rub on your hands before touching the patient.

Lemon juice prevents the formation of the dangerous membrane; use it as frequently as the patient can be persuaded to take it, also squirt some on to the tonsils.

Inhaling steam in which birch leaves, pine needles, cayenne, eucalyptus, camphor or cloves have been placed (or oils of these substances) is very beneficial indeed.

Nettle tea or pure nettle juice should be taken regularly in addition to any other remedies. Nettle tea can also be used as a gargle.

Black molasses and honey should be added to the daily diet. Fruit, particularly grapes and citrus fruits, and salads should replace carbohydrate foods. Otherwise be guided by the whim of the patient. Strawberries are often popular with such patients.

Don't force the patient to recline to sleep, it may choke him/her.

DROPSY

First of all let us understand what it is. Basically it is an abnormal accumulation of fluid underneath the skin or in any part of the body where fluid can conveniently collect. To start with, this is *not* a disease in itself, it is the end-result of one of several conditions. It is a sign that something is wrong with the body, but not the illness itself—however unpleasant it may feel and look.

It is often due to a watery condition of the blood which permits fluid to flow through the capillary walls. Sometimes it appears because there is obstruction to the flow of lymph in the proper channels, or due to general ill-health which promotes a weakening of the capillary walls. Toxins in the blood may cause dropsy, as may obstructions in the veins. It is frequently a by-product of kidney disease (Bright's disease) or heart trouble, cirrhosis, tumours, thrombosis or starvation (malnutrition).

Nevertheless in any cases it is a complication every patient can do without; the undermentioned may bring speedy relief.

Herbal remedy: ½ oz. basil, 1 oz. broom tops, 1 oz. dandelion herb, ¼ oz. Lily of the Valley flowers. Mix the herbs and put into a quart of boiling water; simmer gently until about a fifth of the liquid has boiled away. When cool administer a wineglassful every three hours.

Asparagus should be eaten freely.

Celery and parsley should be eaten raw (washed) as often as the patient can stomach them.

Herbal teas: Birch leaf tea (¼ oz. to 1 pint of water), horsetail grass (1 oz. 1 pint), St. John's Wort (1 oz. 1 pint), tansy (1 oz. 1 pint).

Horseradish shredded up and taken in salads is very beneficial : do not use ready-made horseradish sauce.

Nettle tops can be shredded and added to salads, they are helpful.

Dandelion tea or coffee is recommended instead of ordinary teas and coffee; it is very efficacious over a long period.

Shepherd's purse can be taken as a tea, one ounce to one pint; it was a favourite country remedy.

Lemon juice with or without sweetening is most useful.

DRUG ADDICTS
If one of your children or adolescents comes home under the influence of drugs administer one of the following and send at once for professional advice.

Basil tea. Half a teaspoonful to one pint of water.

Marjoram tea. Half a teaspoonful to one pint of boiling water.

Radiesthesia offers great hope for the recovery of drug addicts, especially in the modern form of *radionics* and an expert should be sought out.

DYSENTERY. *See* the entry under DIARRHOEA.

DYSPEPSIA
This form of indigestion is due to over-eating or malnutrition. If is often a sign that something serious could go wrong with the body if further neglected.

Pineapple eaten regularly at the end of a meal is a wonderful aid to good digestion; this is well known to the Chinese cuisine.

Herbal teas made of caraway, coriander ($\frac{1}{2}$ oz.), fennel, ginger ($\frac{1}{2}$ oz.) golden rod, peppermint or thyme ($\frac{1}{2}$ oz.) can be used to improve digestion; except where otherwise indicated one ounce to the pint is used; it is better to use any of these separately and *not* use the herbs mixed together.

Raw carrots often can be chewed up to prevent digestion.

Apples and cucumber should always be eaten with their peel/rind on, they can be very indigestible if they are peeled before eating! The rinds or peel contain mineral salts which facilitate digestion.

Parsley should form part of the daily diet.

Apple cider vinegar is a great help against indigestion, with or without the addition of honey.

Constipation is sometimes indicated by indigestion; see the entry in this book which gives the appropriate remedies.

EAR : ABSCESS
This is very painful, and if the swelling cannot be clearly seen it can be most definitely felt by the patient.

Peppermint oil or *rosemary oil.* Apply a half teaspoonful of the oil to a basin of boiling water, the patient shall sit with the abscessed ear over this, the head covered by a thick towel, but his nose and mouth need not be in the steamed area.

EAR : ACHE

The above remedy is often successful.

Teeth and gums should be brushed or massaged with cinnamon or oil of cloves (powdered cloves).

Marigold juice and an equal part of warmed olive oil can be dropped into the affected ear.

Olive oil warmed slightly can be poured into the ear slowly, *one drop* of oil of peppermint, or oil of cloves, could be added to an eggcupful of warmed olive oil.

EAR : BOILS

Treat as for ABSCESSES, see above!

EAR : CATARRHAL DEAFNESS

Cut open a clove of garlic, rub the point of half the length of garlic into the ears gently. Another clove of garlic should be chewed slowly; although not pleasant it is a very reliable remedy.

EAR : FOREIGN BODY IN THE EAR

Dropping warm olive oil into the ear usually causes the foreign body to float to the exit on the oil. Never put any pointed object into the ear, it could perforate the ear drum and cause irreparable harm.

EAR : WAX

Use an infra-red-ray lamp at three feet from the patient's head, preferably with the patient reclining. Simple, very effective *oil and water* mixed together and both warm can be employed to drop into the ear and wash it out, only one drop of one of the powerful oils would be used—peppermint, eucalyptus, rosemary, etc. But more parts of olive oil could be used.

ECZEMA

A scaly and fissured inflammation of the skin is characterised by sticky fluid discharges which carry the infection further.

Marigold tea should be drunk warm and applied as a cold wash to the skin; one uses the flowers at the rate of 1 oz. to 1 pint.

Bilberry juice is an excellent medicament to paint on the sores.

Watercress is an essential item of diet for sufferers from eczema.

Walnut leaves can be applied $\frac{1}{2}$ oz. to 1 pint, this is *for external use only.*

Slippery elm soap is probably the best soap to use, although if any purely herbal soaps are available they will do as well; avoid soaps with animal fats or chemicals in them.

Lemon juice can be taken at regular intervals and applied to the sores.

Constipation is invariably present and this must be cleared up (see the entry under that heading in this book). *Carbohydrates,* sugars, fats and starches must be rigorously pruned back and more proteins, fruit and vegetables eaten. One meal a day should be a pure salad.

Slippery elm and honey mixed with warm water and a pinch of cayenne pepper should be taken every morning before breakfast; use a dessertspoonful of each ingredient, three of water.

EPILEPSY

So many families are grief-stricken if one member develops this dread 'falling-sickness'. Take courage much can be done to heal and help.

Firstly, dosing the patient with drugs which dull the nervous system suppress the symptoms and do little to establish a permanent cure.

The patient usually utters a cry or a scream and falls as if in a fainting fit; it is an uncontrolled explosion of energy which convulses the entire body. Insert a strong rubber or something which will not break the patient's teeth, but will prevent him/her from biting the tongue during the convulsions. Do not panic if the patient emits blood-flecked foam from the mouth, the bleeding is invariably harmless. The contents of the bladder and of the bowels are sometimes voided, this is unpleasant, smelly and annoying, but the patient has no control, do not blame him/her.

Herbal recipes which have been recommended by herbalists over many decades :

(*a*) 1 oz. black horehound, 1 oz. mugwort, 1 oz. pellitory of the wall, 1 oz. skullcap, 1 oz. valerian, 1 oz. vervain, 1 oz. wood betony. Mix the herbs, put into 5 pints of water; simmer until one pint has evaporated. When cold administer one wineglassful every three hours.

(*b*) 1 oz. burdock herb, 1 oz. pennyroyal, 1 oz. valerian, 1 oz. vervain, $\frac{1}{2}$ oz. cayenne pepper (added last). Mix the herbs and put into one quart of boiling water. Simmer down to slightly over one pint. When cool add the cayenne pepper, stirring in well. Administer one wineglassful every three hours.

Expecting an attack. Many sufferers have a premonition of an attack. Loosen all clothing, especially around the neck, waist, etc. Administer one of the recommended herbal drinks.

Silica deficiency is common among epileptics, and the following foods rich in that mineral should be taken as much as convenient : barley, cabbage (raw), cauliflower (raw, chopped), figs, lettuce, oatmeal (especially as a breakfast food), spinach and strawberries. See the note below.

Horsetail grass, a much despised herb, is the richest source of natural silica known to man, it makes a quite delectable tea, using one ounce to one pint.

White sugar and bread must be avoided, only raw brown sugar, honey or black molasses should be used, and wholemeal, stone-ground bread should be taken.

Salt may be lethal to epileptics, and only sea-salt or *Bios* is recommended. *Alcohol* is also toxic to epileptics. *Constipation* is often an irritant cause. I have never found any epileptic who did not suffer from constipation. See the entry in this book.

Heartsease makes a valuable remedy for this condition; many old herbalists claimed to have cured it with this herb alone.

Black molasses is an essential item of the daily diet.

Bladder and kidneys must be kept in first-rate condition, preferably by use of salads in the diet; I have often found epileptics refuse the fresh green food which offers them the best cure.

Olive oil is the safest fat to use, better than butter or margarine.

Elderflower tea, made with $1\frac{1}{2}$ oz. flowers to one pint boiling water, is a helpful substance which, if persevered with, should bring a marked relief and improvement in the patient, three cups a day for three months; use it instead of any other Indian tea or any coffee.

Dandelion coffee may be used, ordinary coffee not.

Chocolate is strictly forbidden to all epileptics.

Sauces, mayonnaises, curries, and all spiced foods are out until cured.

Massage and chiropractic services are helpful.

A warm bath before bed, followed by milk and honey, is helpful.

Liver troubles are common among epileptics. This was discovered, believe it or not, by the neglected and despised phrenologists over a century ago, they discovered many things which mankind could ill-afford to forget. I was talking to a Swiss friend who has made a specialised study of epilepsy, and he was astounded to learn that his years of research had already been done, proved—and forgotten! Mankind does not learn too well, often taking two steps backwards for every three forwards.

ELECTRIC SHOCK

If the patient cannot stand start artificial respiration. If the patient seems dead do not panic, this is more often than not only shock. Carry on with artificial respiration. People have recovered after fantastic shocks of thousands and more volts.

Burns. If there are burns, when the patient has recovered you can treat according to the suggestions given under that heading in this book.

EYES

One of the most overworked and generally neglected parts of the human body; the unimaginative do not realise how valuable our sight is until it becomes affected.

Rose petals were placed on tired and strained eyes (shut) by old Turkish *hakim*; the flowers are good for the nerves and contain substances which are not fully understood, the remedy is worth a try.

Apple pulp made from crushed fresh apples can be placed over the closed lids and left on for an hour or two while the patient rests and then rinsed off with cold water. The fruit is extraordinarily rich in mineral salts. Pure *apple juice* will also serve.

Eyebright is one of the oldest herbal standby remedies for all manner of eye troubles. I have used it myself for eyestrain, and for a burst bloodvessel in the eyes, and found it most efficacious : many herbalists make up their own eye lotions containing this.

Puffy eyes indicate often a lack of protein or kidney disorders.

Chickweed, that 'weed' you have probably spent so much time killing (may God forgive you) is one of the most valuable herbs for healing *styes and ulcers*, one places the freshly washed herb on the stye or ulcer, binds it into place with a firm but not tight bandage and leaves it on for three or four hours at a time, then after an hour's interval it is replaced—chickweed tea should also be drunk during this treatment (one ounce to a pint). Chickweed leaves can be eaten in salads, and very nutritious they are.

Groundsel is another despised plant which is essential to heal many different eye ailments (you never find wild rabbits with bad eyes, and they eat masses of groundsel); apply the crushed leaves at once to the closed eyes, bandage it on and leave it; in severe cases mix the groundsel with warm milk and apply.

Special herbal remedy for inflammations of the eyes : 1 oz. raspberry leaves, 1 oz. marshmallow herb, $\frac{1}{2}$ oz. groundsel. Put the mixed herbs into one and a half pints of boiling water; simmer them gently until about one pint remains. When this is cold strain, then use it as a lotion to apply by eyebath.

Eyebaths should be held as close as possible up to the open eye, and then look North, South, East and West; change the contents for each eye! **Fingers** weren't made for pushing into the eyes, keep them out of it.

Watercress and parsley, honey and black molasses should figure in the daily diet. *Yoghourt* with breakfast is also advisable.

Conjunctivitis is often alleviated by using boiled poppy seed heads (one ounce in a pint of water), when suitably cooled, as an eye lotion. Try sassafras lotion.

Cataract was formerly treated by simmering the blossoms of St. John's Wort in a mixture of almond and olive oil; and using it when it was cold to apply to the damaged eyeball via an eyebath. **Always wash your eyes with clean water** every morning, use an eyebath.

Increase vitamin A, B (complex) and D intake if suffering from eyestrain. Rutin has been used for haemorrhage of the retina. Agrimony, anemone leaves and celery were also used for cataract.

FACE PIMPLES

Treat as for ACNE (*see* entry). Sarsaparilla percolated like coffee; ½ oz. to one pint boiling water, is a very useful help, being taken for about a week.

FAINTING

Is a symptom that something is wrong inside the body or that exhaustion is setting in.

Alcohol should not be given to a person recovering from a faint, herb teas are much safer and more nutritious.

Hold the head down between the knees, this restores the blood circulation to the brain and brings the patient round.

Honey and cinnamon, a dessertspoonful of the first, a pinch of the second, given in fairly hot water and well mixed, are advisable.

Peppermint tea if handy is a good restorative.

Aspirin-type drugs are not recommended by me; indeed in Sweden such drugs are considered dangerous enough to be available only on a doctor's prescription.

Burnt feathers (from a pillowcase or eiderdown) may be an old-fashioned treatment, but they can still bring a fainting person round quickly.

Eau de Cologne rubbed into the temples and held beneath the nose also acts as a restorative.

Rosemary tea with a pinch of lemon juice is excellent, one ounce to a pint.

Lavender water acts just as well as eau de Cologne.

Sage tea or St. John's Wort tea make good drinks for a recovered person after a faint—use in each case one ounce to one pint boiling water, sweeten only with honey or rough brown sugar.

FEET

If you want to get the best out of them give them the best treatment. *Cold feet* are a sure passport to an illness; whatever you do keep your feet warm in winter *and in wet weather. Stockings and socks* should never be worn longer than 48 hours, and if possible should be changed every 24 hours. Avoid running dyes in your hosiery.

Lemon peel is useful to rub over tired feet, do not throw it away.

Onion or garlic can be used to rub over badly aching feet; this remedy is said to go back to the Roman Legionaries.

Baths of hot water containing birch leaves, pine needles or ordinary mustard powder are very refreshing.

Sweaty feet demand increasing your intake of silica foods and of sulphur-containing foods: cabbages and figs contain both of them.

Feet with aching joints. See the entry ARTHRITIS.

FEMALE COMPLAINTS

From Germany I learned to use a herbal tea made of *hollyhocks,* one ounce to one pint of boiling water. Very few of the flowers and plants that our clever forefathers grew were just grown by accident or for fun. The emotional and snobbish attitude of many of our 'Clever Dicks' (as my grandmother used to call them) prevented them from ever learning anything from the old country-folk, whose secrets too often went with them to the grave—Humanity being the losers. One or two of us listened patiently to our grandparents and absorbed the lore of centuries—even so it was nearly 40 years before I fully realised that everybody did not know such things and decided to write down my acquired knowledge in books.

Sage tea should be used freely. 1 oz. to 1 pint.

Thyme tea is also valuable. (*See Herbal Teas for Health and Pleasure* for further information on thyme tea).

See entries under BREASTS, CONSTIPATION, CHILDBIRTH, ETC.

Old herbal recipe: 1 oz. bistort, $\frac{1}{4}$ oz. cinnamon, $\frac{1}{8}$ oz. cloves, 1 oz. cranesbill, 1 oz. golden seal, 1 oz. white poplar bark. Mix herbs and put into one quart of boiling water, simmer for 15 minutes. Add honey to taste. Take one teaspoonful in $\frac{1}{2}$ cupful warm water every four hours.

FERTILITY

Most of the problems associated with this are of a psychosomatic origin. Some are glandular, and these are said to be helped by the powdered bark of *Dichrostachys nutans*; the Dichrostachys are mostly found in Angola.

FEVERS

When there is a feverish condition and you are not sure what it is there are one or two useful things you can do at once.

Yarrow tea given in the strength of one ounce to one pint boiling water.

Lemon juice and honey can be taken as strong or weak as thought necessary, as often as the patient likes.

Apple cider vinegar and honey could also be used.

Never panic; the presence of fever shows that the human body is giving battle to invading, alien organisms which cannot stand the increase of heat too well; the effort of fighting them does weaken the body generally. Never try to suppress a fever, you could kill the patient! Lessen it a little but don't suppress it.

Herbal recipe: ½ oz. powdered quinine (Peruvian bark), 1 oz. powdered pleurisy root, 1 oz. skunk cabbage, ¼ oz. ginger, 2 oz. yarrow. Mix the herbs, add them to one quart of boiling water, and simmer for 10 minutes very gently. Give one wineglassful with a little honey every three hours, or one teaspoonful every hour.

Marigold flower tea is a very beneficent agent. One ounce to one pint.

Countryfolk used to bathe a fever patient in milk and wash it off every six hours; I have no experience with this method.

Balm melissa or tansy tea are excellent helpful drinks. One ounce to one pint.

'FLU

Most people call it "Flu" and not 'Influenza', so here we are.

Keep calm is the first rule, it can be defeated.

Old herbal recipe: 1 oz. boneset, 1 oz. mullein, 1 oz. sage, 1 oz. vervain, 1 oz. yarrow. Mix the herbs, put them in ½ gallon boiling water; simmer gently until only half the quantity of liquid remains. When it is cool give one wineglassful every three hours.

Garlic, however badly it smells, helps your patient more than most cures.

Raw onions, cut open and fresh, should be placed around the patient's pillow; this helps to protect the other members of the household.

Vapour baths. Inhaling eucalyptus or clove oil under a heavy towel clears the blocked passages.

My first herbal tea for 'flu cases: ½ oz. elderflowers, ½oz. peppermint, ½ oz. yarrow. Put into a teapot, cover with 1½ pints of *boiling* water, leave 10 minutes after covering up teapot. Drink when the right temperature—as much as you feel like. Sweeten only with honey.

Honey and lemon juice should be taken every hour.

Citrus fruit as much as the patient can eat.

Cinnamon and milk warmed up makes a nice drink.

Salt-water gargles are excellent. Repeat frequently.

Mustard baths, sometimes with a pinch of cayenne added, bring feelings of relief.

Phlegm, etc., must be *burnt. Constipation* must be avoided. *See* the appropriate entry in this book.

FIBROSITIS.   *See* the article on ARTHRITIS.

Consult my book entitled : *How to Defeat Rheumatism and Arthritis.*

FLATULENCE.   *See* DYSPEPSIA.

FLEAS

They detest wormwood and an old herb called Fleabane; if you wash your clothes in water containing either herb fleas will trouble you no more. Other herbs used against fleas were alder, asarabaca and camomile flowers.

FLIES

Are harbingers of disease, they are the filthiest of all insects; owing to their smallness and their numbers it is rather exhausting to go around with a swotter or a rolled-up newspaper killing them by ones or twos. It is even more dangerous to use DDT or one of the sprays on sale, because the chemicals are no respecters of persons and if some of them spray down on to your food they may do you more harm than they do the flies. (*See* Rachel Carson's book *The Silent Spring*).

All flies and insects seem to hate the herb TANSY whether it is fresh or dried, many cottagers grew it at the kitchen door for this reason. Countryfolk would also sprinkle their rooms with the remains of white horehound tea.

In a sickroom expose some eucalyptus in a saucer, the fumes will drive flies away. You could also pour some on a handkerchief and wave it about vigorously to spread the fumes.

Bunches of mignonette, nettles or walnut leaves hung up near a window keep flies from coming in.

Heat a poker or a knife and apply it to a piece of solid camphor, once this has been done a room will keep fly-free for several days.

Cedar-wood oil keeps away flies and moths.

Ox-eye daisies grown in a window box usually keep flies away from the window.

Oil of lavender also deters flies, it is quite a pleasant perfume for us.

Elder flowers are reputed to drive flies away if hung up in bunches around a room.

FRACTURES (SUSPECTED)

The golden rule is this—however uncomfortable the patient looks or feels, do not move him/her; leave them lying, and never touch the leg or part of body which looks as if it may be fractured, if you do so you may cause the flesh and skin to break open, admitting air-borne bacteria which will complicate the matter and could end in the death of the patient.

Send for professional advice. If this is a long time coming, keep the patient warm with blankets, etc. In case an operation is required do not give the patient anything to eat, a little warm water with a teaspoonful of honey might be given once. If a very long wait is anticipated, apply comfrey leaves which have been dipped in boiling water (quickly) to the area of pain, bandage on lightly.

FRECKLES

Let us face it, they do mar one's appearance.

Cowslip tea is used cold to wash the face and arms affected. Half ounce to one pint.

Elderflower tea, made half ounce to one pint, is used cold to wash freckled skin.

Cucumber juice is very useful for removing freckles.

Sorrel leaves may be eaten; this is supposed to cure freckles, but I have no personal experience of it.

GALLSTONES

Pain in the region of the gall-bladder, high temperature and shivering take place. A spasm of pain often starts under the lower right rib and may shoot up as high as the shoulder blade. There is often sweating, vomiting and a cold sweat.

If no professional advice is available, try one of the following :

Broom tops (spartium scoparium) can be used, a few teaspoonfuls of them (three or four) to one pint of boiling water, simmer for 10 minutes. When cool give one wineglassful every three hours. Remember this—the body allowed the stone to form—by reversing the type of nutrition and by use of certain herbs the same stone can be dissolved !

Hot fomentation applied to the main area of pain brings relief.

Epsom salts (originally found naturally in the water supply of Epsom (which means the 'hame' or home of the Saxon King Ebba) and since found elsewhere) bring some relaxation of the pain, but one dose is usually enough. *Do not use any purging medicines.*

Lemon juice and olive oil should be taken alternately, one a few minutes after the other; if you take the oil first—a tablespoonful, the lemon juice will take away the taste of it. Repeat the dose every quarter of an hour until about six or eight ounces of oil and the juice of several lemons has been consumed.

Herbal recipe: 1½ oz. powdered bitter root (*apocynum androsaemifolium*), 2 oz. powdered poplar bark, 2 oz. powdered golden seal, ½ oz. powdered black root (*leptandra virginica*), ½ oz. powdered cayenne pepper. Mix the five different powders together and then give enough to go on a saltspoon every three hours for the first day, and every six hours on the following three days.

GASTRITIS.   *See* the entry under DYSPEPSIA, and treat the same.

GIDDINESS.   *See* the entry under ANAEMIA.

Lily of the Valley. Place one stalk of flowers in a pint of boiling water; take a wineglassful when desired, and one more the night and morning of the next day.

Rosemary tea is very helpful. Half ounce to one pint boiling water.

Lemon juice and honey is very restorative.

Beetroot juice has also been found of some value.

GLANDULAR TROUBLES

Not always easy to diagnose what is really happening but for first aid you can use the following :

Dandelion tea. One ounce to one pint boiling water, drink as much as desired, sweeten the drink with a little honey.

Mullein tea. One ounce to one pint boiling water. Put some hot on a handkerchief and apply to the swollen glands, and drink a wineglassful every hour.

Nettle tea. One ounce to one pint boiling water. Drink half a teacupful every hour. Sweeten with brown sugar or honey. *Rue* is a plant which was especially favoured and blessed by the prophet Mahomet; only in recent times have chemists discovered that it possesses remarkable properties of healing a very large number of diseases affecting the heart, circulation and the glands. It is very powerful. Half ounce (not more) to one pint of boiling water, simmer for three to five minutes. When cool administer half-a-wineglassful every three hours.

Violet leaves plucked fresh and washed carefully under the tap are helpful; *eat four to six leaves only,* twice a day.

Glands swell up to hold back toxins from entering further into the body, try to help them win their fight, not weaken them. Cut out most of your carbohydrates, go on to fresh green salads, fruits, etc.

Lemon juice and orange juice are very helpful, so are *grapes.*

GOITRE

Swelling of the thyroid gland, visible in the neck, often affects the eyes, giving them a bulging-out appearance.

Horsetail grass tea one ounce to one pint boiling water. Drink a wineglassful every three hours.

Colloidal iodine is obtainable from most chemists, rub a little into the swelling round the throat every night before retiring.

Seafood is essential. In Iceland fresh, raw fish is eaten for this condition. *Kelp tablets* are advised.

Runner beans contain iodine as does *agar-agar;* eat plenty of them.

Garlic, chew one clove a day slowly.

GOUT. *See* the entry under ARTHRITIS.

Consult my book *How to Defeat Rheumatism and Arthritis* which deals with Gout in full detail.

Herbal recipe: 1 oz. broom tops, 1 oz. juniper berries, 1 oz. buchu, 1 oz. parsley piert. Mix the herbs and put them into one quart of boiling water, simmer the whole down to one pint. When cool give one wineglassful every three hours.

Celery leaf is very helpful, so often this is wasted and only the stalks eaten, this is quite wrong; the leaves help gouty patients.

Uva ursi tea is often a great relief. One oz. to one pint.

Alcohol and meat must be cut out of the patient's diet; meat can be given later, but as for alcohol only a nettle beer or dandelion wine would be permissible.

Pears should form part of the daily diet for gouty patients.

Tansy tea is an old gypsy remedy for gout. One oz. to one pint.

GUMS

For gumboils and for ulcerated gums and inflammations of one kind or another the following recipes will be found most helpful. A word of advice: **Take care of your gums and your teeth will take care of themselves.**

Sage tea—from half-ounce to one ounce to one pint of boiling water. Use when warm as a drink, and when cool as a mouthwash, very effective.

Constipation must be cleared up, see the appropriate entry in this book.

Lemon juice should be used to massage on to the gums every night and morning. Take plenty of natural lemonade made with fresh lemons and honey.

Tormentil root should be simmered for an hour and used as a mouthwash, it is very helpful especially where there is bleeding from the gums.

Scurvy grass can be boiled for 10 to 15 minutes in a pint of water, when cool it is an outstandingly good mouthwash.

Buckbean leaves should be washed and chewed as long as possible : the juice has a purgative effect compared to none, so it is best to spit it out rather than swallow it.

Marigold tea is very beneficial. One ounce flowers to one pint boiling water. *Golden seal* can be used if no marigolds are available. One ounce to one pint.

Gingivitis and pyorrhoea can be treated with a wash of eucalyptus oil into which two or three drops of clove oil have been poured. Rinsing the mouth out with lemon juice every hour is also very good, otherwise witch-hazel can be used. Visit your dentist as soon as possible, but try to clear up the condition first.

Fruit and salad diets are essential, but lightly boiled fish, chicken and lean meat are permissible. No sweets, no cakes and pastries, no white bread, no white sugar.

Black molasses should be taken at least a dessertspoonful twice a day.

HAIR

Blonde hair needs a chamomile shampoo. *Dark hair* needs an elderberry wash. *Reddish/ginger hair* needs a henna wash.

The condition of your hair is a very good sign of the health of your body, if you are out of sorts it will show on your hair. *Silica* deficiency is a common cause of falling hair.

Nettle juice invigorates the scalp very well.

Sage tea, one ounce to one pint, makes a good hair lotion.

Rosemary and thyme mixed together in equal parts in a pint of water so that the total herbs come to one ounce to one pint of water. Can be used to apply morning and night to refresh and strengthen the hair follicles.

Greying hair is often a sign of serious copper and iron deficiency. Visit a professional dietician or herbalist. Prunes, radishes, onions, lentils, raspberries and rye bread should be included in the diet.

HAYFEVER

The pharmaceutical industry has made a very big thing of the allergies which go to create Hayfever, but we must first ask ourselves : *What is wrong with my body to allow this allergy to act?*

Elecampane tea, made one ounce to one pint boiling water, can be drunk, half a wineglassful every four hours. While some of it is still hot it can also be used as a vapour inhalation, taken while the patient covers the head with a thick towel draped also around the basin holding the steaming herbal tea.

Try large doses of vitamin A.

Mignonette can also be used to make a tea, it is a small, pretty plant but one that has remarkable curative properties. One ounce to one pint boiling water. Drink one wineglassful every four hours.

HEADACHES

These are not usually an illness but just a serious symptom that something is wrong with the body and your diet.

Chamomile tea is a good standby, a little marjoram can be added. Half ounce to a pint of boiling water. Drink as much as desired.

Limeflowers are much used in Germany and Switzerland for nervous headaches, they call it *Lindentee*; I recommend one ounce to one pint boiling water.

Elderflowers can be used in the same proportion instead of lime-flowers.

Ground ivy has also been used for the same sickness; same portions. Most of these teas can be drunk half a cupful at a time, but it is often easier to make the tea half strength ($\frac{1}{2}$ oz.) and drink a full cup or two when thirsty.

Lavender water or *eau de Cologne* applied to the temples helps.

Liver trouble is often first indicated by repeated headaches.

Make a pot of *Indian tea* and put in two or three cloves; it brings a noticeable relief.

HEARTBURN.   *See* the entry under DYSPEPSIA.

HEART TRANSPLANTS

During the 1967–68 period, out of 21 cases 10 survived an average 5·8 days; five survived 4·2 hours, six lived slightly longer. These figures cover S. Africa, U.S.A., and other countries.

Heart diseases were first described by Marie in 1896 and clinically recognised by Herrick in 1912. Heart disease is frequently concommitant to diabetes, bladder and gall-disease, ulcers and high blood pressure. Obesity and heavy smoking are bad for cardiac conditions.

The Californian San Diego Heart Centre has established that gentle but increasingly active physical exercise is good for heart patients. To blame a high fat diet is not always fair : the Eskimos eat a very high fat diet, but match this with mineral-rich marine foods which are full of unsaturated fatty acids.

A substance called *rutin* is found in elder flowers, forsythia, violets and buckwheat. This is very effective when mixed with yerba maté. Herbalists have long used it for *high blood pressure, varicose veins, atherosclerosis* and for *haemorrhage of the retina*. All the above conditions require vitamins B^{12}, C, K and P. Calcium, iron, magnesium and potassium are essential in the diet as are adequate proteins and plenty of chlorophyll foods.

HEART TROUBLES

Many heart weaknesses are caused by psychosomatic things, and a visit to an analyst or a minister or priest may do a lot more good than a great deal of medication.

Roses are very good for heart patients, and their room should have these flowers in them as much as possible. Rose-petal jam is also very good for the patients, it is a Bulgarian speciality, but is nowadays exported to most countries and easily obtainable.

Motherwort tea is an uncommon blessing for sufferers. One ounce to one pint.

Hawthorn leaf tea is my own favourite recipe. Take two teaspoonfuls of dried hawthorn leaves, cover with a pint of boiling water—in a teapot, cover up, allow to draw, and then drink instead of ordinary Indian tea; milk and brown sugar or honey are permitted.

Camphor may be sniffed to restore a patient who is feeling very bad.

Watercress and parsley should figure prominently in the diet.

Holy thistle is a herb which is specific for heart cases. A tea made from it, one ounce to one pint of boiling water. Drink half a cupful every four hours.

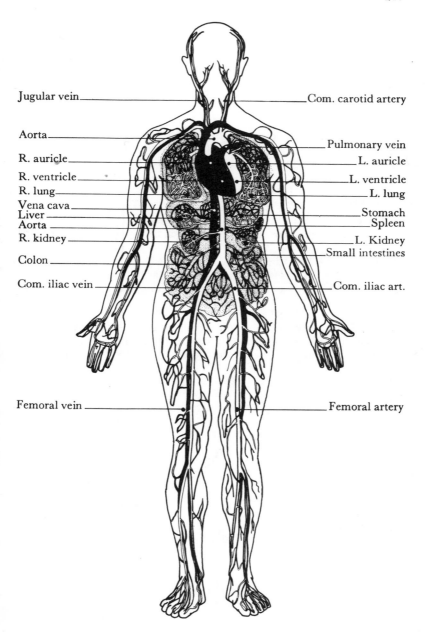

Jugular vein

Aorta

R. auricle

R. ventricle

R. lung

Vena cava

Liver

Aorta

R. kidney

Colon

Com. iliac vein

Femoral vein

Com. carotid artery

Pulmonary vein

L. auricle

L. ventricle

L. lung

Stomach

Spleen

L. Kidney

Small intestines

Com. iliac art.

Femoral artery

COURSE OF THE CIRCULATION OF THE BLOOD

Breathing exercises and fresh air are essential to heart sufferers. *The heart* is the strongest muscle of the body; even when damaged, with reasonable care and common sense, it will regain its efficiency.

Cholesterol is the biggest enemy the heart has; avoid fats and all foods which increase the cholesterol of your body, particularly animal fat foods.

Do seek professional advice.

HICCOUGHS

Hold the right hand above the head and press the thumb tightly against the middle finger tip and hold the position until the hiccoughs stop—it works! I learnt the remedy from a Flemish friend many years ago.

Herbal recipe: 1 oz. powdered rhubarb, ¼ oz. powdered cinnamon. Mix well, take one teaspoonful with honey.

Chew mint leaves.

Apple cider vinegar taken with a pinch of raw brown sugar helps.

HOARSE THROAT

Use *sage tea* or *apple cider vinegar* as a gargle.

Yarrow tea. One ounce to one pint boiling water is very helpful.

HOUSEHOLD PESTS

Ants : Soak a sponge in water, wring it out gently, then sprinkle liberally with sugar. Leave it where the ants appear. When it is covered by ants plunge it into a bucket of boiling water. Ants detest wormwood.

Beetles : Detest cucumber peel.

Crickets : Detest cucumber in any form.

Flies : Get a sundew plant in the house. This flower will make a meal of them, and reward you by brightening up your rooms. The sundew (*Drosera Rotundifolia*) is stocked by many florists. Flies can also be trapped by a mixture of black pepper, sugar and water.

Insects generally detest pennyroyal or oil of peppermint.

Mice : Rarely venture where oil of peppermint has been sprinkled.

Moths : Have a fear of camphor, cedarwood or even sawdust made of cedar.

Spiders : Dislike pennyroyal.

Quassia chips can be boiled in water. The mixture can then be sprayed on your rose bushes to keep them free of insects.

HYDROPHOBIA

If the patient can stand it a sauna bath (100° C.) is recommended. Steam baths are also helpful. If no professional aid is available, try :

Herbal recipe: ¼ oz. cayenne pepper, 1 oz. skullcap, ¼ oz. rhubarb powder. Mix the ingredients and add to one pint of boiling water;

when it has simmered for ten minutes, remove and before cooling ¼ oz. tincture of myrrh. Administer one dessertspoonful every hour.

Onion poultices made of freshly-cut onions can be bound on to the point of initial infection.

Garlic or onions can be chewed.

Chickweed tea is very good, and after it has been made the boiled leaves can be applied as a poultice.

HYSTERIA

Keep calm yourself, however great the strain.

Chamomile tea, valerian tea, limeflower tea. Any of these teas can be given. One ounce to one pint of boiling water. Half a cupful at a time, more if desired.

St. John's Wort tea is very valuable. One ounce to one pint of boiling water.

INDIGESTION. *See* the entry under DYSPEPSIA.

INFLUENZA. *See* 'FLU.

INSECTS. *See* the entries under FLEAS and FLIES.

INSECT BITES

Apply any one of the following remedies :
Onion juice from freshly-cut onions.

Pennyroyal or *buckshorn plantain juice.*

Wasp bites respond to *lemon juice or apple cider vinegar.*

Bee stings. Apply sal volatile or bicarbonate of soda, then dock or plantain leaves.

Mosquitoes and gnats. Apply Feverfew juice.

INSOMNIA

Do not take sleeping pills, too many accidents occur.

Honey in hot milk with a pinch of nutmeg or cinnamon is a very good nightcap.

Garlic, just a pinch of it, will help you sleep; in the south of Calabria they rub it on the feet to help sleep. I do not know the origin or the logic of it, but Italians say it works.

Hops put into the pillow case are said to aid peaceful sleep.
An old Frisian proverb says :

> 'Hest du din Dagwerk richtig dan
> da kommt de Slap von sülvst heran.'

(If you have done your day's work well sleep comes easily enough).
Mustard baths for the feet help you sleep.

INWARD BLEEDING
Send for professional advice.

Comfrey tea drunk cold is helpful; one ounce to one pint.

Iceland moss. Take one handful of the moss, soak in a pint of warm water. Administer cold. No hot drinks allowed.

JAUNDICE
Indicated by the yellowing of the skin and the white parts of the eyes. The urine turns a dirty dark brown. Tongue furred, appetite falls off, sickness experienced and malaise.

Asparagus should form a frequent item of diet.

Agrimony tea, one ounce to one pint of boiling water. Drink as required.

Cinquefoil, one ounce to one pint. One wineglassful every two hours.

St. John's Wort, one ounce to one pint. One wineglassful every three hours.

Lemon juice should be administered frequently.

Kelp in any form is helpful.

Apple cider vinegar in water is often very beneficial.

Salads and fruit should form a large part of the diet.

KIDNEY COMPLAINTS
Although there are many different kinds, I think we can lump them together insofar as the ordinary mother and housewife can do anything to bring relief. **Seek professional advice.**

Pains in the back, in the thighs, difficulty in urinating, turbid urine, headaches, etc., are symptoms that something is wrong with the kidneys. Wasting away, loss of weight and dropsy (*see* the entry in this book) are often further symptoms of kidney ailments. **Cut out meat** from the daily diet until there is some alleviation of the symptoms, then a little may be taken. Boiled fish or lightly boiled chicken may be taken.

Fruit and salad diets are essential.

Sugar and sweets must be avoided.

A valuable herbal recipe: 1 oz. burdock seed, 1 oz. dandelion, 1 oz. marshmallow root, 1 oz. tansy, 1 oz. uva ursi. Mix the herbs well, put them into $\frac{1}{2}$ gallon boiling water; simmer until slightly more than half remains. When cool administer a wineglassful every two hours the first day and every three hours on succeeding days.

Buchu, a useful herb from South Africa, is very helpful for many kidney ailments. A tea made of one ounce to one pint boiling water; one wineglassful when required.

Parsley piert makes another valuable herbal tea. One ounce to a pint.

Watercress should be eaten frequently; *parsley* often.

Carrots and celery should be taken chopped and raw in salads very often.

Constipation must be avoided, see the entry in this book.

Lemon juice and orange juice should be made freely available.

Grapes are a valuable item of the sufferer's diet.

Gypsy recipe: Nettles (a handful), tansy (a handful). Put into about a quart of boiling water, leave for ten minutes. Strain and drink when the liquid is cool, a cupful at a time.

St. John's Wort tea. One ounce to one pint boiling water. Half a cupful at a time, three or four times a day.

Runner beans lightly boiled are very beneficial and soothing.

Dandelion, broom top, fumitory and ground ivy can all be used to make teas for sufferers of kidney complaints; except the broom tops ($\frac{1}{2}$ oz.) all the others are used at one ounce to a pint of boiling water.

KNEE (HOUSEMAID'S)
It can happen to elbows too. *Rest* is essential. Don't fight it or you'll really land in trouble—if not in hospital.

Witch-hazel soaked cloths can be applied to the suffering joint.

Constipation must be eradicated, it is nearly always present.

Dieting must be strict, watch the carbohydrates, try to keep to fruit and salads, more protein foods are needed.

Silica foods, listed under the entry CHILBLAINS, must be taken.

LARYNGITIS
Inflammation of the throat. Huskiness of voice—even temporary loss of voice, pain in swallowing, difficulty in breathing. Expectoration of vast quantities of matter. Occasionally laryngitis that will not heal up may be symptomatic of tuberculosis or of syphilis, but never panic!

Apple cider vinegar or *malt vinegar.* Use either of these to soak a handkerchief and pack it externally round the throat; use a loose but sufficiently firm bandage.

Lemon juice can be taken as often as the patient can drink it, mix with a little honey. *Spray the throat* with lemon juice, it relieves the tension and aids better breathing.

Herbal gargle: One teaspoonful cayenne, two teaspoonfuls salt, two teaspoonfuls vinegar (any vinegar). Add this to half a pint of warm water and use a wineglassful at a time to gargle with, make sure that you convey the liquid to the back of the throat.

Constipation is often present and must be cleared urgently; see the entry under this heading in this book.

Garlic cloves chewed one every two hours works wonders in clearing up this dangerous and unpleasant condition.

Raw onions or leeks may be chewed, but they are not so quickly effective as the garlic.

Sage tea with honey should replace ordinary drinks; *nettle or yarrow* teas can also be mixed with a little *thyme*; in general, whatever the mixture, make one ounce of herb up with one pint of boiling water, and cover over in the teapot, leave to draw and cool before use.

Fruit, salads and protein must form the major part of the diet. Cut out starches and sugary foods, alcohol and tobacco, etc.

Salt-water gargles are very effective, and each one should be followed by a drink of lemon juice or orange juice.

Slippery elm mixed with one teaspoonful of cayenne pepper to three of slippery elm, with a little honey and four or five teaspoonfuls of warm water added (mix it into a thick paste) should be swallowed every morning and evening—before breakfast and after supper.

LEPROSY

This is a disease not usually found among Europeans but *a very infectious one*. You must send for professional advice. The most effective medicine in the world is a herbal substance which is greatly prized and valued : *Chaulmoogra oil (gynocardia odorata)*. Of similar value is the oil of *Hydnocarpus Wightiana*; both of these grow in the Far East : they are normally available only to medical practitioners.

First aid would consist of applying a poultice of *oil of bay (laurus nobilis)* mixed with oatmeal to the sores. Every dressing should be scraped off with a piece of wood; that and the dressing must be burnt immediately.

Do not try to treat the illness yourself—only apply aid until professional help arrives.

See section TROPICAL HERBS.

LEUCORRHOEA

A white, catarrhal pus follows the menstrual flow. Pain is often felt in the lower back. Weariness is often present. *Douche* with cold water into which one dessertspoonful of witch-hazel (per pint) has been added. *Sexual intercourse* should be avoided until the condition has cleared.

Old herbal recipe: 1 oz. cinnamon, 1oz. *euonymus atropurpureus, 2 oz. *aletris farinosa, 1 oz. golden seal, 2 oz. castalia odorata. Mix herbs, put them into ½ gallon boiling water; simmer until only one quart remains. Add honey to taste, drink one wineglassful every three hours. If the items marked with an asterisk are difficult to procure (mostly coming from U.S.A. or Canada) leave them out and substitute one ounce of fluid extract of echinacea, and one ounce of tincture of myrrh.

Tonics such as sage tea, thyme tea, dandelion coffee or tea, and nettle tea (all one ounce to one pint) are to be recommended.

Fruit, salad and high protein diet are also recommended.

LIFESPAN
Average lifespans are as follows :

Giant tortoise	300	years
Pike	250	years
Elephants	150	years
Crocodiles	100	years
Man	64	years
Horse	30	years
Dogs	12	years
Cats	10	years

LINEN
Linen is always nicer when scented by laying sachets of herbs in the linen-cupboard—lavender, rosemary, rose petals, thyme, etc. Just sew little net bags—about as big as your hand—and fill them with dry herbs, sew up the mouth of the bag, and it is ready to use.

LIPS CRACKED
Apply cold marigold tea. Marshmallow ointment or chickweed ointment. Butter can be used in an emergency.

LIVER COMPLAINTS.   *See* the entry under JAUNDICE, you can apply the therapeutic suggestions made there.

Carbohydrates (sugars, fats, starches) must be reduced. *Salads and fruit and high protein diet* followed.

Exercise is essential for liverish patients.

Apple cider vinegar with a very little honey; say a dessertspoonful of vinegar, half a teaspoonful of honey to one cupful of warm water. Repeat this dose every three to four hours.

Lemon juice to be taken as often as required.

Tansy tea is one of my first and best treatments. One ounce to one pint.

St. John's Wort can also be used, in the same proportions.

Valuable herbal recipe: 1 oz. agrimony, 1 oz. dandelion, 1 oz. wood betony. Mix the herbs and add to one quart of boiling water; simmer for fifteen minutes. When cooled down give one wineglassful every three hours.

LUMBAGO
This is too complicated to give full details here, and the reader should consult my work *How to Defeat Rheumatism and Arthritis*; this is one of the rheumatic diseases.

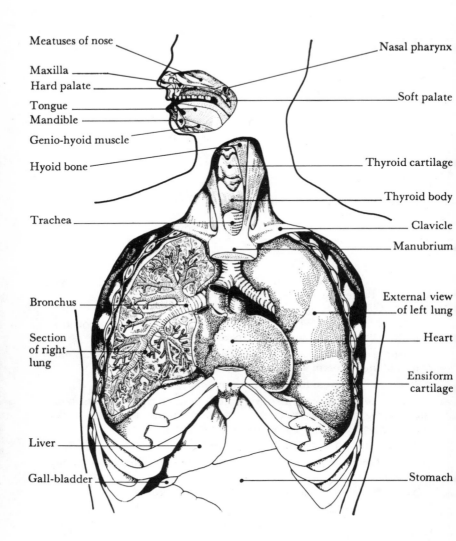

THE RESPIRATORY TRACT

Uva ursi tea brings some relief : one ounce to one quart of boiling water. Drink half a cupful every three hours.

Watercress should be included frequently in the diet.

LUNG COMPLAINTS

These can be very serious and professional advice must be sought. Treat these only until help comes; the suggested recipe can be continued throughout. Herbal treatment never conflicts with any other form of healing, it is nutritive and strengthening.

Raspberry leaf tea with a teaspoonful of cayenne pepper added can be drunk every four hours : use one ounce of leaves to one pint.

Garlic cloves should be chewed at the rate of one every two hours.

Onions can be used if garlic is not available. Spread freshly-cut onion slices around the patient's bed, they ward off the spread of infection, as research at Russian universities has shown.

Useful herbal recipe: 1 oz. coltsfoot, 1 oz. marshmallow, 1 oz. slippery elm bark, $\frac{1}{2}$ oz. thyme. Mix the herbs, put them into three pints of boiling water, then simmer until roughly one pint has evaporated. Give one wineglassful an hour.

Daily baths are recommenled. Keep the patient's feet warm. *Fresh air* is essential.

Fruit, salad and high protein diet. Plenty of halibut liver oil.

LYMPHATIC GLAND DISTURBANCES.   *See* the entry GLANDULAR TROUBLES.

MALARIA

Fever, pains, shivering fits, etc. Seek professional advice.

Pure lemon juice should be given with honey as often as the patient can drink it conveniently.

Herbal recipe: 1 oz. boneset, 1 oz. Peruvian bark chips, $\frac{1}{2}$ oz. quassia chips, 1 oz. sage, 1 oz. skullcap, 2 oz. yarrow. Mix the herbs and add them to three pints of water; simmer for 15 minutes. When cool administer a wineglassful every two hours.

Sage tea should replace ordinary tea and coffee.

MALIGNANT THROAT ULCER

A very severe form of throat disease. Seek professional aid.

Sauna baths or steam baths may be recommended. *Gargle* with wood sanicle tea—one ounce to a pint.

Salt water. Using two dessertspoonfuls of salt to a pint of warm water brings some relief.

Garlic is an essential for this condition. Eat one raw clove slowly every hour, after three hours or four considerable relief should be experienced.

Onions with a pinch of cinnamon are very helpful; they can be served warm, but not boiled, just slightly cooked, so that they are still crisp in shape and not limp.

Honey and cinnamon administered in water, well spiked with the juice of half a lemon, should be served frequently.

Lemon juice should be sprayed down the throat of the patient, especially on the tonsils.

Useful herbal recipe: 1 oz. blackberry leaves, 1 oz. cudweed, 1 oz. golden seal, 1 oz. yarrow. Mix the herbs, add them to three pints of boiling water; simmer for twenty minutes; when cool give one wineglassful every three hours.

Note : A pinch of cayenne pepper and tincture of myrrh can be added for very severe cases.

MEASLES

Keep your patient in a warm but well-aired atmosphere. Wash the patient with a mixture of apple cider vinegar and water.

Send for professional advice if available.

Salad, fruit and *high protein diet* is recommended.

Beetroot leaves make a useful body wash, mixed with warm water.

Peawater is used in Germany to wash down chicken-pox patients; it could also be tried with measles; when you boil the peas for lunch, keep the water for your patient.

Pleasant herbal recipe: 1 oz. balm melissa, 1 oz. elder flowers, 1 oz. marigold flowers, ½ oz. peppermint. Mix the herbs, add them to one quart of water; simmer for 15 minutes. When cool give the patient a wineglassful every two hours.

Alternative recipe: 1 oz. agrimony, ½ oz. clover heads (red), 1 oz. ground ivy, ½ oz. peppermint, 1 oz. raspberry leaves. Mix the herbs, put them into one quart of boiling water; simmer for 15 minutes. When cool give the patient a wineglassful every three hours.

Citrus fruit juice can be given as often as the patient likes.

Grapes—and only grapes eaten for *one day*—do a good deal to pull a patient round; the fruit is very rich in mineral salts. Do not extend the grape diet for more than one day.

MENOPAUSE

Do not panic, this is a natural process. Keep up a well-balanced diet, take plenty of exercise, and do not forget to investigate how many of the 'pains' are projections of little fears and worries you are thinking up for yourself. Your husband will *not* stop loving you; you are not becoming senile : there is a great relief in the fact that you need no longer bear children; at this age they would be too exhausting for you to cope with; try to look on the positive side, and do not let yourself become introspective. If you have problems go and see a priest, an analyst, or one or two good friends.

A tea can be made of an American plant called Cohosh, or in Latin (for ordering it from a supplier) *caulophyllum thalictroides*. Dr. Alva Curtis assures us that the herb is quite safe to eat. 'I handled it and ate it in my boyhood enough to know that it is not a poison. I therefore invite my friends in the practice to try a tea of the root in the cases above mentioned. . . .'

Indian women used it to make childbirth easier. It is said to relieve all sorts of spasms and lessen sudden pains. From a half ounce to a whole ounce to one pint of water; if you haven't used it before start with a half ounce. One wineglassful night and morning when required.

Pennyroyal tea is another great help, and easy to come by. One ounce to a pint.

Tansy tea was a favourite gypsy remedy for menopause flushes. One ounce to a pint.

MENSTRUATION—EXCESSIVE

Indicates that the body is trying to rid itself of an accumulation of toxins. See the entry for Leucorrhoea and follow the treatments suggested there.

Silverweed tea, one ounce to one pint, is very helpful; take it lukewarm, drinking a wineglassful whenever required. During a bad session a glassful every two hours will help.

Raspberry-leaf tea is also a help, use the same proportions as for the above tea.

Pleasant herbal remedy: 2 oz. comfrey, 1 oz. quassia chips, 1 oz. tansy. Mix the herbs and add them to one quart of boiling water; simmer until about a quarter of the liquid has steamed off. Allow to cool and administer one wineglassful every three hours.

Lady's mantle can be chewed up; put a few leaves with a salad of fresh green vegetables, chopped carrots, apples etc.

Mugwort grows all over the temperate zone countries. It is often a neglected, although beautiful plant; I have dealt at length on the astonishing virtues and medicinal properties of this herb in my book *Herb Growing for Health*. It is one of the finest teas which any woman with menstual difficulties of any kind can use. One takes one ounce of the dried leaves and puts them in the teapot, covering them with a little more than a pint of boiling water, add a little honey—and you have a very valuable therapeutical agent in your hands—drink from half a cup to a whole cupful when it is cool enough to enjoy. Some old herbalists used it successfully against some tumours, but what sort they did not specify.

A powerful herbal recipe: 1 oz. bistort, 1 oz. cranesbill, 1 oz. cudweed, 1 oz. raspberry leaves, 1 oz. tormentil. Mix the herbs; add them to $\frac{1}{2}$ gallon boiling water; simmer this until nearly a pint has evaporated. When cool give one wineglassful three times daily.

Constipation must be avoided. *See* the appropriate entry.

MENSTRUAL PAD SUBSTITUTE

In earlier times sphagnum moss, kapok or milkweed floss were used.

MENSTRUATION—PAINFUL

Fennel tea is an ideal treatment to start with, it is so pleasant to taste, being a cross between peppermint and liquorice; one half ounce to one pint makes a strong tea. Do not sweeten before tasting or you may swamp the taste : honey, not sugar, please. *Another herbal tea* made of ½ oz. pennyroyal, and ½ oz. tansy, to one pint of boiling water will often solve the patient's problems quite easily.

Difficult cases are advised to sit over a bowl of steaming tansy or yarrow herb tea, or a mixture of both. An old-fashioned remedy, but thoroughly recommended down the ages. These olden remedies from bygone ages may not appear very elegant, but they do not produce any queer, frightening side-effects like many of the antibiotic and sulfa drugs which are in common use.

Useful herbal drink: 1 oz. catmint, 1 oz. germander speedwell, 1 oz. pennyroyal, 1 oz. southerwood, 1 oz. tansy. Mix the herbs, put them into three pints of boiling water, simmer for 10 to 15 minutes slowly; when cool give one wineglassful every three hours.

Safflower seeds—quarter ounce to one pint of boiling water, cover teapot up and allow to draw. Drink a wineglassful every five hours.

Chamomile tea can be used the same way as the above tea, but one ounce of flowers would be used to one pint.

MIGRAINE

This is partly psychosomatic and nearly always associated with some Liver complaints, see the entry in this book accordingly and clear up the liver complaint first of all. *See also* entries on HEAD-ACHES and CONSTIPATION.

MILK FLOW FOR MOTHERS

This can be helped by the use of some very simple well-tried herbal remedies.

Dill, widely used by Swedish women all throughout the rolling countryside of Central Varmland, Kopparberg and Jämtland. Take about an ounce to a pint of boiling water, make and use just like an ordinary tea, drink half a cupful a time, three times a day.

Fenugreek seeds are used to make a tea; it is thought that this was a herb used by the ladies of Ancient Rome for this purpose. Its use goes back to antiquity. One ounce to one pint suffices. Drink one wineglassful every four hours.

Holy thistle, about half an ounce in a pint of boiling water—the tops and youngest leaves are used.

MORNING SICKNESS

Be more careful of the diet you are taking. This is usually a sign that the diet is wrong; too short of mineral salts, vitamins, trace elements, too short of proteins especially. Get a professional dietician or herbalist to help you. Basically you need more fruit and salad foods every day.

Watercress and parsley should be taken as often as you can get them.

Lemon juice allays the unpleasantness.

Apple cider vinegar mixed with a dessertspoonful of honey in a little warm water is an excellent restorative; use from one to two dessertspoonfuls of the vinegar.

MOUTHWASHES

Can be made of salt and water; apple cider vinegar and water; sage tea (cold); lemon juice with or without water; eucalyptus and water or one or two *drops* of oil of cloves with water. Try 5 drops of myrrh tincture mixed with eucalyptus and water.

MUMPS

Fatigue, feverishness, sore throat, parotoid glands and sub-maxillary glands swell, temperature rises. *Highly infectious.*

Bed rest essential. **Seek professional advice.**

Constipation must be avoided, see the entry on this subject.

Flannel can be torn into strips, warmed and placed against the painfully swollen glands.

Pleasant herbal recipe: 1 oz. chamomile flowers, 1 oz. marshmallow. Mix and put into a tea pot, pour a little over a pint of boiling water, leave to draw; when cooled, give half a cupful with a tiny pinch of nutmeg, cinnamon or ginger and a dash of lemon and honey. Every hour if patient is thirsty.

See the entry GLANDULAR TROUBLES in this book.

Cudweed leaves can be used to make a decoction, part of which can be drunk as a cold tea, the other part can be painted over the swollen glands. I recommended it first in my work *Herbs for Cooking and Healing.*

MUSCULAR PAINS, ACHES, SPRAINS

Tired muscles: Rub with oil of comphor or with a clove of garlic.

Sprains: Witch-hazel is marvellous, use it freely.

Aches: Firstly a good bath, a sauna if possible—the finest cure for all muscular discomforts. Then a rub down with a good towel and a light massage with olive oil, spread very thinly.

NAILS

When they are brittle or in bad condition they are a useful indication that the general health is breaking down—never neglect this warning. All serious illnesses come about because we neglect the first indications that our health is not in good order. Attend to the smallest symptoms promptly and you will avoid worse consequences. A mineral-salt enriched diet is essential to increase the salad and fruit diet; by the way, avoid salad creams and mayonnaise when you take salads, they are mostly indigestible. Do not cover your nails with chemicals to make them look prettier—just try to keep healthy and then they will, of their own accord, look their best.

NAPKIN (DIAPERS) SUBSTITUTE FOR BABIES
In olden times kapok, milkweed floss or sphagnum moss were used.

NARCOTICS.   *See* the heading under DRUG ADDICTS.

NASAL CATARRH.   *See* the entry CATARRH.

NAUSEA
Peppermint tea, unsweetened, is a good standby for sickness. Tansy tea also helps, do not use sweetening with it. Both teas would be made with ½ oz. herb to one pint boiling water.

Apple cider vinegar, a dessertspoonful in cold water is helpful.

NEPHRITIS
This is a kidney complaint as is *Nephrosis. See* the entry KIDNEY COMPLAINTS in this book.

NERVOUS COMPLAINTS
This covers a vast range of illnesses, most of which require professional advice, nevertheless there are some first-aid measures which a housewife and mother can take.

Balm melissa is your best friend; use just three teaspoonfuls for a teapot and pour over it a pint or a little more of boiling water, allow to draw a few minutes, pour out and drink as much as you feel like. Use only honey for sweetening please, milk may be added.

Basil and sage is another mixture in which you place your trust. One teaspoonful of basil, two of sage, pour on the boiling water, cover up the teapot, allow to draw, pour and drink as much as you fancy.

Heather and lavender. Two or three sprigs of fresh heather, one head of lavender. Make like the other teas described in this section. Drink as required. Brown sugar may be used to sweeten.

Clover and marjoram is a delightful tea with very soothing properties for the nerves. Take a heaped dessertspoonful of fresh red clover heads and a half teaspoonful of dried marjoram. Put into the teapot, pour on a pint or a little more of boiling water; allow to draw. Drink as much as you fancy, it is very beneficial.

Tansy and thyme can be prepared in exactly the same way as the above tea.

Valerian and rosemary is another similar tea.

NEURALGIA

This is a nervous pain associated with toothache, gout, rheumatism and even with some forms of anaemia. Check to find the cause and deal with that. *Bathe* the area where there is most pain with warm water. *Apply* a poultice of chamomile flowers warm to the area and bandage on loosely.

Banana peel can be used for a poultice, it appears to have some peculiarly beneficent properties of its own.

Hops make another poulticing agent. *Hops and valerian* tea bring considerable relief. A tablespoonful of hops and a teaspoonful of valerian, cover with a pint or more of boiling water; add sweetening, and drink as required.

Try some of the remedial teas listed under the entry NERVOUS COMPLAINTS.

Garlic can be rubbed gently over the area giving pain.

NETTLE RASH

Amusingly enough, the best remedy is nettle tea, made with four teaspoonfuls of nettles to one pint of boiling water, and served with honey. Drink as much as you like.

NEURASTHENIA AND NEURITIS

Related to an imbalance of mineral salts and vitamins. Attend to your diet, call in professional help if the condition persists. Try the remedies listed under NERVOUS COMPLAINTS, they are very effective.

NIGHTMARE

Chamomile tea, $\frac{1}{4}$ oz. to one pint served with honey and a pinch of cinnamon.

NIPPLES SORE

Either cold marigold tea or an ointment made of marigold flowers. Powdered gum acacia could be used, but I would normally recommend marigold wherever possible, it is a very safe herb, one of the finest natural antiseptics in the world.

NOSE BLEEDING

Put a cold key down the back of the neck, a little cotton wool lightly up the nose. It does not usually harm anybody to let the nose bleed freely for a few minutes, the blood often removes germs and impurities the body is desperately anxious to get rid of, so do not worry unless the bleeding goes on for more than five minutes. Do not try to stop it before three minutes are up. Lie on the side with some paper handkerchiefs to catch the blood, do not lie down on your back. Generally speaking, when this occurs frequently there is a very serious shortage of mineral salt balance in the blood.

Nettle juice held in the mouth usually stops nose bleeding quite quickly, the herb is very rich in mineral salts.

Nettle tea made half ounce to one pint of boiling water is advisable for all people who suffer frequently from nose bleeding.

NOSE POLYPI

These can occur only if the 'soil' is right for them. An unhealthy body allows any form of disease to happen, some more nuisance than others.

Constipation is often present, eliminate it by following the advice given under that heading in this book. One of the most highly valued herbal remedies is a coniferous plant which is native to Canada, but which will sometimes grow in parts of Europe, its leaves have remarkable medicinal properties, it is *Yellow Cedar* (*Thuja occidentalis*), and an extract made by soaking the tips of the leaves in pure alcohol (or brandy if this is not available) for two weeks can be used to paint on to polypi, warts or any similar fungoid development. At the same time treat the patient with the remedies given under the entry Catarrh, because this is invariably present in such cases.

Buttercup juice can also be used, paint it on carefully.

OBESITY

Too much is written about this by people who know too little. It reminds me of the rat in Kipling's story who found a single piece of Turmeric and shouted 'I will open a grocer's shop'. Firstly, do not be entranced by enthusiastic articles in newspapers and magazines, they are all-too-rarely written by professional dieticians or people without any medical background. Obesity occurs because there is a breakdown of the body's metabolism. Your body is receiving food, not using all of it properly, and for any one of a dozen reasons storing it in excess of all reasonable needs. There is no single cause for fatness, but much of what we call 'fat' is stored water. Clean out your bladder, your kidneys and your liver and you will be delighted to find how much more efficiently your body starts working. There is a lot of truth in the old adage that most people dig their graves with their teeth!

By cutting out all fats or all carbohydrates you will definitely make matters worse—so don't try that stupid gimmick, it is too dangerous. *Time* is what you need first, time to sit down and consider whether you are eating nutritional foods or mere 'filler' fodder to avert the feeling of hunger. It is amazing how many overweight people are constantly feeling hungry—why? Because they are starved of some particular minerals or vitamins which they simply do not get, or which are found in foods they do not 'like'. Seek expert advice. The following will help you to start off right :

No white bread, no white sugar, no pastries; no midday snacks, have proper meals at proper meal times, try to make sure that every meal is balanced with proteins, mineral salts, carbohydrates, roughage and vitamins.

Bladderwrack tea tastes terrible, but it does rid your body of excess fluids. Half ounce to one pint of boiling water, and do not try to sweeten it. Drink one wineglassful every three hours.

Nettle tea. One ounce to a pint is helpful, drink *half a cupful* every three hours.

In order to slim you need a lot more herbs in your cooking, and my work *Herbs for Cooking and Healing* will be found very helpful indeed.

Fennel and rosemary tea made of two teaspoonfuls of fennel and one of rosemary will provide a very satisfying substitute for the mid-morning cup of coffee. One pint of boiling water to the teapot.

Bay and dandelion tea is a mineral-rich substitute for the odd cups of tea with which we so often while away the afternoons; take one or two bay leaves, and two teaspoonfuls of dandelion herb, mix in the teapot, add a pint or more of water. Sweeten with honey. Drink as much as you want.

Watch your cooking fats. Take my tip and cook only with olive oil, sunflower seed oil or maize oil; they are less fattening than any other—especially so than animal fat oils.

OVERFEEDING

Don't ever force a child to stuff itself, allow the child's instincts to have some play. The child's metabolism may be quite different to your own. Watch the mineral and vitamin intake, don't fuss over quantity. The fewer sweets your child eats the healthier it will be, and the longer it will keep its own teeth. When the child wants a sweet give an apple, orange, grapes, dates, figs, dried bananas, etc. You'll help it more that way to live a good, normal, healthy life.

PAIN

Do not be in a hurry to rid yourself of pain. Sorry, but it is quite true. Many modern medicines promise you instant relief from pain, but all they do is to suppress the pain, to deaden the symptom. Pain is a symptom that something is wrong; by thinking carefully about it you can find out a great deal about what is wrong. Seek to remove the cause, then you will really heal.

PALPITATIONS OF THE HEART. *See* the entry HEART TROUBLES.

The following herbal treatments can also be recommended.

Old herbal recipe: 1 oz. centaury, 1 oz. dandelion, 1 oz. marigold, 1 oz. motherwort, 1 oz. mugwort. Mix the herbs, add then to three pints of boiling water; simmer slowly for 15 minutes. When cooled down give the patient a wineglassful three times daily.

Read the entries in this book for DYSPEPSIA and CONSTIPATION.

Chamomile and valerian tea makes a good standby remedy. Take two spoonfuls of each herb, pour a pint of boiling water over them, cover your teapot, and when it has had time to draw drink as much as you feel like. Sweeten only with a little honey or rough brown sugar.

PARALYSIS
It is the accepted opinion nowadays that little or nothing can be done for cases of paralysis. I believe this is because the lines of research are strictly limited, and the less known (unorthodox) avenues are never fully explored.

Ancient Greek physicians used to massage paralysed limbs with alternate rubs of olive oil and of rough wine (neither sweetened nor chemicalised, i.e. home-made wine of grapes); they claimed it was often successful, I have no experience of this but mention it in case it can help.

Apply some of the remedies listed under the heading NERVOUS COMPLAINTS.

Build up the general health of the patient, include plenty of olive oil and the herb basil in the diet. Seek advice from a chiropractic specialist, from a radiesthesia expert, from every source possible; try acupuncture, this ancient Chinese form of medicine has often succeeded where others have failed. Spiritual healing should also be tried. Never give up hope.

PHARYNGITIS. *See* the treatments listed under LARYNGITIS, this illness usually succumbs to the same treatments.
Garlic cloves chewed one every hour are very beneficial.

PILES
A worrying condition but it can be cured fairly quickly.

Garlic is the almost infallible remedy here. A peeled large clove should be inserted in the rectum just after passing motions, and left in until next time motions are passed, then a fresh one should be pushed up. The disinfectant, bactericidal and antiseptic value of this herb make it worthwhile any inconvenience.

Wash the affected area only with witch-hazel.

Lesser celandine, sometimes called pilewort, can be applied directly to the painful area—using the washed leaves and flowers.

Plantain juice can be painted on the rectal area if no witch-hazel is available; country people also used to drink a tea made of *Plantago major,* half ounce to one pint boiling water. Drink a wineglassful every four hours when the mixture has cooled down; this was held to be very efficacious against piles.

PIMPLES

Apply the treatments outlined under the head ACNE.

PLEURISY

Try some of the recipes listed under BRONCHITIS. This is basically an inflammation of the walls of the lungs.

If no professional aid is available try

Pleurisy root was the popular herbal remedy—one ounce of shredded root to one quart of boiling water; simmer this for 20 minutes. When cool give the patient a wineglassful every two hours; it can be flavoured with lemon, orange or grapefruit juice and honey.

Black molasses should be fed to the patient, a dessertspoonful every three hours for the first day, every six hours on succeeding days.

Salads and fruit are advisable, as much as the patient will eat.

Constipation must be cleared quickly; it is often present.

Old herbal recipe: ½ oz. cayenne pepper, 2 oz. raspberry leaves, 2 oz. yarrow. Mix the herbs, add to three pints boiling water; simmer for 30 minutes. When cool give the patient a wineglassful every two hours.

Keep your patient's feet warm; do not force to lie down if he/she can breathe more easily sitting up. While keeping the patient warm make sure that there is fresh air in the room.

Elder flowers make a very good tea, one ounce to one pint, give to the patient as often as he/she feels like a drink.

PNEUMONIA

Call in professional advice as quickly as possible.

Honey and lemon juice every half-hour, a dessertspoonful of honey to the juice of half a lemon.

Yarrow tea, one oz. to one pint. A wineglassful every hour.

Herbal recipe: 1 oz. boneset herb, 1 oz. mallow leaves, 1 oz. pleurisy root. Mix and add to quart of boiling water; simmer 15 minutes; when cool give with a pinch of cayenne—half a wineglassful every 30 minutes.

Slippery elm powder mixed with honey and a teaspoonful of cayenne pepper, and warm water. Use three dessertspoonfuls of slippery elm powder. Administer twice daily at six-hour intervals.

Constipation must be avoided at all costs, see the heading in this book.

Black horehound and wild cherry bark make a very beneficient drink; one ounce of each; two pints of water; simmer; when cool give the patient a wineglassful every four hours.

Cinnamon and lemon juice make a very effective gargle for pneumonia patients and bring much relief.

Delightful and helpful herbal recipe: 1 oz. agrimony, 1 oz. salad burnett, 1 oz. meadowsweet, 1 oz. raspberry leaves, 1 oz. wood betony. Mix the herbs and add them to one quart of boiling water; simmer for twenty minutes; when cool administer one wineglassful every hour. Sprinkle with cinnamon and a few drops of lemon-juice before serving.

Keep the sickroom well aired, but make sure the patient does not feel any chill.

Bathe the patient in warm water in which a tablespoonful of apple cider vinegar has been poured. Dry with paper tissues and burn these after use.

POISONING

Send for professional advice at once. First-aid and treatment depends greatly upon what type of poison has been taken.

Acids: Carbolic, hydrochloric, nitric sulphuric, etc. (found in industrial and household materials). Give magnesia or chalk, then olive oil (several spoonfuls) or milk. *Prussic acid, cyanide of potassium,* etc. Alternate hot and cold sponges applied to heart; apply artificial respiration, if possible induce vomiting. If ammonia is available allow the patient to inhale the fumes. Put your finger down the patient's throat to encourage quick vomiting.

Aconite: Give brandy, wash the stomach out with a drink of water in which one or two specks of permanganate of potassium have been dropped; do get help, this is a difficult thing to handle alone. Children sometimes suffer from this if they have not been disciplined about putting berries in their mouth, the berries of wolfsbane are often thought to be 'pretty'—pretty deadly!

Alcohol: Wash out the stomach; expect plenty of vomit, be prepared; alcohol destroys vitamin B like fury; as soon as there is some improvement feed the patient on toast (dry) and then yeast tablets; no sugar at all, no sweetening. Black coffee, not too strong, no sweetening, no milk.

Alkalies: Caustic soda, caustic potash, ammonia, etc. Give apple cider vinegar, or diluted malt vinegar, in water; lemon juice is good; afterwards a little olive oil or linseed oil.

Aniline dyes: Keep patient warm; artificial respiration; a little brandy.

Antimony: Very strong Indian tea (for its tannic acid), brandy: keep the patient warm; do send for help.

Arsenic: Emetics, castor oil, wash out the stomach with barley water.

Aspirin: Overdose. Coffee; bicarbonate of soda; tannic acid (heavy tea).

Barbiturates: Try to empty out the patient's stomach, send for help quickly.

Belladonna: Tannic acid, coffee or brandy in small doses, artificial respiration.

Benzine: Dilution by oil; evacuation of the bowels. If the poisoning has occurred by inhaling fumes give artificial respiration and stimulants.

Boric acid: Evacuate the bowls, give fluids.

Bromides: Coffee and salt.

Cannabis (marijuana): Evacuate the stomach. Send for an expert.

Chloral hydrate: Empty the stomach, apply warmth to the extremities; artificial respiration and massage.

Cocaine: Stimulants, artificial respiration; unless a doctor is called a fatality can easily follow.

Corrosive sublimate: Camphor inhalation, tannic acid (heavy tea), wash out the stomach with strong tea.

Creosote: Empty the stomach and give diluted alcohol.

Cyanide: Act quickly! Clean the stomach out with a few specks of permanganate of potassium—in a lot of water. The speed of a doctor's arrival is essential.

Digitalis: Evacuate the stomach; rest in bed; plenty of liquids, no food.

Ether: Wash out the stomach, give cold douches.

Formaldehyde: Give raw eggs.

Hypnotic drugs: Anything (such as dandelion tea) which encourages urination; try inhaling camphor.

Insulin: Orange juice and grape sugar.

Iodine: Empty the stomach, starch (flour).

Lead: Stomach emptied; Epsom salts; milk.

Mushrooms: Emetics; a doctor will probably inject dextrose. Try to keep the patient awake.

Opiates: Empty the stomach, keep the patient awake and walking; cold and hot alternate baths; a little coffee; external warmth and artificial respiration if needed.

Phosphorus: Wash out the stomach with a weak solution of permanganate of potassium in water, then liquid paraffin. Do see that medical help is hurried to the patient.

Ptomaine: This comes about from bad meat, fish, tinned food, etc. Emetics immediately; apple cider vinegar in water is very useful; later on castor oil.

Strychnine: Evacuate the stomach; give strong tea; artificial respiration.

Sulfa drugs: Plenty of fluids.

Turpentine: Emetics, then magnesium sulphate and milk.

PSORIASIS

Rough, reddish areas of skin, white or silvery scabs form; usually appearing at the back of the elbows or the knees. A sign of a general collapse in health; often indicative of a rheumatic disease developing. The cure is effected by attention to diet, rest, hygiene, plenty of fresh air and exercise.

Witch-hazel can be used to wash the sore places.

Slippery elm and honey taken with warm water first thing in the morning and last thing at night.

PYORRHOEA

Massage the gums frequently with the fingers using eucalyptus oil with a drop or two of oil of cloves; use witch-hazel as a frequent mouthwash. Biochemic salts help a lot, particularly cal. sulph.

QUINSY.   *See* the entry MALIGNANT THROAT ULCER.

RABIES.   *See* the entry HYDROPHOBIA.

RATS

Rats positively hate catnip. Hang it round the room. If possible plant it as close as possible to the walls of your house—especially near the kitchen.

RHEUMATISM

This is a very wide range of diseases too readily grouped under a collective name; even sciatica is a form of them. My book *How to Defeat Rheumatism and Arthritis* deals with the entire range of problems these diseases bring about, and offers a wide range of known, reliable remedies.

Nettle tea is a good emergency treatment, one ounce to a pint. *Nettles* can also be used fresh to massage into the limbs affected; yes, indeed, the cure does hurt, but nowhere near so much as does rheumatism in any form.

Herbal tea for first aid: 1 oz. broom tops, 1 oz. buchu, 1 oz. parsley piert, 1 oz. juniper berries, 1 oz. stinging nettles. Mix the herbs, put them into one quart of boiling water; simmer for 15 minutes; when cool give the patient one wineglassful three times a day (about four hours' interval).

Mustard and cayenne baths are very helpful, put a dessertspoonful of each into the bath water, it tones the skin up very well.

Massage affected limbs with a mixture of wintergreen and olive oil in equal parts, especially valuable before going to bed.

RICKETS
Vomiting, diarrhoea, sweating at night, restlessness, bronchial disturbances and occasionally convulsions indicate that a child may be suffering from this deficiency disease.

Beans, runner or broad, etc., very lightly cooked so that they are still firm and crisp to taste, should be in the daily diet.

Halibut liver oil must be given daily; the chemist or supplier will advise you how much, according to the age of the child.

Minerals and vitamins are best found among fruits, salads and in a high protein diet. Avoid sweets, pastries, and sugary things, most of which fill the child's belly and let it starve—there is a wide difference between fodder and food.

RINGWORM
Red patches on the skin, usually round scaly margins.

Iodine applied night and morning and at midday usually kills the infection off quite quickly.

Clothing must be washed in disinfectant, the infection is capable of staying through an ordinary wash and reinfecting the patient.

Lemon juice can be applied neat to the patches, every four hours.

Herb Robert juice or the juice of *Rue* can be applied directly to the itching patches, every four hours.

RUPTURE
If a rupture has just happened there are a number of things that an intelligent housewife can do to help. Firstly get the patient to lie flat and *relax* the stomach muscles, if the extrusion does not sink back, press it gently with the fingers, it will usually go back quite gratefully into its rightful place.

Secondly, apply poultices of the following herbs, any one will do :

Comfrey, two dessertspoonfuls of herb, soak in boiling water, remove after two or three minutes, allow to cool and then apply.

Rupturewort (herniara glabra), the same procedure.

Horsetail grass, the same procedure. Whichever herb you use bandage it on with a pad, pressing against the place where the rupture occurred; use a rolled-up handkerchief to make the pad.

Constipation and coughing must be avoided at all costs.

A rupture is essentially a collapse of the muscle fibres due to a severe mineral salt deficiency; if prompt action is taken the patient may find that the condition cures itself after a week in bed.

A tea of whichever herb is being used should also be made and drunk one wineglassful every three hours. One ounce to a pint. The patient can get up to go to the toilet, but should be taught to crouch native-fashion on the lavatory, not to sit—this strains the stomach muscles too much.

Gentle stomach exercises can be performed wholly in a reclining position after a week or so if the rupture does not protrude again.

SCALDS.   *See* the entry BURNS.

SCALP

All the conditions applying to diseases of the scalp are dealt with in my work *How to Keep Your Hair On*. However, for first-aid treatment try some of the following :

Rosemary tea, cold (one ounce to a pint boiling water), massage into scalp. Extract of rosemary in alcohol is even more effective.

Nettle juice is very good for invigorating the scalp; cases are known where hair has started growing again after its use.

Garlic rubbed on the scalp is very good for cleaning it up.

Apple cider vinegar rubbed in neat is very invigorating and cleansing. Because it is rich in mineral salts it strengthens the hair follicles; do not apply more than twice a week, water it down according to your estimate of your own needs.

SCARLET FEVER

Seek professional aid. A highly infectious condition. Take precautions to isolate your patient. Symptoms are usually shivering, sore throat, vomiting, increased pulse rate, occasionally convulsions. A rash appears within the first two days showing on arms, chest, neck, and eventually all over the body. Tonsils swell up, submaxillary glands swell up, scales form and there may be kidney trouble.

All the symptoms show that there are serious toxic substances which the body is trying to fight off. A fever is a sign that the body is fighting back; do not suppress the symptom, try to help the body win its battle !

Three weeks' bed treatment may be anticipated. Keep the patient from all contacts other than those absolutely necessary—one case is quite enough to handle.

Food will consist mostly of fruits, salads and liquids, adequately enriched. *Constipation* must be avoided at all costs; use plenty of : —

Slippery elm and honey, three dessertspoonfuls of powdered elm, and two of honey, mix with warm water, and add a well-stirred-in half teaspoonful of cayenne pepper before administering.

Black molasses should be given once or twice a day, a dessertspoonful at a time.

Vomiting. Do not worry if the patient does vomit; if it is anticipated keep plenty of newspaper handy. Afterwards give *lemon juice* and a little water.

Garlic cloves should be chopped up and chewed by the patient, they are very good to clear the breathing tubes, throat etc. The disinfectant power of garlic is rivalled only by that of the big 'Spanish' onion.

Onions should be sliced open and placed around the bed of the patient, they help ward off infection. The patient should be encouraged to eat *onion soup* made of finely sliced onions, water, and a finely shredded paprika.

Lemon juice and cinnamon in warm water should be constantly available for the patient, and if he/she will take it, given every hour.

Spray the patient's throat with pure lemon juice at hourly intervals.

A valuable herbal tea: 1 oz. ginger, 4 drachms quinine, $\frac{1}{2}$ oz. cayenne pepper, 2 oz. yarrow; and if available from your herbal suppliers add : 4 drachms powdered snake root, otherwise omit it. Mix the herbs, add to one quart of boiling water; simmer for 15 minutes. Give the patient a wineglassful every hour.

A very old herbal recipe: 1 oz. catmint, 1 oz. chamomile, 1 oz. elderflowers, 1 oz. skullcap, 1 oz. yarrow. Mix the herbs; add them to one quart of boiling water; simmer for 15 minutes; give the patient half a wineglassful every hour.

Fruit juices, finely chopped (easy to swallow) salads, and protein enriched soups (some are ready-mixed and sold in shops) are the best dietetic items. Do not let the patient lose strength, if the patient specifically craves after some sort of food, see how you can best prepare it so that there is no ensuing constipation or choking.

Alcohol and smoking are tabu.

SCIATICA. *See* the entry for ARTHRITIS and apply the same remedies, there is another entry for RHEUMATISM with several useful remedies.

SCROFULA

There is a hardening and swelling of glands.

Burdock seeds mixed with yarrow make a very efficacious tea, one ounce to one pint.

See the entry for GLANDULAR TROUBLES.

Mineral salts and vitamins should figure more prominently in the diet.

SCURVY

Basically caused by a lack of fresh green vegetables, vitamin C, fruits etc. Plenty of lemon juice daily. This is purely a question of diet; increase the citrus fruit intake, have at least one fresh, green salad every day; get more protein and the ailment should clear up without any complications.

Celery is useful; so is *watercress*.

SEASICKNESS

Most people get seasick because they get very cold on board ship; unless they are used to the sea they do not realise that the sea is always cooler than the land; many are travelling with pent-up excitement or some other tensions—sooner or later they get what Mark Twain described as the 'Oh My' feeling. Keep yourself occupied. Keep yourself warm. Eat a good meal, don't think you'll prevent seasickness by not eating : that is the surest way to get it! I spent one part of my life at sea, I know.

SENILITY

'Grow old with me—the best is yet to be,' wrote Browning. Getting older does not mean collapsing on to a bed and decaying. Professor Clements climbed Mount Kenya when he was over 60, still performs a back somersault off a five metres diving board, and as I write is on his way to Nepal for some more climbing. You are what you eat—physically, that is. So watch the mineral salt, vitamin and protein intake.

Hydrocotyle asiatica, powdered, is a very good herbal tea for those who feel the weight of their years.

Social activities are essential, nobody gets senile who has plenty to do; they say the 'older the fiddle the better the tune' or as the Finnish proverb has it : *Ilta on aamua viisaampi*—the evening has learnt more than the morning knew!

Balm melissa is a delightful tea which will make many older citizens feel much younger for drinking it. Take two or three teaspoonfuls of the herb, put into a teapot, cover with a pint or more of boiling water, sweeten as required, milk may be added if wished.

SEXUAL APATHY

Drinks made from eryngo (sea holly) leaves were long held to help this condition. A course of vitamin E is a preferable treatment. One ounce of herb to one pint of boiling water is enough; of this a wineglassful drunk three times a day is the usual dose.

SEXUAL ORGANS

Can be washed with cold marigold tea (1 oz. to 1 pint) or with witch-hazel. Paper tissues are best, they can then be burnt.

SHINGLES

This is basically an inflammation of the nervous system although it shows itself in the physical sign of a series of pus-bearing vesicles circling round half the chest.

Walnut leaves used 1½ oz. to one pint of boiling water, simmered for 10 minutes. Allow to cool, then apply as a wash **Externally**; the mixture is not to be taken internally. *Sage tea* is a must. One ounce to a pint of boiling water.

Nettle tea can be used jointly with sage tea, the two herbs can even be mixed to make one tea.

Camphor and menthol mixed together form a beneficial rub to apply to the affected areas. Burn any scabs which come off, they carry germs.

Keep the patient warm, give plenty of rest. A visit to a professional analyst often reveals some deep-rooted psychosomatic reason for the upset.

SHOCK
Apply the remedies given under NERVOUS COMPLAINTS.

Sage and basil tea is a good standby, a teaspoonful of basil, two of sage, cover up with one pint of boiling water, allow to draw, drink as much as you like.

SINUS TROUBLE. *See* the entry under CATARRH.
Elecampane can be used as a vapour bath, with a towel draped over the head of the patient and a small basin of boiling water, into which the herb has been placed.

Eucalyptus or *birch leaves* can be used the same way.

SKIN TROUBLES
A full list of skin diseases would occupy not one book but about three volumes; it is clearly possible to give only some general recommendations for first-aid treatment, which are, nevertheless, very efficient and highly recommendable.

Chickweed, that much neglected but most valuable 'weed', is one of the very best plants for the treatment of a large variety of skin diseases. It can be eaten as an element of salad, or made into a tea, about half an ounce or an ounce to one pint of boiling water in a teapot; this can be drunk at the rate of one cup three times a day; when it is cold it can be used as a lotion to wash over the skin.

Dock (Red or Yellow): Use the top leaves—one ounce to one pint of boiling water; drink one wineglassful every three hours. Either the juice or the fresh leaves can be applied to the skin.

Elder leaves make a lotion, 2 oz. to one pint of boiling water, this can be painted over the skin area affected.

Honeysuckle leaves from $\frac{1}{2}$ oz. to 1 oz. to one pint of boiling water. Applied externally.

Marigold flowers. Half-a-dozen fresh flowers to half pint of boiling water; if flowers are in short supply use the newest leaves. Apply leaves or flowers to the skin.

SLEEPLESSNESS
Never take any pills or pharmaceuticals for this condition. It is invariably caused by serious mineral salt deficiency.

Honey and hops make a useful goodnight drink. $\frac{1}{2}$ oz. hop extract and two dessertspoonfuls of honey in a beerglassful of warm water.

The hops should be put into boiling water and simmered until only half of it remains.

Honey, milk and a pinch of *nutmeg* help; a glassful of warm milk with a dessertspoonful of honey and the nutmeg or cinnamon stirred in.

Chamomile and elder flowers can be mixed, a teaspoonful of each, and put into your teapot, pour on the boiling water, and serve with a little honey just last thing at night.

Lime flowers and basil. Take a teaspoonful of lime flowers, half a teaspoonful of basil, pour a pint of boiling water over them in the teapot; serve with honey last thing at night.

SLIMMING

My first word of advice is *don't*. What you need is to discover what your correct weight should be. This varies according to age and height. Do not go by enthusiastic articles written in magazines and papers by 'terrified amateurs'. Health is essential. In general if you feel you are overweight cut down on carbohydrate foods— but never cut them out completely—that would rob you of strength and energy and definitely make you fatter. Do not worry too much about calories—pay more attention to your body's intake of mineral salts and vitamins—if these are correctly balanced the body will do its own work, get its metabolism working correctly and restore you to your right size. Avoid salt, white sugar, and white bread. Take lots of salads, meat and fruit.

SLIPPED DISC

The so-called disc is like a washer between each pair of the bones in the spine (vertebrae). It acts as a shock-absorber—no athletes or parachute jumper could live if these shock-absorbers were not there. If the health is so poor that the disc slips from its position it can jam up against the spinal cord canal, in which all the nerves leading from brain to body (and back again) are situated—apart from disability this can cause extreme pain.

The treatment combines heat, massage and use of comfrey as an external poultice (changed every 24 hours); this herb should also be taken in strong tea form.

SMALLPOX

Constipation, intense thirst, stiffness and temperature rising up to 104; headache, sickness, pain in the back and sometimes there are convulsions to distinguish an attack of smallpox. Eruptions usually appear about the third day, on the forehead, hair roots, and the more exposed parts of the body. The pocks become surrounded by red, intensely-inflamed skin swellings. Mouth, throat and nose are also affected by the poisonous matter; there is a distinct danger that sight may be lost if care is not taken. **Do not try to treat this yourself unless help is unobtainable.** This is an infectious disease, take precautions. Be well prepared for nervousness, irritability and unreasonableness on the part of the patient—the nervous system is also under attack from the sickness.

Darkened room is essential, keep the patient away from direct light, this lessens the strain on the eyes and nerves, and induces more restfulness. There is no proof that vaccination is the answer to this disease which thrives on outward uncleanliness (however momentary) and internal toxins in the weakened body.

Paper sheets, pillow cases, tissues, are essential, replace them every day, burn the old ones.

Constipation must be cleared first, do make sure that the patient has a fair chance of eliminating waste products and poisons from the body.

> *Figs, honey and hot water* should form the only meal until the bowels have moved; prunes could also be used :
>
> *Special herbal recipe:* ½ oz. powdered cascara sagrada, ½ oz. liquorice, a few cardomon seeds. Put these into half a pint of boiling water; simmer for 10 minutes; when cool (but not cold) give the patient a wineglassful every hour until the bowels pass motions.
>
> *Senna pods and ginger* can also be taken, four pods to one cupful of boiling water; cover over with a saucer, allow to draw, add a pinch of ginger, stir well and administer warm.

Lemon juice should be sprayed down the throat every half hour. The patient can drink as much lemon juice as he/she likes (unsweetened).

Garlic should be finely sliced and the patient persuaded to chew as much as he/she possibly can, it is extremely valuable to keep open the breathing passages.

Apple cider vinegar and water can be used to wash the skin. Throw away the liquid and the flannel or paper tissues used to bathe the skin (burn them if possible).

Solid foods are usually inadvisable. Finely grated salads (passed through a mincer) are all right, but if you have a juicer in the house administer even salads and fruit through it until the patient shows signs of mending. If the patient expressly asks for some solid food, a little porridge, well mixed with honey or black molasses could be given; bread puddings with plenty of milk and cinnamon can be given; sago pudding, tapioca (very milky and weak, otherwise it may constipate) with powdered cloves and lemon juice is also acceptable.

Yarrow tea, balm tea or tansy tea should be the main drinks given to the patient, half ounce to one pint boiling water; serve with honey or a little black molasses. As much as the patient wants.

Marigold flower tea should be administered every three hours, one wineglassful. Use flowers and/or top leaves with one to one and a half ounces of herb to one pint of boiling water which is then immediately simmered for 10 minutes on the lowest possible heat.

Golden seal is highly recommendable for smallpox cases—use from $\frac{1}{2}$ oz. to 1 oz. (judging by the severity of the case) and give the patient from half to a full wineglass of the liquid resulting from boiling the powdered root for 10 to 15 minutes. Some herbal suppliers will supply the tincture and advise you how to use it. The mixture, when cool, makes an excellent wash for the skin. Professor England and the early Thomsonians (pioneers of non-toxic botanic medicine) regarded this as one of the most important herbs for the treatment of smallpox. Usually the patient recovers within two to three weeks. Take great care not to weaken the patient with a diet lacking in mineral salts and vitamins; keep up the patient's strength as best possible, especially with fruits and salads in one form or another; special protein soups can be bought from most health shops, and these can also be used. If the patient fancies a little bread—use only wholemeal, stoneground, natural bread. If the patient should desire meat, use fresh mince only. **Do send for help if at all possible. Treat the disease yourself only if no help is available.**

SNAKE BITE

In Brazil the Indians have made good use of a plant classified as *Pareira Brava*, applying the bruised leaves directly to the bite, and drinking an infusion made from the roots. Most snake bites destroy some constituents of the blood, many affect the nervous system—some as quickly as 15 minutes after the bite, so that paralysis, difficulty in breathing, faintness and convulsions take place. A tight band should be applied above the bite, an incision should be made about $\frac{1}{2}$ inch deep and 1 inch long. Press, wash and suck the wound (sucked-out material to be spat out). Professional advice should be sought if available.

SPLENIC FEVER

Inflammation of the spleen is concommitant to or a result of anthrax, leukaemia, plague, rat-bites, typhoid or malaria. *Ceanothus americanus* has been known to bring relief.

SPLINTERS

An old-fashioned remedy was to cover the area with a piece of linen, put some powdered resin over that, and drop hot candle grease on to the resin—it was said that this would remove any splinter, however deep it had gone.

Needles should be sterilised in the flame of a lighter or by soaking a few moments in some antiseptic lotion.

Hot fomentations often draw out an awkward splinter.

Comfrey leaves bruised until the juice runs can be put straight on to a splinter (especially wood or thorn) and the flesh soon pushes the offending piece out.

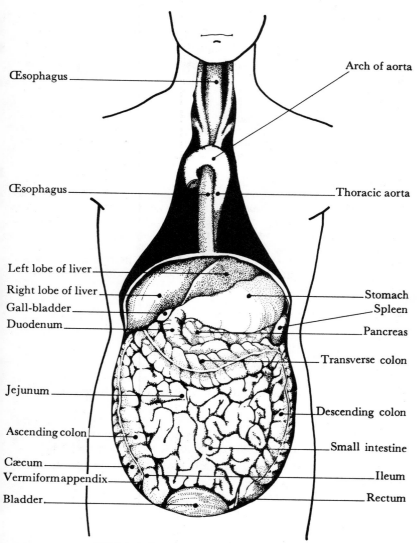

Œsophagus

Arch of aorta

Œsophagus

Thoracic aorta

Left lobe of liver

Right lobe of liver
Gall-bladder
Duodenum

Stomach
Spleen
Pancreas

Transverse colon

Jejunum

Descending colon

Ascending colon

Cæcum
Vermiform appendix

Small intestine

Ileum

Bladder

Rectum

THE ORGANS OF DIGESTION, ETC.

SPRAINS

As soon as possible after the accident occurs apply some *comfrey leaves*, just bruise them slightly to make the juice run, then bandage them on to the hurt. Very efficacious.

Bladderwrack will do the trick if you are on the seashore.

Elderberry juice is not too bad, provided it is applied quickly.

Parsley can be crushed and bandaged round any sprain or strain.

St. John's Wort is another most useful herb to wrap round the hurt.

STITCH

Put a leaf from a fresh cabbage to the side—said my grandfather —I've never tried it myself, it is usually a sign of some mineral salt deficiency, and a dose of black molasses or honey will do much to relieve it—if desired take with a little warm water.

STOMACH COMPLAINTS

See the headings ACIDITY, BOWELS—INFLAMMATION OF, CANCER, COLIC, CONSTIPATION, DIARRHOEA, DIGESTIVE TROUBLES, DYSPEPSIA, GALLSTONES, JAUNDICE, KIDNEY COMPLAINTS, LIVER COMPLAINTS, OBESITY, OVERFEEDING, PILES, RUPTURE, and STITCH.

For first aid try one of these : *Fenugreek, pennyroyal* or *peppermint tea*. Take two to three teaspoonfuls of the herb, put into a teapot, pour on it a pint of boiling water and leave it to draw. Drink as much as you want.

STONE. *See* the entry GALLSTONES.

STYES

A serious symptom that something is wrong with the health, that there is a general breakdown of health pending; act at once, increase the intake of mineral salts, vitamins; more protein is required, and less fats, sugars and starches. Rest more, try to get a change of air.

Chickweed or *tansy tea* : Use three teaspoonfuls of herb, put into a pot, cover with a pint of boiling water, leave to draw, drink three cups a day. Some of the cold tea can be used to wash the stye.

Witch-hazel can be used to wash the stye, do not get it in the eye itself.

Hot fomentations applied on a small corner of cloth to the stye help, don't put the hot cloth into the eye.

SUNBURN

Use a mixture of a little *elderflower tea*, lemon juice and eau de Cologne.

Lemon juice and milk mixed çan be applied to sunburn. So can *white pond lily leaves*.

SWELLINGS. *See* the entries under CANCER, DROPSY, GOUT, KIDNEY COMPLAINTS, LYMPHATIC GLANDULAR DISTURBANCES.

TEETH

Clean your teeth with *lemon juice and water* mixed in equal parts. *A useful tooth powder* can be made of equal parts of cinnamon, arrowroot and salt.

Rose petal powder and arrowroot make another tooth powder.

All teeth require plenty of fruit, salads and high protein; starches, sugars, and fats are very dangerous for the health of teeth.

An apple at night before you go to bed cleans your teeth and massages your gums very well. *See* the entry in this book under GUMS.

TEETHING TROUBLES

There may be a lack of mineral salts, especially calcium and phosphorus in the child's diet. A little honey may help.

TETANUS

If help is available *do* send for professional aid.

The traditional treatment by herbal methods was to administer *cayenne pepper*, one teaspoonful (levelled) in a cupful of warm water, drink as quickly as possible to avoid burning the mouth with the pepper. A steam bath or a sauna bath is essential. After this rest in bed and keep the feet warm. I have no experience of this treatment. It is best to send quickly for professional advice. Clean the wound and encourage bleeding, apply *freshly sliced onions* or *garlic*, and get the patient to chew either raw onions or raw garlic.

THROAT. *See* the entries LARYNGITIS and MALIGNANT THROAT ULCER.

THROMBOSIS

Rest is essential. *See* the entry under HEART TROUBLES.

THRUSH

A patched white, spotty appearance on the mouth, tongue, etc. Indication of fungus having taken root in the mucous membrane, due to imbalance of mineral salts and vitamins.

Plantain is the answer, if you haven't destroyed all of it on your garden lawn with 'weedkiller'; it is surprising how we kill the weeds that heal us! One ounce to one pint of boiling water. Make in the teapot, leave 15 minutes to draw. Half a cupful at a time, well flavoured with a heaped teaspoonful of honey stirred into every dose, add a small pinch of cinnamon!

Constipation is invariably present, this must be cleared; see the entry in this book.

Old herbal recipe: ½ oz. Peruvian bark (quinine), ½ oz slippery elm. Mix these powders well then add them, slowly stirring, to half a pint of hot water in which a few drops of tincture of myrrh have been poured; stir vigorously and when the mixture cools down give half a wineglassful as a gargle and mouthwash; use this every two hours.

Blackcurrant juice is the best drink to administer when the patient is thirsty.

THYROID TROUBLE
Often associated with defective kidney action (*see* the heading in this book KIDNEY COMPLAINTS). If the body is misusing the juices that the thyroid gland produces it will not be long before it misuses the artificially introduced 'thyroid extracts' that the medical profession tend to favour. The art lies in curing the cause of the disease.

Horsetail grass tea, three teaspoonfuls of dried herb, one pint of boiling water, make it in the teapot and drink as much as you like, at least three cups a day, sweeten it with black molasses or honey.

Bladderwrack tea. One ounce to a pint. Apply externally to the goitre before going to bed; drink a half cupful of the tea to which water has been added.

Dandelion tea, one ounce to a pint, is very useful indeed.

Parsley and watercress must be eaten frequently, a little every day.

Black molasses—at least two dessertspoonfuls a day. *See* the entry LYMPHATIC GLAND DISTURBANCES.

TONICS
If you feel down in the dumps, don't wait for anything to develop, make yourself a good tonic tea. All the following are made with a total of three teaspoonfuls (level) of herb to one pint of boiling water—in the teapot, and drunk sweetened with honey or raw brown sugar.

Dandelion and basil; peppermint and tansy; fennel and thyme (two parts fennel, one part thyme); *Sassafras* (powdered) *and sarsaparilla* (powdered); *golden rod and marshmallow; nettle and balm melissa.*

TONSILITIS. *See* the entries LARYNGITIS, MALIGNANT THROAT ULCER.
The same remedies can be used. Spray the tonsils frequently with lemon juice.

TOOTHACHE
Keep your gums in good health and you are unlikely to have any real damage to your teeth. Massage the teeth with your finger, using one of the recipes given under the entry TEETH, or a natural toothpaste. Many modern toothbrushes do more harm to the soft

material of the gums than they ever do to help the teeth. If you've
toothache go to a dentist at once, the chances are he can make a
simple, painless filling in a few minutes, and if you leave it the
tooth may have to be extracted!

In emergency there is a simple herbal remedy you can try:
cloves or oil of cloves allay the pain of toothache, but do not act as
a substitute for a dentist's attention.

Eat more fruit and less chocolate and sweets.

TORTICOLLIS
A stiff neck is a form of cramp; see the entry under that heading.

TUBERCULOSIS
Seek professional advice if available.

Tuberculosis is a disease of malnutrition (you can be overfed
and still suffer from malnutrition if the mineral salts and vitamins
are not balanced), and it is also a psychosomatic disease often
associated with a despairing unhappiness. The patient must be made
happy, encouraged to look on the bright side, want to get better,
make plans and expect a brighter future. I have *never* met any
TB patient who was not suffering from a chronic lack of silica, and
the silica foods listed under the entry for chilblains should figure
in the daily diet of the patient.

Fruits, salads and high protein diet are essential.

Halibut liver oil must feature in the daily diet of the patient; if
not available use cod liver oil. Most chemists sell these oils in convenient capsules, the TB patient needs double the normal dose of
these oils. *Constipation* must be avoided.

Fresh air—however cold—night and day is needed. Shut the
windows only if fog is expected, and then not completely. Keep
the patient warmly wrapped up; bed rest has cured an enormous
number of TB patients.

Sleep. Eight to nine hours sleep is needed each night, and two
extra hours during morning and afternoon are also recommended.

Liquorice can be taken, as much as the patient accepts of it; it
is very beneficial.

Comfrey, coltsfoot, horsetail grass, powdered bugleweed, can all
be used individually to make teas at half ounce to the pint of boiling water in the family teapot. *Comfrey is essential; failing that
horsetail grass.*

Old herbal recipe: 1 oz. black horehound, 1 oz. marshmallow,
1 oz. hyssop, ¼ oz. cayenne pepper. Mix the herbs and put into
one pint of boiling water; simmer them for 10 minutes; when cool
give one wineglassful every three hours.

Meat broth helps keep the patient's strength up, but give plenty
of vegetables with it; stews with original gravy help; salads, fruit,
etc., as much as the patient wants. Hunger is a good sign for the
TB patient.

No white bread, white sugar, etc., only raw sugar, *honey*, *black molasses*, and wholewheat bread. The italicised items must be taken every day. Do try to get the advice of a professional herbalist, dietician, etc. Spiritual Healing often helps this disease when the situation seems desperate.

Recipe to be given every second day: ½ oz. slippery elm, ¼ oz. cayenne pepper. Stir these ingredients into one pint of hot water, adding the powders very slowly. Then stir in one dessertspoonful of honey and the juice of one lemon. During the course of the day the pint should be drunk in three cupfuls, spaced about four hours apart.

Golden rule: All sputum must be burnt. *Paper* sheets, pillowcases, handkerchiefs should be used as much as possible, and burnt after use.

Spitting blood is often a sign that the patient is getting better and by no means a cause of despair.

Milk should be taken cold and never boiled for TB patients; it loses much of its virtue if boiled.

Cheese and free-range eggs can be given, as much as the patient fancies them. Eggs, lightly boiled, and cheese accompanied by lettuce or chopped raw cauliflower.

Gentle walks graded 5, 10 and 15 minutes may be taken twice a day as the patient recovers strength.

Direct sunlight is not always good for TB patients, and sunbathing is not usually so beneficial as in other cases.

Cultivate a positive frame of mind. Too many TB patients have a negative outlook—mind and body relationship is very important in this disease.

Garlic or raw onions should be chewed twice a day.

TRANQUILISERS

These medicines are widely advertised, and for the most part vastly over-valued. There are a number of conditions which are lumped together as requiring tranquillisers. Here are some healthy, natural means of fighting these conditions.

Chamomile. For children whose teeth are coming through. Stomach troubles, nervous sleeplessness and in combination with honey for neuralgic pains. One ounce of herbs to one pint of boiling water, simmer for five minutes. Drink a wineglassful as required when the mixture is cool.

Cohosh. Long recommended for women's nervousness, periodic upsets and hysteria. One ounce to a pint—recipe as for chamomile.

Hops. In my grandparents' days fresh hops were put into a pillowcase to ensure blissful repose. One ounce to a pint—recipe as for chamomile.

Horsetail grass. Extremely useful for mentally disturbed, neurotic and highly excitable patients. One ounce to a pint. Recipe as for chamomile. Cases of hormonal disturbance and glandular disorders often react favourably to this herb.

A simple household remedy made in an instant: Take one large dessertspoonful of pure honey. Add a generous pinch of cinnamon, and cover with warm *but not boiled* milk.

TUMOURS. *See* the heading CANCER.

TYPHOID

Send for professional help as soon as the disease is suspected.

Also known as Enteric Fever, symptomised by headaches, feeling of disinterest, lassitude, slight feverishness and restless sleep; often there is bleeding at the nose without any blow or apparent cause. The temperature varies considerably, rising and falling evening and morning respectively. After a week the patient usually wants to rest in bed. The course of the illness takes about a month, occasionally less. The stomach swells, there may be a pain in the groin; there is marked drowsiness; diarrhoea is often present; spots on the stomach, chest and the back; occasionally there is constipation instead of diarrhoea.

Sheets, towels, cloths, handkerchiefs should be of paper and burnt after use : at least they must be sterilised.

Raw fresh onions cut open should be placed around the sickbed, in saucers or paper plates. This minimises the risk of infection.

Barley water, beef tea, chicken broth, milk (only a cupful at a time) form the main items of diet; but for the first three days the patient is advised to *fast* lightly, using only fruit juice from fresh fruit, juiced vegetables, and a little milk. A juicing machine is the most valuable possession a household can have for fever patients, because the mineral salts and vitamins can be turned into liquids and easily absorbed by the weakened body.

This illness should be treated at home only if no medical help is available.

Old herbal recipes:

(1) 4 oz. bayberry bark (powdered), ½ oz. cayenne, ½ oz. cloves (powdered), 2 oz. ginger, 2 oz. pinus canadensis (powdered bark). Mix the powders carefully and thoroughly, then give a level teaspoonful in a large cup of warm water, if necessary sweeten slightly with honey or black molasses or rough brown sugar. Give twice daily, at six hours' interval.

(2) 3 oz. bitter root (powdered), 1 oz. cayenne, 1 oz. culvers root (powdered), 4 oz. golden seal (powdered), 4 oz. poplar bark (powdered). Mix the powders, give 10 grains after each meal.

(3) ½ oz. agrimony, ½ oz. burnet (Great), ½ oz. meadowsweet, ½ oz. raspberry leaves, ½ oz. vervain, ½ oz. wood betony. Mix the herbs and put into two pints of boiling water, then simmer carefully until about half a pint has steamed away; allow to cool and give a wineglassful every 30 minutes. Sweeten with

honey or brown sugar, add a pinch of cinnamon or a few drops of lemon juice to vary the taste.

Apple cider vinegar, one dessertspoonful to a bowl, should be used in water for washing down the patient's face, hands and body. Cold-water washes are usually more comforting to the patient than warm.

Bilberries have long been considered a tonic medicine for typhoid in some parts of Scandinavia.

Yarrow and bayberry teas can be given ½ oz. to one pint.

TYPHUS
THIS SHOULD BE TREATED AT HOME ONLY IF NO PROFESSIONAL HELP IS AVAILABLE.

Headache, prolonged shivering bouts, feeling of malaise, and sleeplessness, temperature rising to 105°F. Constipation is nearly always present and the kidneys do not function too well. Towards the end of the first week the patient shows a mottled series of brown to purple blobs on the limbs, stomach, back and flanks. If untreated the patient may show an apathy, staring into space, prostrate, and may become delirious. It is a great strain on the heart. Isolate the patient at once, keep the sickroom well aired, use blankets to keep the patient warm, the window open wide at all times.

Juiced vegetables and fruits, chicken broth, and milk are allowed.

Constipation is best eliminated by the administration of *slippery elm.* Two dessertspoonfuls, half a level teaspoonful of cayenne, two dessertspoonfuls of honey, and warm water given first thing every morning—most effective.

The fever usually takes a turn for the better about the end of the second week, provided nursing has been careful.

Garlic or raw onions must be chewed by the patient every day. *Sliced onions* should be placed around the patient to minimise infection.

Wholemeal, stoneground bread can be given in small doses; no white bread, white sugar, and only correctly balanced salt.

Camomile tea mixed with equal parts of *vervain* makes a good drink for the patient. One teaspoonful of each herb, a pint of boiling water, make it in the teapot, and drink as much as required, spice it with a little cinnamon and sweeten as required.

Boneset tea (Indian Sage) was one of the herbs most favoured by the herbalists to cure typhus. One ounce to one pint of boiling water, allow to draw for 10 minutes. Sweetening may be required, the taste of the herb is, to say the least, unusual. The Amerindians of North America are recorded as having cured typhus with this herb.

Old herbal recipe: 1 oz. bayberry, 1 oz. bitter root, ½ oz. cayenne, ½ oz. Peruvian bark (quinine), ½ oz. rosemary, 1 oz. vervain. Mix the herbs, put them into a quart of boiling water then simmer for

15 minutes. When cool give the patient a wineglassful every three hours.

Remember that this is an infectious disease, and do get professional advice if possible.

ULCERS

Internal ulcers can be successfully treated only by a change to a strictly controlled diet, and expert advice from a professional is required. Milk foods are usually recommended, and frequently *slippery elm* mixed with honey and milk is recommended—three times a day.

External ulcers fall into several different groups. *Varicose* ulcers form on varicose veins. Do not scratch a varicose vein, the harm may be irreparable. The tendency is to rest a varicose condition far more than it needs, regular exercise is needed. Increase the intake of vitamin E and consult a doctor.

Trophic ulcers are due to nervous conditions. *See* the heading NERVOUS COMPLAINTS.

Callous ulcers, the most usual kind, distinguished by a hardened edge around the area, the discharge is often slight. *Slippery elm and eucalyptus* mixed together can be applied to such ulcers.

Bread (stoneground wholemeal) in hot milk can be applied hot to an ulcer, it is an age-old and effective recipe.

Comfrey and marshmallow, soaked a few minutes in hot water, can be applied directly to an ulcer.

Witch-hazel should be used to wash ulcers. *Onion* slices, freshly cut, should be applied directly to an ulcer; I have often used this method myself, and recommend it; bandage the onion slice on and renew every 12 hours.

Red clover flowers, soaked in hot water for a few minutes, can also be bandaged on to an ulcer. So can *figs*, lightly boiled.

URAEMIA.   *See* the heading KIDNEY COMPLAINTS.

URINE DISORDERS.   *See* the entry KIDNEY COMPLAINTS.

Shepherd's purse tea, one ounce to a pint boiling water is very helpful.

UTERINE AILMENTS

Call in professional advice. If it is slow in coming you could try the following if there is an inflammation of the womb : 1 oz. buchu, 1 oz. comfrey root, 1 oz. pellitory, 1 oz. uva ursi, 1 oz. white poplar bark. Mix the herbs and put into three pints of boiling water; simmer for 15 minutes, then allow to cool and give the patient one wineglassful every three hours.

Feverfew and horsetail grass tea; mixed in equal parts, two teaspoonfuls of each of the dried herbs, mixed in a teapot, one pint of boiling water, allow to cool slightly, drink as much as you feel like.

See the entries FEMALE COMPLAINTS and LEUCORRHOEA.

VARICOSE VEINS

This is a sign of long neglect. Standing rather than walking damages the veins; standing for long periods is neither healthy nor natural.

Fruit and salad diet is essential; for quite a few weeks this must be the basis of all meals. Starches, fats (except olive oil), and sugars must be rigorously reduced (but not entirely eliminated from meals). Alcohol, coffee, curries, spices, sauces, rich food, tea, etc., must be cut out altogether, although one cup of weak tea could be allowed at tea time.

Scratching of irritable veins may result in severe blood-poisoning.

Witch-hazel can be used to wash the affected veins; always move the hand upwards along the veins—towards the heart, never away from it.

Jack-by-the-hedge can be used, in the form of a cold tea, one ounce to a pint, to massage varicose conditions, in the manner described above. *Also see* : HEART TRANSPLANTS.

VENEREAL DISEASES

These should not be treated at home but handled by a professional man, do call in advice. No venereal condition ever 'goes away by itself'. Garlic should be eaten daily, several cloves.

VERTIGO

Cold valerian tea helps. This is often a psychosomatic ailment, but may be caused by mineral salt deficiencies. *Diet* must be checked. A little apple cider vinegar mixed with a teaspoonful of honey in warm water is a great help.

VOICE, LOSS OF. *See* LARYNGITIS, MALIGNANT THROAT ULCERS, etc.

VOMITING

The first rule is allow the patient to vomit in comfort, the body is trying to get rid of poisonous material this way, don't stop it. Afterwards give a litle apple cider vinegar or lemon juice in water.

WARTS

Old-fashioned people would rub a little common soda on a wart, and said that this would cure them in just over a week. I have never tried that method.

Buttercup juice (celandine) can be squeezed on to a wart, this usually cures it within a few days. External application only.

Dandelion juice is used externally only on warts.

Pineapple may be rubbed on to a wart, or a small piece bandaged over a wart; in spite of the pleasant taste it contains a powerful acid.

Tormentil leaf leaf, moistened in hot water, can be bandaged on to a wart and *yellow cedar* can be painted on.

Figleaf juice squeezed from a freshly plucked leaf is a popular cure among the peasants of Piedmonte.

WHITLOWS

Squeeze on *groundsel juice,* bandage and leave. Repeat every 12 hours. *Comfrey poultices* work well. Soak two or three comfrey leaves a few minutes in hot water, then apply hot to the whitlow, and bandage on. Check your diet for shortages of mineral salts.

WHOOPING COUGH

Distinguished by the 'whoop' or gurgling noise made while coughing. Treat as for CATARRH; many of the recipes given under BRONCHITIS will be very helpful.

WORMS

An Italian method to kill all worms parasitic to man is to chew up a clove of garlic and to insert another in the rectum . . . they claim it is infallible.

Thyme eaten raw (a pleasant taste) and followed only by a drink of pure lemon juice is very effective. Repeat three times a day, fasting.

Pumpkin seeds can be eaten, they are specifically good against the tapeworm. It is as well to fast for a few hours while the medicines take effect.

WOUNDS

Rule 1—Stop the haemorrhage, there's no good tending a wound if the patient quietly bleeds to death. If you must fix a tourniquet (by twisting a pencil or piece of wood through a bandage and tightening it) remember you *must* put a label on the tourniquet with the exact time it was applied, and the tourniquet *must* be opened to allow some flow of blood every 12 minutes afterwards.

Rule 2—Clean the wound, using witch-hazel or apple cider vinegar mixed with equal parts of water; get as much grit, dirt, grease and any foreign bodies out of the wound as quickly as possible. If nothing else is available use salt and water, the patient will most likely twitch if you do this, but better to have him alive and twitching than not moving at all. Do *not* normally apply iodine, it may slow down the healing processes.

Chickweed poultice or tea can be applied to a wound, and renewed every six hours; it tends to attract a lot of toxic matter, and should be burnt after removal.

Golden rod leaves, groundsel leaves, St. John's Wort or *yarrow leaves* can be washed in warm water and put on to a wound.

If there is any fracture of bones, suspected or definite, do send for professional medical advice quickly. Give the patient comfrey tea when he is recovering.

RAPID GUIDE TO CHILDREN'S ILLNESSES

Description	*How long?*	*Complications*
MEASLES		
Nine to 16 days after exposure. Child loses appetite, seems to have feverish cold. Eyes pink and watery, hard, dry cough. Blurred pink spots behind ears appear about fourteenth day, when fever high. Over next two days spots enlarge, darken, spread on face and body.	About a week from first cold symptoms. Child can play outside one week from appearance of rash if all symptoms have subsided.	Most common complications are ear abscesses.
GERMAN MEASLES (rubella)		
Twelve to 21 days after exposure. Child may complain of sore throat, have low fever and swollen glands behind ears and sides of neck towards back. Flat pink spots usually cover body on first day, then run together and fade so body looks more flushed than spotty.	Often under a week, though swollen glands may last longer.	Danger is for women in first three months of pregnancy, since unborn child could suffer.
MUMPS		
Two or three weeks after exposure. Swelling under ear or side of throat hurts during chews or swallows. Puffed face and climbing fever.	A week to 10 days.	Encephalitis in teenage boys. Can affect testicles but sterility rare.

Description	*How long?*	*Complications*
CHICKENPOX		
11 to 19 days after exposure. First signs pimples surrounded by a reddened area of skin. The pimples are small, with tiny yellow blisters which break within a few hours and dry to a crust.	About a week. Child can mix with others out of doors two days after last pox has appeared.	Boils, which come from infecting pox by scratching.
ROSEOLA		
Rarely found in children over three years. High fever for three or four days without feeling of cold or sickness. A pinkish, flat rash appears and subsides in a day or two.	About a week.	None.

Bibliography

Leechbook of Bald, tenth century (British Museum).
Meddygon Myddfai, fourteenth century (British Museum). Welsh.
Loeb Classical Library. Bilingual versions of : Hippocrates, Galen, Dioscordies, Pliny, Celsus and Theophrastus (Heinemann, London).
The Greeks. Prof. H. Kitto. Penguin Press.
Greek Science. Benjamin Farrington. Penguin Press.
The Roman. R. H. Barrow. Penguin Press.
Moslem Spain (A study in the effect of monotheism on social welfare and human progress). J. A. Lawrence, M.Ph.A., F.I.A.L.
Botanical Materia Medica. Jonathan Stokes, M.D. 4 vols. 1812.
Flora Medica. John Lindley, Ph.D., F.R.S. 1838.
Vivisection Revealed. John Morgan, M.Ph.A.
The Death Doctors. Dr. A. Mitscherlich (Elek Books, London, 1962).
Green Medicine. Dr. Margaret Kreig (Harrap, London, 1965).
Grundlagen der Heilkunde. Dr.med. et phil. Otto Leeser (Stuttgart, 1926):
De Taal der Kruiden. Mellie Uyldert (Strengholt, Amsterdam).
Integraçao Portuguesa nos Tropicos. Prof. Gilberto Freyre (Lisbon, 1961).
Revolution in Medicine. Brian Inglis.
Drugs, Doctors and Diseases. Brian Inglis.
The Silent Spring. Dr. Rachel Carson.
Brave New Victuals. Elspeth Huxley (Panther, London).
Deine Seele, Dein Korper. Dr.med. Flanders Dunbar (Ullstein, Stuttgart, 1955).
At Home in the Woods. V. & B. Angier (Hale, London, 1953).
In Few Hands. Estes Kefauver (The Kefauver Senatorial Report).
Ressources Medicinales de la Flore Française. Drs. Garnier, Bezanger et Debraux (Vigot, Paris).
Un Médecin aux Champs. Prof. Léon Binet (Plon, Paris).
Die Heilwerte Heimischer Pflanzen. Dr. Wolfgang Bohn (Hedewig, Leipzig).
Welche Heilpflanze ist das? Dr. Schoenfelder Fischer (Kosmos, Stuttgart, 1965).
Heilpflanzentaschenbuch. Dr. Oertel-Bauer (Thomas, Kempen, 1963).
Plantes Medicinales. Dr. Eugene Fischer (Lausanne, 1966).
Botanic Guide to Health. Aloysius Browne.
The Badianus Manuscript. An Aztec Herbal of 1552. E. W. Emmart (Baltimore, John Hopkins, 1940).
The Golden Bough. J. G. Fraser (Macmillan, 1911).

Gerards Herball. Edited M. Woodward. 1927.
Primitive and Archaic Medicine. H. E. Sigerist (Oxford, 1951).
Folk Medicine. Dr. D. C. Jarvis (Holt & Co. Pan Books, 1958).
Indian Uses of Native Plants. Edith van Allen Murphy (Desert Printers, 1959. Calif.).
The Family Herbal. Sir John Hill, M.D. 1812.
The Greek Herbal of Dioscorides. R. T. Gunther (Oxford, 1934).
Arabian Medicine. E. G. Brown (Macmillan, New York, 1921).
A Minnesota Doctor's Home Remedies. John Eichenlaub, M.D. (Prentice Hall, 1960).

FOR IDENTIFICATION OF HERBS
The Concise British Flora in Colour. W. Keble Martin.
Oxford Book of Wild Flowers.
Wayside and Woodland Flowers. Fr. Warne & Co.
Observer Book of Wild Flowers.

Various Copies of *Natural Therapeutics, Phrenosophical Medical Journal* and other journals, etc.

Herbs Mentioned in the Text and their Latin Names

When ordering a herb from a supplier, or identifying it when out on an expedition to collect herbs, you should check the Latin name (and quote it on any order form). These names are international and used for your safety.

Agrimony	*Agrimonia eupatoria*
Angelica	*Angelica archangelica*
Balm melissa	*Melissa officinalis*
Balmony	*Chelone glabra*
Basil	*Ocimum basilicum*
Bay	*Laurus nobilis*
Bayberry	*Myrica cerifera*
Betony	*Betonica officinalis*
Birch	*Betula alba*
Bistort	*Polygonum bistorta*
Bitter root	*Apocynum androsaemifolium*
Blackroot/Culvers	*Leptandra virginica*
Bladderwrack	*Fucus vesiculosus*
Bogbean/Buckbean	*Menianthes trifoliata*
Boneset	*Eupatoria perfoliatum*
Broom	*Cytisus scoparius*/or *Spartium scoparium*
Buchu	*Barosma betulina*
Buckbean/Bogbean	*Menianthes trifoliata*
Burdock	*Arctium lappa*
Calamint	*Calaminta officinalis*
Calamus	*Acorus calamus*
Chamomile	*Anthemis nobilis*
Catechu	*Acacia catechu*
Catnip	*Nepeta cataria*
Cayenne	*Capsicum minimum*/or *C. frutescens*
Celandine	*Chelidonum majus*
Centaury	*Erythraea centaurium*
Chaulmoogra	*Gynocardia odorata*
Chickweed	*Stellaria media*
Clivers	*Galium aparine*
Clover	*Trifolium pratense*
Cohosh	*Caulophyllum thalictroides*
Coltsfoot	*Tussilago farfara*
Comfrey	*Symphytum officinale*
Cowslip	*Primula veris*
Cranesbill	*Geranium maculatum*
Cudweed	*Gnaphalium uliginosum*
Culvers/Blackroot	*Leptandra virginica*
Daisies	*Bellis perennis*
Dandelion	*Taraxacum officinalis*

Devil's bit	*Scabiosa succisa*
Dock (red)	*Rumex aquaticus*
Dock (yellow)	*Rumex crispus*
Dogwood	*Cornuus sanguinea*
Echinacea	*Echinacea angustifolia*
Elderberry	*Sambucus nigra*
Elecampane	*Inula helenium*
Eyebright	*Euphrasia officinalis*
Fennel	*Foeniculum officinalis*
Fenugreek	*Trigonella foenum graecum*
Feverfew	*Chrysanthemum parthenium*
Fleabane	*Erigeron canadense*
Fumitory	*Fumitoria officinalis*
Garlic	*Allium sativum*
Germander speedwell	*Teucrium marum*
Ginger	*Zingiber officinale*
Golden rod	*Solidago virgaurea*/or *S. odora*
Ground ivy	*Glechoma hederacea*
Groundsel	*Senecio vulgaris*
Guiacum	*Guiacum officinale*
Hawthorn	*Crataegus oxycantha*
Herb Robert	*Geranium robertianum*
Hollyhocks	*Althea rosea*
Holy thistle	*Carduus benedictus*
Honeysuckle	*Lonicera caprifolium*
Horehound	*Marrubium vulgare*
Horsetail grass	*Equisetum arvense*
Hyssop	*Hyssopus officinalis*
Iceland moss	*Cetraria islandica*
Juniper	*Juniperus communis*
Knapweed	*Centaurea nigra*
Lady's mantle	*Alchemilla vulgaris*
Lavender	*Lavendula vera*/or *L. spica*
Lily of the Valley	*Convallaria majus*
Limeflowers	*Tilia europaea*
Linseed	*Linum usitatissimum*
Liquorice	*Glycyrrhiza labra*
Maidenhair fern	*Adiantum capillus veneris*
Marigold	*Calendula officinalis*
Marjoram	*Origanum vulgare*
Marshmallow	*Althea officinalis*
Meadow fern	*Comptonia asplenifolia*
Mignonette	*Reseda lutea*
Mint	*Mentha viridis*
Motherwort	*Leonurus cardiaca*
Mugwort	*Artemesia vulgaris*
Mullein	*Verbascum **thapsus***
Nasturtium	*Tropaeolium majus*/or *T. minus*
Nettles	*Urtica dioica*
Oak	*Quercus robur*
Parsley	*Petroselinum sativum*
Parsley piert	*Alchemilla arvensis*

(N.B. The two preceding plants show the danger of old country names; although the names are similar in English these plants are not at all related!)

Pellitory of the wall	*Parietaria officinalis*
Pennyroyal	*Mentha pulegium*
Plantain (quite a family of them)	*Plantago major, P. lanceolata*, etc., etc.
Pleurisy root	*Asclepias tuberosa*
Poplar	*Populus tremaloides*
Prickly ash	*Zantherzylum americanus*
Primrose	*Primula vulgaris*
Purple loosestrife (Willowherb)	*Lysimachia salicaria*
Purslane	*Portula sativa*
Queen of the Meadow	*Eupatorium purpureum*
Raspberry	*Rubus idaeus*
Red dock	*Rumex aquaticus*
Rhubarb	*Rheum palinatum*
Rosemary	*Rosmarinus officinalis*
Rupturewort	*Herniara glabra*
Safflower	*Carthamus tinctorius*
Sage	*Salvia officinalis*
St. John's Wort	*Hypericum perfoliatum*
Salad Burnett	*Sanguisorba officinalis*
Sarsaparilla	*Smilax ornata*
Sassafras	*Sassafras variifolium*
Scabious	*Scabiosa arvensis*
Skullcap	*Scutellaria galericulata*
Skunk cabbage	*Symplocarpus foetidus*
Slippery elm	*Ulmus fulva*
Solomon's seal	*Polygonatum multiflorum*
Sorrel	*Rumex acetosa*
Southernwood	*Artemesia abrotanum*
Stramonium	*Datura stramonium*
Tansy	*Tanacetum vulgare*
Thyme	*Thymus vulgaris*/or *T. serpyllum*
Tormentil	*Potentilla tormentilla*
Uva ursi	*Arctostaphyllos uva ursi*
Valerian	*Valeriana officinalis*
Verbena	*Verbena officinalis*
Violet	*Viola odorata*
Willow	*Salix alba*
Wood betony	*Betonica officinalis*
Wormwood	*Artemesia absinthium*
Yarrow	*Achillea millefolium*
Yellow cedar	*Thuja occidentalis*
Yellow dock	*Rumex crispus*

Welsh Names of Herbs

To Mrs. Eluned Roberts of Tywyn
who gave me my first lessons in Welsh
and respectfully to the *Merched y Wawr*.
I append the names of some important herbs in Welsh

Gorau cyfoeth-iechyd,
Gorau arf, arf dysg.
A fynno iechyd, bid lawen;
Plant gwirionedd yw hen ddiarhebion.

DONALD LAW

AGRIMONY	Llysiau'r Dryw
ALDER	Gwern
ALEHOOF	Llysiau'r Nepeta
ALEXANDER	Persli yr anialwch
ANEMONE	Blodyn y Gwynt
APPLE	Afal
ASH	Onnen
ASPEN	Aethnen
ASTER	Sêr-flodau
BARLEY	Haidd
BAY	Llawryf
BEECH	Ffawydden
BIRCH	Bedw
BLACKBERRY	Mwyar duon
BLACKTHORN	Draenen ddu
BOX	Pren bocs
BURDOCK	Cedowrach
BUTTERCUP	Blodeuyn yr Ymenym
CHAMOMILE	Camri
CAMPHOR	Camfwr
CANTERBURY BELL	Canterburyn Clychau
CARNATION	Carnasiwn
CEDAR	Cedrwydden
CENTAURY	Ysgol Fair
CHESTNUT	Castan
CINQUEFOIL	Pumbys
CLOVER	Meillionen goch
COLUMBINE	Troed y Glomen
COMFREY	Llysiau'r Cwlwm
CORNFLOWER	Llysiau'r Grawn
COWSLIPS	Briallu Mair
CYPRESS	Cyprewydden
DAFFODIL	Cenhinen Bedr
DAISY	Llygad y Dydd
DANDELION	Dant y Llew

DILL	Llysiau'r gwewyr
ELDER	Ysgaw
ELFWORT	Clafrllys mawr
ELM	Llwyf
EYEBRIGHT	Effios
FERN	Rhedynen
FIG	Ffigysen
FIR	Ffyniddwyden
FLAG	Enfys elestr
FLAX	Llin
FORGET-ME-NOT	N'ad fi'n angof
FOXGLOVE	Bysedd Cochion
GARLIC	Garlleg
GERANIUM	Mynawyd y Bugail
GOLDEN ROD	Y Wialen aur
GORSE	Eithin
GRAPE	Grawnwin
HAWTHORN	Ysbyddaden draenen wen
HAZEL	Collen
HEATHER	Grug
HELLEBORE	Hydyf
HOLLY	Celyn
HONEYSUCKLE	Gwyddfid
HOPS	Hopys
HYACINTH	Clychau'r Gog
IVY	Eiddew
JESSAMINE	Siasmin
LAVENDER	Lafant
LEEK	Cenhinen
LETTUCE	Letys
LILOCK	Lelog
LILY	Lili
LILY OF THE VALLEY	Lil'r dyffrynnoedd
LIVERWORT	Llysiau'r afu
LOTUS	Alaw'r dwr
LUPIN	Bys y blaidd
MAIZE	Grawn yr India
MANDRAKE	Mandragora
MAPLE	Masarnen
MARIGOLD	Gold Mair
MARJORAM	Mintys y Graig
MARSHMALLOW	Mallws
MELISSA	Balm Triagl
MIMOSA	Mimws
MINT	Mintys
MISTLETOE	Uchelwydd
MULBERRY	Morwydden
MYRRH	Myrr
MYRTLE	Myrtwydd
NARCISSUS	Croeso'r Gwanwyn
NUTMEG	Nytmeg
OAK	Derwen
OATS	Ceirch
OLIVES	Olewydden

ONION	Wynwynyn
ORANGE	Oraens
PAEONY	Rhoysn y Mynydd
PALM	Palmwydden
PANSY	Pansi
PASSION FLOWER	Blodeuyn y Dioddefaint
PEACH	Eirinen wlanog
PERIWINKLE	Gwichiad
PEACH	Eirinen
POMEGRANATE	Pomgranad
POPPY	Pabi
PRIMROSE	Briallu
ROSE	Rhoysn
ROSEMARY	Rhos Mair
ROWAN	Pren Criafol Cerdinen
RUE	Rhyll
SAFFRON	Saffrwm
ST. JOHN'S WORT	Dail y Fendigaid
SCARLET PIMPERNEL	Brithlys
SNOWDROPS	Eirlys
SORREL	Suran y coed gyffredin
SUNFLOWERS	Heulflodyn
SYCAMORE	Sycamorwydden
VALERIAN	Triaglog
VERBENA	Llysiau'r hudol
VIOLET	Fioled fer
WALLFLOWER	Llysiau'r fagwyr
WALNUT	Cneuen Ffrengig
WORMWOOD	Wermod Lwyd
YARROW	Milddail
YEW	Yw

Reader's Notes

Reader's Notes

Reader's Notes

Reader's Notes

Reader's Notes

Reader's Notes